# Pachyderm
# and the Rat

*For Bill,*
*Enjoy!*
*'Rat'*

# Pachyderm and the Rat

Flying with the "Big Boys" in Vietnam

HARRY R. NEVLING

ISBN: 1539949788
ISBN-13: 9781539949787

# Dedication

*I wish to dedicate this story to my classmates from Fort Wolters, Texas and Fort Rucker, Alabama, who did not return. Some were on a second tour but gave their all. These men succeeded in the struggles of flight school and helicopters. I wish I had adequate words to describe my sense of loss of these men.*

# Classmates Killed in Vietnam

| RANK | NAME | INCIDENT DATE | FLIGHT CLASS | TAIL NUMBER | UNIT |
|------|------|---------------|--------------|-------------|------|
| WO1 | ARVIDSON, James W. | 08/2/68 | 67-25 | 66-15055 | B/1/9 CAV 1 CAV |
| CW2 | BURNS, Ernest D. | 07/14/69 | 68-501/68-1 | 62-02063 | C/1/9 CAV |
| WO1 | CARPENTER, Walter. A. | 03/08/69 | 68-501 | 66-07823 | B/7/17 CAV |
| WO1 | DUNEMAN, Allen E. | 11/27/68 | 68-501 | 65-09620 | 187 AHC |
| WO1 | ENGSTROM, Loren E. | 11/13/68 | 67-25/67-23 | 11-15163 | 170 AHC |
| WO1 | FAVERTY, Alvis R., Jr | 08/18/68 | 68/501 | | 240 AHC |
| WO1 | GROTH, Dennis A. | 10/19/68 | 68-1/6725 | 66-17010 | 82 MED DET |
| WO1 | HAGGARD, Darrell L. | 12/20/68 | 68-501/67-25 | 67-16367 | 1/40 ARTY |
| CW2 | HOLDITCH, Robert W. | 07/2/69 | 67-503/67-25 | 67-17694 | B/2/17 CAV 101 ABN |
| WO1 | JACOBS, Thomas C. | 09/13/68 | 67-25 | 66-14412 | A/7/17 CAV |
| WO1 | JOHNSON, Jerry H. | 06/13/68 | 67-25 | 66-01016 | 174 AHC |
| WO1 | KOPPPEL, Redlick S. | 09/08/68 | 68-501 | 67-17149 | 155 AHC |
| WO1 | KOSLOSKY, Walter, N. | 01/06/69 | 68-1/67-25 | 67-15582 | A/3/17 CAV |
| 1LT | MACNEIL, Douglas, G. | 04/07/70 | 67-25 | 69-15038 | 159 MED |
| WO1 | MCPHAIL, Franklin L. | 09/30/68 | 68-501/68-1 | 62-02009 | B/2/20 ARA |
| CW2 | PAWLAK, Richard V. | 03/03/70 | 67-25 | 68-15571 | B/4/77 ARA 101ABN |
| CW2 | PETERSON, Stephen R. | 04/23/69 | 68-501 | 66-15203 | B/1 AVN 1INF |
| CW3 | POWERS, Lowell S. | 04/02/68 | 68-3/67-25 | 67-18523 | A/159 ASHB 101ABN |
| WO1 | RILEY, Richard S., Jr. | 10/24/68 | 67-503/67-25 | 66-16121 | C/101 AVN 101 ABN |
| WO1 | ROHTVALI, Arvi | 06/25/68 | 68-3/67-252 | 66-16206 | 240 AHC |
| WO1 | ROLF, Tommie A. | 05/20/68 | 68-501/68-1 | | C/2/20 ARA 1 CAV |
| WO1 | ROLLINS, William P. | 09/29/68 | 68-1/67-25 | 66-00523 | ACT/11 ACR |
| CW2 | SAPP, William, D | 02/15/71 | 67-503-67-25 | 68-15835 | A/159th ASHB 101 ABN |
| WO1 | SILVERBURG, Arvid O., Jr. | 01/23/69 | 68-1/67-25 | 66-16217 | 383 MED DET |
| WO1 | SONNKALB, Charles, D., Jr. | 08/16/68 | 68-501/68-1 | 67-16015 | C/19/CAV 1 CAV |
| WO1 | TOMLINSON, David C. | 07/12/68 | 68-501 | 64-14037 | A/2/20 ARA 1CAV |
| WO1 | TURONE, Norman M. | 06/05/68 | 68-501/68-1 | 65-10019 | 191 AHC |
| CPT | VEHLING, Robert W. | 01/11/72 | 68-501 | 65-09543 | 162 AHC |
| WO1 | WILLIAMS, Floyd L. | 05/24/68 | 68-501 | 66-17752 | B/7/17 CAV |

Twenty-nine classmates killed in action

(We graduated 9 April 1968 and lost our first classmate on 20 May 1968, forty-two days following graduation.)

In all, 2,165 pilots and approximately 2,735 crew were lost in Vietnam. Being a helicopter pilot was the most dangerous job in-country. We had a significantly higher casualty rate than any other MOS (military occupational specialty or job).

# Acknowledgments

I wish to thank all my buddies and friends from my flying days for being there. There were days that their just being there was a comfort. Sometimes it was their insights, sometimes their explanations, sometimes it was their humor. They were, for the most part, a great bunch to be around.

Many of us stay in contact after all these years. There is a special bond among those who have shared the experiences of combat.

I'd like to thank J. Andrew Belmont, Andy, for his support and stories that he shared with me for this book. I'd like to thank Tom Andrews and Andy Belmont for some technical information I had forgotten and had lost my -10. operator's manual for the C model Chinook. I'd like to thank Larry "Lurch" Hines for his support and some details. Eric Van Opstal provided some valuable information as well.

I'd like to thank my wife for putting up with me spending the time and effort to write this book.

"Pachyderm" was a great bunch of guys trying to do a good job in support of the troops on the ground. Many of us had been there ourselves. Andy Belmont had been a crew chief on Hueys as had Lowell Powers. Lurch Hines had been an infantryman. So had Tom Sheff. I had been a radio operator.

Most of the guys, even if they hadn't been there before, would do whatever they could for the guys on the ground. I think we were all happy we weren't down there!

Those who didn't do their jobs to the fullest know who they are—so do we. We don't have to live with it; they do.

So, here's to my friends, my colleagues, my comrades-in-arms. Thank you!

A Pilot's Prayer

God, grant me the eyes of an eagle,
The judgment of an owl,
The quickness of a hummingbird,
The reflexes of a cat,
The radar of cave bat,
The heart of a bull, and
The balls of an army helicopter pilot.
                    Anonymous

# Introduction

This is the tale of Harry R. Nevling—"Rat"—and flying with the "big boys" in Vietnam. There are two reasons I wanted to write this book. First was to tell people I know something about what it was like in Vietnam for the average Joe. The second is that of all the books about helicopters in Vietnam, I don't know of any telling what it was like flying the CH-47 Chinook. It was a lot different than flying the smaller birds.

Some of the information contained herein may not be accurate, but any errors are unintentional. The information provided is from my memory—with the help of some very good friends. If I accidentally offend someone, it is not my intent; it is simply my recollections. However, there are intentionally derogatory things contained herein, but they are justly deserved. Most of the men I served with were brave and honorable men. They were more than a bit crazy and got the job done. Others, not so much. One soon learned which side of the chicken wire a pilot was on. Then again, perhaps it was just sanity.

First, why the big boys? Well, the CH-47 Chinook is a large helicopter. When running, the blades occupy a space that is sixty feet wide and nearly ninety-nine feet long. The fuselage is twelve feet five inches wide by fifty feet nine inches long. The front rotor head is ten feet eleven inches off the ground, while the aft head is eighteen feet eleven and a half inches high. It could carry a load of twelve thousand plus pounds.

In comparison, a UH1-H Iroquois (Huey) Slick has a main rotor space of forty-eight feet, and from the tip of the main rotor to the tail rotor, it is fifty-eight feet four inches long. It is twelve feet five inches tall with a fuselage width of three feet ten inches. It can carry a load of four thousand pounds. The Chinook has a fuselage four times the size and four times the load capacity of the Huey. Overall it is about 25 percent wider, 50 percent taller, and nearly 70 percent longer than the Huey. It was a big boy. In combat there was a crew of five: an aircraft commander, or first pilot; a pilot; a flight engineer (universally referred to as chief and normally on the floor looking down at the load); a crew engineer (usually manning the machine gun in the right door); and a gunner (manning the left machine gun).

The Huey UH-1 is the most identified helicopter of the Vietnam War. While there were a lot of other helicopters there, most people identify the UH-1 with the conflict. The Huey had a crew of four: aircraft commander, or pilot (usually in the left seat); pilot (normally in the right seat); crew chief (occupying the right door machine gun); and door gunner (manning the left door machine gun). It had a maximum seating of thirteen in addition to the two pilots. This was rarely used, as the two outward-facing two-man seats were occupied by the crew chief and gunner. I don't know that the Huey would actually lift that much in the air of Vietnam. A Chinook has a crew of five. In addition, it has seating for thirty-three, and the gunners do not take up any of that space. I have personally had over three times that many combat marines on board when evacuating a fire support base. We had some difficulty but got them all out and back to their base at Vandergrift. It was a big boy.

The Chinook could carry a variety of internal loads in addition to the thirty-three-troop arrangement. It could also carry two 105 mm (millimeter) howitzer cannons, or two jeeps, or one three-quarter-ton truck. While the pilots did not like internal loads because they could not be jettisoned if something went south, there was a lot of room in the cargo cabin. It was a big boy.

The Huey had one engine, two main rotor blades, a tail rotor, and five interconnected fuel cells. It had a fuel endurance (flight time) of about two hours. It was also equipped with synchronized elevators (stubby wings) on the tail boom that pushed the tail boom down and allowed the aircraft to be closer to horizontal when flying relatively fast. The A and B model Chinooks had two engines, six main rotor blades on two rotor heads, and two interconnected fuel cells located on the sides of the main fuselage. It had a fuel endurance of about two hours. The C (or C-) model that I flew with Playtex and Pachyderm had four additional smaller fuel cells, also located on the sides of the main fuselage. The C model had a fuel endurance of about three and a half hours. It was equipped with speed ramps that adjusted the rotor head at higher speeds to keep the aircraft nearer to horizontal. The Huey had a maximum airspeed of 124 knots (135 mph) while for the Chinook it was 174 knots (just over 200 mph). It was a big boy.

The C Model Chinook had two Lycoming T55-L7-C engines. Each of these produced up to 2,850 foot pounds of torque, making the aircraft capable of lifting thirteen thousand pounds or six and a half tons. It was a big boy.

# Author's Note

I was on active duty for six years, five months, and ten days. During six years and ten days of that service in the US Army, I held nine ranks in three grade structures. I think that may be a record.

## Enlisted

| | | |
|---|---|---|
| Basic Pay Entry Date | | |
| (BPED) | 16 Nov 65 | Pvt-E-1 |
| Promotion | 21 Jan 66 | Pvt-E-2 |
| Promotion | 15 Jun 66 | PFC-E-3 |
| Promotion | 13 Nov 66 | Spc4-E4 |
| Promotion | 25 May 67 | Spc5-E5 |
| (Unsure of exact date.) | | |

## Warrant Officer

| | | |
|---|---|---|
| Assigned Warrant | 9 Apr 68 | WO1 |
| Promotion—Chief | | |
| Warrant Officer 2 | 9 Apr 69 | CW2 |

# Commissioned Officer

| Direct Commission to 1LT | 6 Aug 70 | 1LT-O2 |
| Promotion to captain | 26 Nov 71 | CPT-O3 |

I was awarded the following medals:

Distinguished Flying Cross
Bronze Star (two)
Air Medal with Valor device and twenty-two oak leaf clusters (still trying to find the orders for the OLCs)
Army Commendation Medal
Good Conduct Medal
National Defense Service Medal
Vietnam Service Medal with silver service star (five awards)
Vietnam Campaign Medal
Republic of Vietnam Cross Gallantry with Palm (two awards) (unit citations)
Republic of Vietnam Civil Actions Honor Medal First Class (unit citation)
Three Overseas Bars (worn on right sleeve of uniform blouse)
Expert Marksman Badge (M-14 rifle, .45-cal. pistol, and .38-cal. pistol)
Army Aviator Badge (wings!)

# Steinbeck on Helicopter Pilots

On 7 January 1967, Steinbeck was in Pleiku, flying with Shamrock Flight, D Troop, Tenth Cavalry. He wrote:

Alicia, I wish I could tell you about these pilots. They make me sick with envy. They ride their vehicles the way a man controls a fine, well-trained quarter horse. They weave along stream beds, rise like swallows to clear trees, they turn and twist and dip like swifts in the evening. I watch their hands and feet on the controls, the delicacy of the coordination reminds me of the sure and seeming slow hands of (Pablo) Casals on the cello. They are truly musicians hands and they play their controls like music and they dance them like ballerinas and they make me jealous because I want so much to do it. Remember your child night dream of perfect flight free and wonderful? It's like that, and sadly, I know I never can. My hands are too old and forgetful to take orders from the command center, which speaks of updrafts and side winds, of drift and shift, or ground fire indicated by a tiny puff or flash, or a hit and all these commands must be obeyed by the musician's hands instantly and automatically. I must take my longing out in admiration and the joy of seeing it.
—John Steinbeck

# DA NANG, REPUBLIC OF VIETNAM

The cabin temperature was cool in the US Air Force C-141 Starlifter. The cabin was dim, with the cabin lights set low so the men could possibly sleep. The men were mostly of C Company, 159th Aviation Battalion (Playtex) of the 101st Airborne Division. They had formed up at Fort Sill, Oklahoma, over the summer and fall of 1968. This day's activities started at Fort Sill, with the men loading on transportation in the afternoon for Tinker Air Force Base (AFB) in Oklahoma City. There they boarded the Starlifter for the flight to Da Nang, Republic of Vietnam. The flight took them to Elmendorf AFB, Anchorage, Alaska (about thirty-seven hundred miles), for refueling around 8:00 p.m. local time, then on to Yokota AFB in Japan for another refueling. By the time they got to Vietnam around midnight, it had been a long day—although because of the International Date Line and all the time zones, it was a day and a half after their departure from Fort Sill.

During this lengthy flight, Harry did not sleep. He pondered how he had gotten to where he was. Some background information may assist the reader with understanding where he was and how his past influenced his actions and behaviors.

Harry enlisted in the US Army effective 16 November 1965. From Rochester, Minnesota, he went to the induction center in Minneapolis, then boarded a train for Fort Leonard Wood, Missouri. The overnight was not pleasant, as there was a steam leak in his compartment, and sleep was difficult. Fort Leonard Wood was not much of an improvement. It was referred to as "Fort Lost-in-the-Woods, Misery."

1

Appropriate. The basic training unit he was assigned to was housed in leftover World War II "temporary" barracks. Clapboard on studs with no insulation. Gaps in the walls you could see light through and *cold*. That miserable, wet cold. The barracks were heated by coal-fired furnaces that leaked coal dust into the barrack bays. His basic training unit had something like 60 percent casualties from upper respiratory infections (URI). He survived the ordeal and came out of basic training as a private first class (E-3). The promotion was because his qualifying as an expert marksman with the M-14 rifle.

Following basic, he went home for a week of leave with his family and friends. He had taken a week at Christmas, so he cut this leave short in order to report to Fort Ord, California, just outside Monterey, with his buddy Tom Luther. Harry and Tom had known each other since they were about five years old. In high school, they were roommates for two years at the Southern School of Agriculture at Waseca, Minnesota. This coed boarding high school was run by the University of Minnesota. They joined the army on the buddy system, which guaranteed them being in the same unit for basic training. That hadn't worked out, but now they were together at the Intermediate Speed Radio Operators School. Fort Ord was again leftover World War II barracks, but the climate was much nicer. The views of Monterey Bay and the proximity of Monterey made it a great place to be. A third friend from Rochester, John Kelly, was stationed there following a tour in the infantry in Vietnam. They had some good times on the weekends.

Both Harry and Tom did well at the school and were promoted to the Radio Teletype School at Fort Gordon, Georgia, just southwest of Augusta. The army contracted with Trans Texas Airways (TTA), called "Tree Top Air." Again, appropriate. Don't think these guys ever got over five hundred feet all the way across the southern states. Part of the orientation to Fort Gordon required all the new arrivals in the replacement depot (repo-depot) to march to a theater and receive indoctrination to Fort Gordon. They presented the services on post and where they were located. Part of this indoctrination was a presentation on warrant officer flight training. This included what was required to get into the school, a bit of the syllabus, and information on becoming a warrant officer helicopter pilot. Harry thought this was pretty neat and signed up. Tom just wanted to get on with things. They had both enlisted as airborne, and Tom was excited to get to jump school.

While at Fort Gordon, learning more Morse code, the radio teletype, and looking forward to going into "the cage" (a *secret* classified compound on the base) to learn about cryptology devices, Harry was called into the battalion commander's office. The CO (commanding officer), a signal corps major, attempted to talk him into going to Signal Officer Candidate School (OCS). Harry politely told him no. He really did not wish to fly a desk but was very interested in flying helicopters. He passed the required Class I flight physical. Then he had to go before a flight board of officers, one of whom had to be a pilot. There were the usual military questions, which he was able to answer appropriately. The zinger—to see if you could think on your feet—was, "You know that Frank Sinatra and Mia Farrow were recently married?" He did. "What do you think of that?" Harry responded, "They are both consenting adults and have enough that they can do about as they please." He continued, "However, if I were Nancy Sinatra, I'd be more than a bit uncomfortable having a mother who was younger than me." Must have been a good answer because he passed on to the final stage, which was a helicopter flight. He went up with a warrant officer in a Bell H-13 Sioux. This was a small "bubble" helicopter, and the purpose of the flight seemed to be if one was susceptible to airsickness, as the pilot "waddled" the aircraft to see if he could get you airsick. He also had Harry try to fly the aircraft straight and level. This was a real challenge, but he must have done well enough to pass. He was informed he had been accepted to Warrant Officer Rotary Wing Flight School. He would not be placed on hold but would instead go whenever the army needed him until a slot opened for him at the school.

Harry finished the training and graduated second in his class. There were no orders, and he was placed on holdover status along with his buddy Tom. During this time, Tom's dad, Benny; his mom, Bev; and his oldest sister, Kathy, came down to visit. Benny invited Harry along, and they all went down to the Atlantic coast of Florida for the weekend. All day on the beach swimming and body surfing in the two foot rollers. Very enjoyable time and a great break from Fort Gordon.

One event that stuck with Harry was when they stopped for breakfast near the Florida border. Benny specifically requested there be no grits on his plate. When the waitress sat his plate before him, there were grits. Benny reacted as if there were a rattlesnake on the plate. His eyes widened, he pushed back from the table, glared at the waitress, and said, "Get those damn grits off my plate!" Benny had been in the air corps during World War II. Must have had a bad experience with grits. No one was about to ask him about it though.

They proceeded to the Atlantic coast in Florida and had a very enjoyable weekend. It was great to be there and to be away from the army for a bit.

Harry finally received orders on an emergency levy to the 4th Infantry Division at Fort Lewis, Washington, south of Tacoma and Seattle. As the 4th was getting ready to deploy at the end of August, Harry was not eligible for any leave. He reported to A Company, 124th Signal Battalion, which ran all the high-frequency radios for the division. The barracks consisted of a cement-block three-story building, and the enlisted bay had a beautiful view of Mount Rainier. Harry was there three days before he saw it because of the low cloud cover. He woke up in the morning, looked out, and there was this beautiful mountain. He said, "There's a mountain out there!" One of the guys came back with, "Yeah, Nevling, we put that there last night to surprise you this morning." Many days it could not be seen because of low clouds.

Fort Lewis was a wonderful post. Beautiful green grass and nice, newer buildings. Duty time was spent getting equipment and vehicles ready for deployment. Off-duty was spent at the enlisted men's club. To get there they had to pass by the airfield. One afternoon there was a practice assault on the sod near the perimeter fence. Several Hueys (UH-1 Iroquois) came into a nice three-foot hover, and the cavalry troops leaped out with their M-16s blazing. They had blank adapters on their rifles, so they would fire on automatic even with the reduced charge in blank rounds. Harry said to the group, "Gee, I wonder if they are going to come into a three-foot hover in Vietnam over the twelve- to fifteen-foot-tall elephant grass?" As he found out later in Vietnam, they did. He heard they had 60 percent casualties on their first combat assault from leg injuries! When he found this out he wondered why he, a lowly E-4, knew this but the army did not. Other questions like this arose. One had to wonder at the level of ignorance.

The day came, and they went to the Port of Tacoma and loaded on the USNS *General John Pope*, a recommissioned World War II Liberty ship. Harry's unit was one of the first to load, which put them just above the bilge at the bottom of the ship. Harry went exploring and found that the ship was not going to be a pleasure cruise by any stretch! The racks were fold-up cots, four high, and just big enough to hold a man. When lying in one, you could tap the head of the man down the row from you, tickle the feet of the man in the other direction, slap the guy next to you in the middle of the chest, and reach across the aisle and pat that guy on the shoulder. If you rolled over, you'd give the guy above you a thrill.

There were guys getting seasick as they crossed Puget Sound. Smooth water. Later when they were near a typhoon, it was very challenging to avoid the discharges.

The ship was followed across the Pacific by a Russian trawler (say "spy ship"). Over the horizon behind them, there was a US Navy destroyer as well.

All in all, it was a pretty interesting and miserable nineteen-day voyage. Between the cramped quarters, seasickness, and food poisoning, it was not pleasant. Oh, and to top it off, Harry lost his twentieth birthday crossing the International Date Line.

They landed at Qui Nhon by landing craft. Down the net, into the boat, and in to shore. Harry got his left foot wet in the landing. Then they hauled themselves and their gear up the beach to a waiting bus. They were taken to a loading area and transferred to duce-and-a-half trucks for the road trip up QL 19, which was mostly a dirt road, not a highway. They went through An Khe (home of the First Air Calvary Division), then through the Mang Yang Pass (where the French Groupement Mobile One Hundred was ambushed and badly mauled by the Viet Minh in late June of 1954) and on to Pleiku. The 4th Infantry Division was at Camp Enari (Dragon Mountain base camp) about ten miles southeast of Pleiku, just northeast of QL 19 and north of Dragon Mountain.

Base camp was tents, GP (general purpose) medium tents, for barracks. Initially dirt floors, but they got wood flooring after a couple of months. There was also a two-by-four frame to hold up the roof of the tent, but someone else used the wood for Harry's tent, so they had tent poles. They ate C rations, leftovers from Korea, for the first few months. The cooks and/or senior NCOs took the fruit and good snack cans so all the men got were the entrées.

A Company was located, along with the rest of the battalion, on the west side of the camp, near the perimeter. It was just below what was called Signal Hill, which was a small hill located inside the camp. There were a lot of radios and radio operators up there.

Harry operated a radio teletype van from base camp, a VRC-29 (vehicle-mounted FM voice radio), and a PRC-10 (backpack FM voice radio) for outside the perimeter. He was on convoys to Quin Nhon and a forward brigade base camp known as LZ 3 Tango. He worked twelve-hour shifts seven days a week at the Division Tactical Operations Center from 8:00 p.m. to 8:00 a.m. for a while. He then went to the top of Dragon Mountain, where he and another man operated an FM voice radio relay site. The two of them shared a GP Small tent. He was there while three others rotated through the other slot. It appeared that a Sergeant Rudi had banished him to the mountain. We won't go into Rudi's capabilities or lack thereof. Eventually the mountain was developed as a major signal center, as it was the highest terrain in the AO (area of operations).

The OIC (officer in charge) was a Captain Lucky. Harry met him one day when there were only three teams of two men each on the mountain. He came walking down the two-rut trail that served as a road. He was wearing silver captain bars on his cap and collar. Not a good idea out in the bush. As he approached, Harry and a member of one of the other teams turned to face him, came to attention, and said, "Good morning, sir." Captain Lucky asked why they hadn't saluted an officer. Harry replied, "Sir, I was told not to salute officers in the field. Do you have any idea what is in those bushes on either side of the road?" After nervously looking around, he said he did not. Harry told him he had no idea, either, but there was nothing stopping Charlie (the bad guys) from walking up that mountain. Captain Lucky told them the plans for the northwest top of the mountain nearest Camp Enari, which was about a kilometer away, in a straight line. Much farther by road. He asked if they would like to be included in the new camp. Harry declined. When asked why, he told Captain Lucky that he was making a target worth walking up the mountain to destroy.

They built the communications center. It was big. They had two seventy-five-foot tall parabolic dishes to transmit back and forth to Ban Me Tout, seventy-seven kilometers (forty-eight miles) south. There were four telephone vans with their antennas, a variety of other radios and their antennas, a Quonset hut mess hall, and another Quonset hut with a television studio and Captain Lucky's quarters and office. The perimeter had been opened by cutting and burning the trees and brush. A nice defensive border was installed consisting of concertina wire, barbed wire, and sandbag bunkers. All except the "back door." Where the road passed through the back of the compound to the rest of the mountain there were simply a couple of two-by-four Xs with another two-by-four connecting the centers and concertina wire. One man could easily move this barrier and gain access to the compound.

Well, Harry's desires were not accepted, and he was ordered to move into the compound. Captain Lucky came by and asked Harry what he thought of the site. OK, you asked. "Well, sir, you have a lot of nice equipment here. You have become a real tempting target. Now there is that nice defensive boundary on the mountain slope. But Charlie is not much for frontal attacks. He's going to walk up that trail we used to get to the bottom of the mountain. He's going to silently kill the sentry at the back door and open it. Then a whole bunch of them are going to rush in, blow this place to hell, and go out through your perimeter from the inside." Captain Lucky did not think that was going to happen.

Harry was now in a bad place. This made him very nervous, as they now became a target worth the climb (walk) up the mountain. He received a radio message that he was to leave the mountain to go back to the States for flight school. He was very happy to get off that mountain. It was, in fact, attacked and destroyed about two weeks after his departure!

Harry went home to Rochester, Minnesota, for a thirty-day leave. Real food, friends, and family. It was a great time!

Flight school! Finally! Fort Wolters, Texas. Harry signed in and found that the class wasn't going to start for a few days, so he was placed in a holding company. He didn't know this was not only students waiting to start but also those who washed out, failed to make it. He checked in and went out and sat on a picnic table to have a cigarette while waiting for the powers that be to decide what to do with him for the day. You couldn't wear anything on your uniform during flight school but the flight school's brass and unit patch. Harry hadn't removed his rank, ribbons, or combat patch yet. A Green Beret staff sergeant came over and sat down. Harry tried opening a conversation by saying, "Looking forward to flight school?" The sergeant replied, "I'm on my way out. Couldn't make it. Those damned things will make you sweat blood!" Harry was to find out he was right.

Preflight was two weeks of "hell week." Mostly BS classes like the History of the Uniform during the day and harassment nights and weekends. They had some attrition during this time, but Harry had seen harassment from experts. The two warrant officer tactical officers assigned to his barracks were no match for what he'd already experienced. Again, into the leftover World War II barracks. Much less uncomfortable than those at Fort Leonard Wood.

On to "The Hill". Once they started flying, the men were housed in three-story cement-block barracks on a hill within the Fort, hence "The Hill". Three men to a room. There were two platoons per company. They were on rotating schedules where one platoon would be on the flight line while the other was in class. Each week they rotated mornings on the flight line, then afternoons in the classrooms, and switching the following week.

Harry's platoon TAC (tactical officer) was CW2 Caulder. The men named the platoon "Caulder's Marauders." The first morning on "The Hill", the men fell into formation in their khaki uniforms. Mr. Caulder introduced himself and gave the men some information about the company and its operations. Then he said, "Whose 'motorcicle' is that in my parking lot?" Harry had purchased a Harley-Davidson Sportster XLCH while on leave and ridden it down to Texas. Nervously, Harry spoke up and said, "That's my bike, sir." Mr. Caulder looked at him and could see the marks on his uniform from the previous rank and ribbons. He mumbled something and dismissed the platoon. Harry breathed a big sigh of relief. That could have gotten nasty.

The initial training, learning how to fly a helicopter, was taught by civilian IPs (instructor pilots). Harry was assigned to a platoon that flew the TH-55, a Hughes 300, a two-seater with a four-cylinder gas engine. It was a very touchy aircraft that you could maneuver just by thinking about the move. When you started, they took you up and had you take over straight-and-level flight. This seemed easy enough. Then they had you do descents, climbs, and turns. A lot more difficult. Then you went to climbing turns and descending turns. Even more difficult. Then the "sweating blood" maneuver—*hovering*! The IP put the aircraft in a rock-solid three-foot hover, told you to maintain this position, then gave you the controls. The rock-solid part lasted a matter of a few seconds, very few! Soon the aircraft started to drift, and you corrected, either over or under, never the correct amount. Soon you were all over the place. Panic started to set in, and the instructor just sat there letting you sweat. Most of them wound up going backward and up until about thirty to fifty feet above the ground, looking pretty much straight down. That's about when the IP said, "I have the controls." He returned the aircraft to its original three-foot rock-solid hover and explained all the things you did wrong. Hovering a helicopter is akin to riding a unicycle, only more difficult, much more difficult. Way too many opposing forces for stability.

Harry's IP had put his hand in the discharge chute of his power mower and clipped the end of a finger. He was grounded. If a student flew with another instructor for three days, he became that instructor's student. So Harry was bounced around the other IPs for the class waiting for this IP to return to flight status. Didn't happen. Harry wound up flying with all the other IPs. This was probably a good thing, as they all had a slightly different way of doing things. Harry tried to learn them all. One day when flying with the assistant flight commander, Harry was doing an approach to a confined area. Not much confinement with tumbleweed and scrub trees. About ten feet from touchdown a jackrabbit jumped up and took off running. The IP said, "See if you can catch him." Immediately Harry rolled the nose over and took off after the rabbit. Now, jackrabbits do not run in a straight line. This one was all over the place, trying to get away from the helicopter. The TH-55 was so agile Harry could keep up with him. Quite an experience in maneuverability. After a few minutes, the IP said, "That's enough. We don't want to run him to death." Harry pulled up, and the jackrabbit probably went somewhere and collapsed for a while.

One of this IP's maneuvers was a different type of autorotation. The army was the only military branch to teach touchdown autorotations. This is a simulated engine failure by rolling all the power off the throttle. The helicopter then has the glide slope of a brick! What you see between your toe pedals is where you are going to land unless you turn. The new spot is still between your toe pedals. Sometimes they would do a simulated forced landing where you recover the aircraft just before touchdown and continue on with flight. Other times you did a full autorotation to the ground.

When you lose power, you immediately have to raise the nose of the helicopter to keep the airflow up through the freewheeling rotor blades and bottom out the pitch so that they can freewheel better. The nose is raised or lowered to keep the rotor rpm desired during descent. Without rotor rpm, you will fall even faster and have nothing to stop you at the bottom. When you get near the ground, you raise the nose a bit more to increase the rotor rpm, then start pulling pitch back in to slow the aircraft. You keep adding pitch to slow the aircraft and allow it to settle onto the ground. This particular IP did not ease the pitch in at the bottom. He waited until about ten feet off the ground and popped enough pitch in to all but stop the aircraft. The he eased in more as it settled onto the ground. Worked extremely well in a small, agile bird like the TH-55. Harry didn't think he'd like to try it in a Huey or a Chinook.

The next phase was tactical flying. How to fly cross-country and land in confined areas and on pinnacles. Not much for pinnacles in that part of Texas (Mineral Wells, west of Fort Worth). Some of the pinnacles were bulldozed mounds of dirt less than ten feet high. You also had to do all the things you had learned in the previous portion of training. This included takeoffs, landings, traffic patterns, cross-country, forced landings, autorotations, and so forth. This was taught by military instructors—pilots who had returned from Vietnam. Harry's IP was a captain just back from Vietnam and just out of the hospital where a twenty-seven foot tapeworm had been removed. He must have been eating local food. Not a good idea.

Harry's first autorotation with this IP was a new experience for him. As the aircraft approached the ground, Harry caught out of the corner of his eye the IP pushing back in his seat as though preparing to crash. Just as he started to reach for the controls, Harry popped in the initial pitch, then followed through with the remaining pitch, and settled in with no forward movement on the ground and a touchdown that couldn't be felt. Smooth and gentle. Harry looked over at the now white-faced

IP, and the IP said, "That was a different autorotation." Harry told him about the assistant flight instructor in the previous phase, and all was well. This phase of flight instruction was also very hard work but a lot of fun. The sweating blood part was mostly past. Now it was just sweat—at times, very serious sweat.

Then on to Fort Rucker, Alabama, for instrument flying and transition to the Huey. Learning to fly a helicopter without being able to see outside the cockpit is a bit of a challenge. Harry made it through this. However, in the beginning, Harry made a real mess of a GCA (ground-controlled approach by radar). When the IP took over, Harry said to him, "Jesus, I really fucked that up. Sorry, sir." Harry did not realize that he was actually transmitting over the radio and not on the intercom. The female controller came on the air and asked, "Aircraft with last transmission please identify yourself." Obviously, she wanted to report whoever had said that over the air. The IP came back and said to her, "Ma'am, he ain't that fucked up." He then warned Harry about language over the air but understood the mistake and did nothing more. As things progressed, Harry got better at it. In fact, one day his instructor had him fly GCA to touchdown on a small cement pad. That was a thrill!

They spent a fair amount of time in a Link Trainer, called "the box." This was a ground-mounted flight simulator in which they practiced instrument flying. The simulators had been converted from fixed-wing trainers and did not simulate rotary winged aircraft flight very well.

The next phase was transition to the Huey. Harry's instructor was a former navy pilot and a real piece of work. He'd set up a trap by giving a forced landing (cutting off the power to the rotor) over a road with a plowed field next to it. If a student went for the road, he'd nail them because of the power lines (which were not in the way). Next time he'd nail them for going for the field, as it was soft dirt from the plowing. No matter what you did, it was wrong. Harry never did get comfortable with the Huey, largely because of that IP.

The final phase was a field test where they went out and lived in tents and operated from a sod landing field. They were trying to give some realism to the training and seeing that you could perform under those conditions.

Just before graduation, orders were provided for the next duty assignment. No one in Harry's class who had been to Vietnam was sent directly back. They all went on to other training or a Stateside assignment. Harry's orders were for the "293rd Aviation Company, MED HEL, Fort Sill, Oklahoma." Hmmm, not good. Harry did not want to fly medevac (medical evacuation) helicopters. He called Fort Sill and found there were no medical helicopter units forming there. Some clerk had messed up the abbreviations, and it should have been "MDM" for medium helicopter not "MED" for medical helicopter.

Harry's mom, older sister, and a girlfriend came down for the graduation ceremonies on 9 April 1968. They had to have their warrant officer (WO1) bars before they could get their pilot's wings so there were two ceremonies the same morning. Following the ceremonies, they all went back to Minnesota for Harry's leave, and then he and his girlfriend went on to Fort Sill.

As the cabin lights came up about halfway, the pilot came over the intercom. "Gentlemen, you may want to start getting up and ready for landing. We are out of thirty-five thousand feet and thirty-five miles east of Da Nang. We should be on the ground in about twenty minutes."

Mike Maloy began to stir, then gagged a bit and said, "My god, what is that smell!"

Rat replied "That, Mike, is Vietnam. Get used to it!"

At seven miles up and thirty-five miles out, yes, they could smell Vietnam—and it wasn't pleasant. The good news was that *everything* stank, so they got used to the smell fairly quickly.

The air force transport landed at Da Nang Main, at the time the busiest airport in the world, and the men off-loaded. There were Chinooks waiting to take them up to Phu Bai, about seventy-five kilometers, or fifty miles, to the northwest. It was night, so there wasn't much to see on the flight to Liftmaster Pad, the heliport for the 159th Aviation Battalion and C Company. A much more pleasant trip than his previous arrival in Vietnam.

# FORT SILL
## (PRELUDE TO VIETNAM)

On the way from Rochester to Fort Sill, following flight school and leave, Harry put on his uniform. He had his combat unit patch on the right shoulder, his ribbons for the medals he'd received, his warrant officer bars, and his aviator wings. He went to Waseca, Minnesota, where he had attended the Southern School of Agriculture, operated by the University of Minnesota. This was a six-month curriculum, coed, boarding high school. Part of the curricula involved three summer projects that were required for graduation. Harry had been cheated out of the credits for all three summers by a teacher we'll call Boyd. Boyd did not like students that were from cities rather than from farms. While Harry had completed twelve years of schooling, he did not have a high school diploma. He went into the school, which was not in session, and chatted with the secretary. This was a very nice woman named Deanne Nelson. She knew full well what had been done to Harry. As they were talking, the superintendent of the school stepped out of his adjoining office. When he saw Harry, his jaw dropped. He also knew full well what Boyd had done to him and condoned it. Boyd seemed to have a lot of power. After stumbling for a bit, he asked Harry how he was doing.

Harry replied, "Just fine. As you can see, I'm an officer in the US Army and a helicopter pilot. I'm on my way to Fort Sill, Oklahoma, to form up with a helicopter unit and go back to Vietnam. Despite Boyd's best efforts, I have made it. If you'd like to clear your conscience, you can send my diploma to this address." Harry handed him a piece of paper with his address at Fort Sill. He then turned back to Deanne, thanked her for her kindness, and left. The next week his diploma arrived at Fort Sill.

Harry reported for duty at the 293rd Aviation Company on 29 April 1968 and found that indeed it was not medical helicopters but Chinooks. When he parked in the lot behind the orderly room (company headquarters), another WO1 came over and asked if he was checking in. Harry told him he was. Mike Layne then introduced himself and told Harry he'd take him to the orderly room. When they approached the stoop at the entrance, a second lieutenant without aviator wings stepped out and asked Layne if he had another newbie. Harry turned a bit so he could see his ribbons and combat patch, and Layne told him, yes, but it was another Vietnam vet. Layne was wearing a 1st Air Cavalry combat patch on his right shoulder. He then said to Harry, "Say good-bye to the nonrated creep."

So Harry said, "Good-bye, nonrated-creep." Then he followed Layne into the orderly room to sign into the unit.

His girlfriend accompanied him to Fort Sill. They were staying at a motel in Lawton, Oklahoma, adjacent to the base. She told him that she would not stay there unless they were married. Harry proposed, and they were married at a chapel near the airfield. Mike Maloy, yet to be named "Flea," which later became "Super Flea," was the matron of honor, and Eugene Collings, about to be named "Pissed Off," was the best man. There were only about a dozen in attendance, and other than the chaplain and the bride, all were WO1 pilots.

# General Information and Preflight

He began the transition into the Chinook and his MOS (military occupation specialty) was changed to 062D effective 8 August 1968.

Compared to the other helicopters Harry had flown, the Chinook was *huge*. Much larger and more complex than a Huey. There were so many dials, switches, gauges, and circuit breakers Harry wasn't sure he'd ever get to know them. Fortunately, he didn't have to know *all* of them.

The Chinook is lifted by two, three-bladed, counterrotating rotor systems. When a blade from the forward head is straight forward from the aircraft, there is a blade from the aft head directly over the fuselage. The forward head rotates counterclockwise while the aft head rotates clockwise. This allows the rotor blades to mesh without striking another blade. The rotor heads are also equipped with speed ramps that tilt the entire rotor head forward when moving fast to allow the fuselage to fly closer to horizontal. Hueys accomplish the same thing with synchronized elevators on the tail boom to hold it down at speed.

Power is provided by two Lycoming T-55 engines. The A and B models were equipped with Lycoming T55-L7C engines producing 2,850 SHP (shaft horse power) each. The C model was to be powered by T-55 L711s producing 3,750 SHP, mainly by adding an additional power turbine stage. It had the transmissions to accommodate the increased power, but Lycoming had problems developing the engine, so L7Cs were substituted in the early models. The C- (C minus) model had added fuel cells in front of and behind the main cells on the sides of the fuselage. This is the bulge one can see on the sides of a Chinook. The added fuel cells increased the fuel endurance from two to three and a half hours. However, with all the pilots being used to flying for one and a half hours or so and having to refuel, it was a long time before anyone got over two and a half, let alone three hours in the air without landing.

They started out learning about the Chinook with ground school. Learning the aircraft, its components and capabilities. These were A model Chinooks with a fuel endurance of about two hours, as with the Huey, the Bell H-13, and the TH-55 Harry had flown. The larger and more complex the aircraft, the more detailed the preflight inspection becomes. There are a lot of things that need to be checked inside and around the lower section of the aircraft. However, the critical items of engine, drivetrain, hydraulics, and rotor systems are on top. To get up there, one has to use toe steps up the right rear of the fuselage, just in front of the number two (right side) engine. You have to lift your foot up and slide in past a hinged door into the toe step. After climbing up these, you are on top of the fuselage and can walk forward to check the forward rotor system and the drivetrain that is along the center under a series of covers. To get up to the aft head, there is a work platform that drops from the upper portion of the aft head housing. Another climb. Another toe step to accommodate your right foot, then swing your left foot up onto the platform. The aft rotor head is eighteen feet eleven and a half inches high. The work platform is about thirteen feet eight inches above the ground. Now, if you have acrophobia (fear of heights) like Harry, this is a very uncomfortable place! How can you be a pilot and have acrophobia? It never bothered Harry while flying. Only when he was on something attached to the ground. Like the roof of a Chinook.

The Chinook has five transmissions. A ninety-degree gearbox at the front of each engine, reducing the rpm from 22,500 rpm to 6,640 rpm and sending the power into a mixing transmission at the front of the aft pylon. This further reduces the rpm, combines the power from both engines, and then powers drive shafts to both rotor heads. There is another transmission at each of the rotor heads that changes the power another ninety degrees and even further reduces the rpm to operating speed for the rotors. The engines are turboshaft jet engines that operate a power outlet shaft that runs back through the engine at about 22,500 rpm. The rotors operate best at 233 rpm. That's a lot of reduction.

The rotor system is extremely heavy and requires hydraulic systems to be able to control the rotors. There are two separate systems, HYD SYS 1 and HYD SYS 2. However, both are powered from a single shaft off the aft rotor transmission. Should that quill shaft break, you could bend over and kiss your ass good-bye!

The engines spin turbines that compress the intake gasses to several atmospheres of pressure. This also increases the temperature to well over two thousand degrees Fahrenheit (1,093 Celsius). The gas is released into a combustion chamber and ignited. The ignited gasses, a fireball, is suspended by incoming gasses so it does not touch the wall of the combustion chamber. It is much too hot to come in contact with any metal at that point. The exhaust gasses are then turned and directed through power vanes at the rear of the engine. By the time the gasses reach the power vanes, they have cooled to about fifteen hundred degrees Fahrenheit (816 degrees Celsius). The power shaft then transfers the power back through the center of the engine to the ninety-degree gearbox at the nose. Each engine produces up to 2,850 foot pounds of torque.

If the pressure in the combustion chamber becomes too high, there is a bleed band around the outside of the engine's combustion chamber that can opened and bleed off the extra pressure. Should this malfunction and bleed band popping occurs, the bleed band continues to pop open and closed and bleeds off pressure, the engine will lose power, the fireball will expand to the combustion chamber walls, and all sorts of nasty things can happen, as Harry would experience later.

Once the preflight check of the aircraft, oil and hydraulics levels, and fuel status are completed, the pilots enter the cockpit. The fuselage or outside doors to the cockpit are emergency exits only. On the inside there is a lever that, when pulled, releases the door, which then springs from the frame. To get into the cockpit one enters from the cabin. There is a small companionway that has a fold-up jump seat for a passenger/observer. There is a small step up into this, then a higher step onto the cockpit level. This puts you behind the center console. You have to lift a leg up over the seat and past the cyclic stick. Then you bring the other leg up over the center console. You have to do this without getting your feet into the flight controls or the console. The pilot's seats are cushioned and comfortable. They adjust up, down, forward, back, and one can change the angle of the seat back and bottom together.

After going through a lengthy preflight check in the cockpit, the engines are started. The engines are big enough that they are not started directly. First an APU (auxiliary power unit) is started. This is a small turboshaft jet engine that produces hydraulic pressure to the flight systems and the engine start systems. It uses hydraulic fluid stored in an accumulator to spin the APU engine up for starting. The process is automated and is accomplished with the flipping of a single switch to START and holding it just beyond that position until the APU reaches 90 percent. Once the APU is running, it pumps hydraulic pressure back into the systems. Now the flight controls can be checked to ensure that the rotor blades are actually doing what the controls tell them to. The cyclic, or joy stick, is controlled by the right hand and controls the direction of the aircraft. It decreases pitch in the blades in the direction of movement and increases pitch on the opposite side. The toe pedals do pretty much the same thing but to turn the aircraft on its axis. Therefore, it will decrease pitch on one side of one of the rotor heads and decrease on the opposite side on the other head. The thrust lever (this is called a collective pitch lever in other helicopters) is controlled by the left hand and changes the pitch in both rotor heads to allow the aircraft to go up and down. It is a bent shaft with a handle on the rear. On the thrust lever are two rocker switches called beep trim switches. This allows the pilot to make minor adjustments in the power output of the engines. The left switch controls engine #1 while the right one adjusts both engines simultaneously. Harry and his companions were taught to "fly the needles"—to keep the needles on the dashboard instrument measuring engine power output together.

To start the engines, the throttle levers are moved from the STOP position to the GROUND position. The throttles in a Chinook do not have gradual adjustments as in most helicopters. There are three positions—STOP, GROUND, and FLIGHT. After placing a lever in the GROUND position, the engines can be started. They will wind up to about 37 percent of power. After they are both running, everything is checked again to make sure all is operating correctly. Then the throttles are moved to 'FLIGHT'. This takes the engines up to about 93 percent of power. The Chinook flies in the upper 7 percent of the engine power output. The APU is shut down by moving the switch to Off.

Now is the fun part—flying! As the Chinook hovers nose-high, you have to put in aft cyclic as you increase power to raise to a hover. If you don't do this, you start moving forward rapidly. Likewise, when landing, once the aft gear is on the ground, you again have to put in aft cyclic as you decrease power, or the aircraft will roll forward. This is counterintuitive and takes some getting used to.

Now you can taxi or hover to a takeoff spot. There is a knob at the rear of the center console that turns the aft left gear for steering while taxiing. There is also a swivel lock to prevent it from turning when you are not taxiing. The takeoff is usually just from a spot. Helicopters do not normally use runways. Any place away from other aircraft, buildings, or people will do. You turn the aircraft into the wind and increase power as you pull back on the stick. As the aircraft comes up off the ground, you push the stick forward to lower the nose. The position of the nose dictates speed, and the amount of power—thrust—dictates rate of climb. With an empty Chinook, one can get a lot of both in a very short time.

Now you're flying. Stick and thrust, stick and thrust. A bit of pressure on the toe pedals to keep it in trim, and you're off. Scan the outside, scan the inside. Keep yoour eyes moving. What are the instruments telling you? Many more instruments than other helicopters. What is outside the aircraft? Altitude, airspeed, trim. Pitch, power, roll, and trim. Engines, transmissions. See what's out there that may be a threat. A lot to keep track of, and it's essential that you do so.

They were trained on the Chinook by instructor pilots (IPs) of the 154th Aviation Company, permanently based at Fort Sill to transition pilots, support the US Army Artillery School, and perform disaster relief in the region.

The IPs trained them to hover the big aircraft on a sod area beside the runway at the airfield. They taught the transition pilots how to turn the aircraft around the front and rear rotor heads as well as on the center of the aircraft. Each of these maneuvers had its own special characteristics with a Chinook two counterrotating, three-blade rotor systems. The need for a tail rotor is removed with this system. It also eliminates the need to push in the left toe pedal when adding power. The aircraft is equipped with a SAS (stability augmentation system) that consists of three static ports on each side of the nose. They constantly measure differences in the static pressures and make minor adjustments to the rotors. Tandem rotor aircraft have an inherent characteristic where the aft rotor always wants to pass the front rotor. It will try to get there any way that it can. Up, down, sideways, or any combination thereof to get in front. The SAS system counteracts this and prevents the pilot from having to constantly fight the aerodynamics of the rotors.

Most of the IPs were really good. They had a lot of hours in the Chinook and were very familiar with the aircraft and the area. They had picked up a saying that Harry took to heart. "There are old pilots and there are bold pilots. There are no old, bold pilots." Harry took this to mean do not do anything stupid or take unnecessary risks. One of the IPs was a bold pilot and got himself killed trying to fly a Chinook back to his base in Vietnam with only one flight hydraulic system. Not a plan conducive to longevity. The other system failed, and he crashed into a tree stump that impaled him.

Most of Fort Sill is artillery ranges, so most of the training took place at either Henry Post Army Airfield, near the southeast corner of the main post, or at the Wichita Mountains Wildlife Refuge, located adjacent to Fort Sill on the north side. It is over fifty-nine thousand acres and has several mountains within its borders. It is home to free-range buffalo, Texas longhorn cattle, prairie dogs, elk, and deer. The high point is Mount Scott, which is 2,464 feet above sea level. Henry Post Army Airfield at Fort Sill is 1,189 feet above sea level so Mount Scott is a thousand feet higher than the surrounding area. A road goes to the top, and cars usually parked there, so we did not use that as a pinnacle very often. However, if we were out early in the morning, we would *buzz* across the parking lot on top at about 150 knots and twenty feet. This would really startle the lovers still there from the night before!

After getting down the very basic maneuvers, they went on to learn how to set the aircraft down on slopes. Left slopes, right slopes, front slopes, and rear slopes. As the Chinook hovers nose-high, setting it down on a front slope can simply be all four gear touching down simultaneously. Rear slope is a challenge. With a side slope, it is four individual touchdown points. They learned touchdown autorotations to the runway. While it can be done, it is all but impossible to set that big thing down without any forward roll. But with a little practice, it can be minimized to about half the length of the aircraft. Harry performed a zero-roll autorotation in a Chinook—once.

Then they started going out to the wildlife refuge to practice pinnacles and confined areas. There were several confined areas that were meadows surrounded by trees that were indeed confined. There was one pinnacle that wasn't much more than a finger sticking up. They had to be able to make an approach as though they were going to place a sling load on top. When you got into that position, you could no longer see the pinnacle, it was below the aircraft and behind the cockpit. It was excellent training for some of the places they would be going to in the mountains of Vietnam.

One of the confined areas was close beside some of the mountains. There was a small band of trees to the north, then the mountains. The trees surrounded the entire meadow. It was about three times as long and twice as wide as a Chinook. Plenty tight enough to learn in. They were taught to do a high overhead observation of the landing area to allow landing in the upper one-third of the space. Then they would proceed downwind of the landing area and approach into the wind with a touchdown approach. One day, with a CW3 IP named Rick Havenstrite, Harry was told to do a setup and approach to this area. Circling above, Harry observed it was clear, and the wind direction was from the west. He proceeded to the east of the area and began a normal approach, aiming at the imaginary line two-thirds of the way into the meadow. It was a beautiful approach. A constant line to the ground, lift the nose, let the aft gear settle in, aft cyclic to keep the gear in place, and reduce power to let the aircraft gently set down. Harry was proud of the job he'd done and looked over at Havenstrite sitting in the left seat. He said, "Pull her up." Harry did. He was about to ask why when this bull buffalo charged under the chin bubble. Had Harry not lifted the aircraft, he would have struck them in the right nose area. Rick said, "This is a really nice practice area for a confined area. However, that buffalo thinks it's his and will charge anything in it. When you land here you have to be prepared to leave quickly." Several days later the same scenario happened to Andy Belmont. He also did a great setup, approach, and landing. However, when the IP said pick her up, Andy looked at him and asked why, knowing that he had done everything correctly. That was about when the buffalo hit the right avionics compartment at the front of the fuel cells. Several thousand dollars of damage and a lesson learned.

One morning, CW2 Rick Havenstrite and Harry were out practicing. Havenstrite told Harry that that today was the day to fly with the SAS off. Oh-oh. He had Harry fly straight and level, then he reached over and flipped the SAS switch to Off. Everything was OK for about two seconds, and then came the back end trying to pass the front up and to the right. Correcting this, Harry found that now it was trying to pass to the lower left. No matter what he did, the aft rotor was always trying to pass the forward rotor. Wrestling a greased pig came to Harry's mind. You can't wait for the aircraft to make any significant move. It requires full concentration and constant minor control adjustments. After about fifteen minutes of this—it seemed like hours—Havenstrite told Harry that he was going to turn the SAS back on. When he flipped the switch, Harry felt a bump in the controls as the SAS took over the minute adjustments to the controls. There was a lot more of this practice until Harry was at least semicomfortable with flying with no SAS. The theory was that if things got nasty in Vietnam and you lost the SAS, you should be at least OK with flying the aircraft. There may be a lot more going on that requires your attention. Harry practiced SAS off flying a lot in Vietnam.

Once the transition was complete, the pilots started flying regular as well as practice missions. The practice missions were taking loads to different locations, including pinnacles and confined areas. The loads were different objects that were salvage items for different weights. The heaviest was the barrel from a 175 mm Long Tom self-propelled howitzer. These were good practice missions.

Other missions were in support of the artillery school. This way both the pilots and the new artillery officer candidates would get experience sling loading 105 mm howitzers. They would tow the cannon to the sod area at the airfield, rig it with slings, and attach the basic load ammo bag. The pilots would hover up to and over the gun. One of the artillery men would climb up on the barrel of the gun and put the "doughnut" for the slings on the cargo hook. This was very demanding and precise hovering. At a hover, the cargo hook is about twenty-five feet behind and five feet below the pilots. The pilots had to get directions from the FE (flight engineer) or CE (crew engineer) to line up the cargo hook over the gun. The artillery men had a grounding stake and a wand to short out the static electricity from the aircraft. If they did not do this and the hook came in contact with skin, the shock would literally knock the man off the gun. The FE would tell the pilot when the load was hooked and guide him up to get the slings tight. More power and liftoff. Then they would have to hover sideways to get over the ammo bag, as it was rigged to hang under the cannon. More guiding and another lift. This was very valuable training for the pilots to learn where the hook they couldn't see was located. Many times they would simply circle the sod area and return. After setting the load back down, another group would take over getting the gun hooked up to the aircraft. One day, Harry was watching other pilots do this. The gun crew failed to ground the hook. Sure enough, the guy grabbed for the hook to attach the load. He landed about six feet from the gun.

Flying in the area around Fort Sill was generally very good. On a bad day, we had about forty miles of visibility. The only bad times were when the occasional thunderstorms would come through. You do not want to tangle with a thunderstorm!

# Firefighting

Some of the more interesting missions involved firefighting. In the summer, things would get pretty dry, and occasionally the artillery would start a fire out on one of the ranges. One of the FEs had designed and built a large conical bucket. It had portholes along the side that had large removable plugs. These could be removed to control the amount of water the bucket would hold. Depending on the density altitude (air pressure, temperature, and humidity), the amount of water in the bucket would vary. It was possible to get more water in it than the aircraft could lift.

The bottom of the bucket had butterfly doors that opened upward and were connected in to the aircraft systems so the pilot could dump the water on the fire. The water would drain out rather quickly. These are the same type of buckets invented at Fort Sill, are the ones that the civilian firefighters now use for fighting forest fires. Once a load of water was dropped, the aircraft was flown to a reservoir, the doors were opened, and the bucket was dunked to refill it. After closing the doors, another trip to the fire was made.

One night Harry was called out to put out a fire on the northwest range. Flying at night in rugged terrain is not a lot of fun. It is very challenging and requires 110 percent concentration. Most people do not know how dark it gets when you are away from all lights. It is *black*.

Filling the bucket from the reservoir in the dark was a new challenge. The pilots used their landing lights to help determine where the water was and surrounding obstacles. Flying over a fire in the daytime presents challenges with the updrafts and downdrafts created by the fire as well as the natural drafts from the mountains. At night, with the lowering temperatures, it is even worse. As you stay fairly high above the fire to drop the load, obstacles are lessened. However, there were small mountains or hills that were higher than Harry wanted to be to have maximum effectiveness for each water drop. After several trips and a lot of bouncing around the sky, the fire was knocked down to where the ground crews could mop it up. Harry had a highly educational evening but was very glad it was over. Perhaps this was a portent of all the night flying Harry would do in Vietnam.

# Firepower Demonstration

Each year the army artillery school hosts a firepower demonstration, presented in conjunction with the US Military Academy (West Point) cadets' rotation through Fort Sill. The cadets go around to the different bases to be impressed by representatives of the different branches in the army who want to attract them into their specific branch. They spend a couple of weeks with the infantry, artillery, armor, and others. The artillery takes the opportunity to invite a variety of other VIPs to attend. Perhaps most notable are the foreign military attachés from the various embassies.

There is a civillian in charge whose sole job seems to be setting up the demonstration once a year. He coordinates all the participants and narrates the actual demonstration. The demonstration is held on the edge of one of the ranges. There is a flat area immediately in front of the grandstand for display of each piece of equipment. Farther out there is a firing platform for actual firing of the different weapons. The presentation starts off with a 105 mm towed howitzer being pulled up onto the display area while another is taken to the firing platform. While the farther weapon is being readied to fire, the narrator goes over the parts of the gun with a soldier at the gun, pointing out these various parts. Upon completion of the description, the farther weapon is fired. The audience can observe the impact of the shell fired. This is repeated with the 155 mm towed howitzer, the 155 mm self-propelled, and the 175 mm Long Tom self-propelled. The finale is the Honest John missile. This is a rocket capable of delivering a tactical nuclear weapon mounted on a military five-ton truck with a launch rail that elevates for firing. After the missile is launched, a nuclear simulator is detonated back in the mountains to simulate the delivery.

With the advent of airmobility, the artillery developed an airmobile 105. It used the same ammunition but was a lighter version of the towed howitzer. When they added this weapon to the demonstration, they put it in right after the towed 105. Harry was picked to do this mission. To accomplish this he had to pick up the gun and crew early and take them behind a ridge near the demonstration area. He set the gun and ammo bag down, then moved to the side and sat the aircraft down. They shut down the aircraft and waited and waited and waited. About a half hour before the time scheduled, Harry started the APU, which provided power to the radios, and checked in with the demonstration control. Everything was on schedule, and shortly before their appearance, they started the aircraft. Control gave them a two-minute warning, they hooked up the gun and ammo bag, and tightened the straps. On cue Harry picked up the gun and ammo bag and rose above the ridge. He flew to the firing platform as another airmobile 105 was towed to the demonstration area. He set down the ammo bag, moved slightly to the side, lowered the gun to the ground, and released it. He then moved farther over, set the aircraft down, and the gun crew ran down the aft ramp to their gun and readied it for firing. Harry went back over the ridge and waited for the demonstration to end to go back and pick up the crew and gun, then return them to the post. Another interesting experience.

# On the Ground at Fort Sill

**M**ost warrant officer helicopter pilots were a rather raucous bunch of men. Some of the guys were quickly given nicknames that were very appropriate, in most cases. There was one called Cruddy Layne, and he was the couth officer, mainly because he didn't have any. Then they had Pissed Off Collings because he was spring-loaded to the pissed-off position. Harry came by his nickname a bit differently, however.

Among the extra duties that were assigned to the officers of the company, WO1 John Michael Weatherly (JM), was their mess officer. By the luck of the draw, Harry was assigned as the insect and vector control officer. He never understood how a rat or a mouse became a vector, but somehow they did.

At a pilots' meeting JM, the mess officer, stood and complained there was a rat at the mess hall. Harry was identified as the insect and vector control officer, and JM demanded that he get rid of the rat. Things were pretty busy, and Harry did not get to do any follow-up on the rat.

The army does not allow kill traps for rodents, as their parasites could then abandon the cooling body and spread germs and disease elsewhere. So, after being educated on the proper method of trapping the rodents, Harry and his NCO (non-commissioned officer—sergeant) went scrounging for live traps and an empty barrel. After they trapped the varmint, they were going to put in some water and a few ounces of JP-4 (jet fuel for the helicopters) in the barrel. This would form a skin on the surface of the water to hold in and kill any parasites. The live trap was then to be dropped into the barrel of water and JP-4. The rat would drown, and the parasites would do the same. Problem over. At that time they had just transitioned into the CH-47 and were spending a lot of time practicing field maneuvers to try to develop their skills in the Chinook. Amazingly enough, those duties had a higher priority than trapping rats did.

The next week at the pilots' meeting, JM again got up and complained that the rat was still in his mess hall. He accused Harry, jokingly of course, of looking out for his "brother rat." During his comments the term "rat" came up pretty often, so Harry was stuck with Rat as his nickname.

After the meeting, Harry went over to the mess hall, which would have been midafternoon by then, to look for evidence of the rat's nest. As he was looking under the mess hall near the side door, the mess sergeant came out with a small bowl and asked what he was doing. So, Harry told him he was trying to trap the rat that the mess officer had been complaining about.

At that point, the mess sergeant laughed and told Harry there were no rats around there. He explained that he had a pet ground squirrel (chipmunk) that he had been feeding. Then the NCO sat down on the steps and threw some of the morsels from the bowl on the ground, just under the edge of the mess hall. Sure enough, out came a chipmunk, and it started eating!

Harry waited for the next pilots' meeting to publicly tell JM that his rat was actually the mess sergeant's pet chipmunk. Then all the officers had a good laugh about the whole thing. However, the nickname Rat for Harry never lost its luster. He decided that if he was going to wear that nickname, then he would embrace it, especially around his military friends.

While the transition to the Chinook and forming a new unit was a lot of work, there was time for relaxation. Most of the warrant officers were single and lived on post in the BOQ (bachelor officers' quarters). There was no on post housing available for those who were married, so they rented places in Lawton, immediately adjacent to the south of Fort Sill.

The BOQs were quite comfortable. There was an entryway with a unit on either side. When the door opened, you were in a living room with a large picture window overlooking the parking lot and a kitchenette beyond with a small table and a refrigerator/sink/stove/oven unit on the inside wall. There were two bedrooms with a bath in between. Harry thought every one of the pilots was assigned a non-rated (not a pilot) roommate. Most of them were second lieutenants (2LT) and there to attend the artillery school. They thought they outranked the warrant officers, and technically, they did. However, with flight pay and prior service, most of the warrants made more money than they did. This upset them. So did the lack of respect for their rank. Many of these "butter bars" felt personally offended by the warrants. The pilots gave them good reason to. Several of the pilots would gather at Tom Andrews's BOQ for a beer after the duty day. They had a ritual where they would slap on the door twice and enter. Without saying anything they would proceed to the kitchenette, open the refrigerator, and take out a beer. After opening the beer and having a big swig, they would say hi to Tom and have a conversation. If the fridge were out of beer, the pilot or pilots would leave, again without saying a word, and go to the PX picnic store and bring back a case of beer, always Lone Star draft in cans.

One afternoon, Harry and one of the other pilots approached the door and went through the ritual. As they entered, a new roommate was just rising from the couch to answer the door. They proceeded to the fridge, which was empty, so they left. The new 2LT roommate just stood there with his mouth open, wondering what was going on. Upon their return, they completed the ritual. As Tom had gotten home, he introduced them to his new roommate. This one was from Kansas City and very proud of it. He even had a small plastic model of the Gateway Arch sitting on the coffee table and would tell anyone all about it, even if you didn't ask. This got pretty old so one of the guys painted it yellow and attached a McDonald's logo from a bag of fries. The roommate got a transfer to another unit.

The large front window was about three feet high by five or six feet wide. The guys started stacking the Lone Star beer cans in it. It was nearly full by Christmas. Tom's new roommate threw all the beer cans away while they were on leave.

One day on their way into the officers' mess, Mike Layne and Harry walked past a couple of 2LTs. They stopped after they'd passed, and one loudly said, "Hey, don't you salute commissioned officers?"

Without missing a beat, Mike hollered over his shoulder, "Yeah, majors and above, and captains by request." He turned back, and they proceeded into the mess hall.

The pilots with prior service got a bit tired of the 2LTs thinking they were hot shit. So they started saluting them on the way in and out of the officers' mess. Only they did it with their left hand. The 2LTs knew they had done something to them but none of them ever figured out it was a left-handed salute.

Several of the guys spoke highly of a restaurant in Meers, Oklahoma. Meers is a tiny town (three buildings) on the north side of the Wichita Mountains Wildlife Refuge. They just thought the catfish and hush puppies there were fantastic. One evening Harry went with Tom Andrews and several of the guys to see what all the rave was about. Catfish and hush puppies—you've got to be kidding! Good? That stuff was terrible! Catfish is a warm-water fish and mushy. It's a bottom feeder and tastes like mud. Eating catfish is like eating a deep-fried mud pie! And hush puppies? Corn meal rolled into a ball and deep fried. Greasy corn meal mush. Yuk! Man, that was a disappointment. Harry guessed that it was an acquired taste, one that he would never acquire!

Much more fun was had at the Blade and Wing, an officers' club annex near the airfield. The main O Club was a rather stuffy affair. Coat and tie required, unless you were a West Point Cadet. There was Fiddlers Green in the basement, but the Blade and Wing was much closer, and one didn't have to deal with the cannon cockers (artillery men).

One evening at the Blade and Wing, things were getting a bit raucous. It was full of pilots, mainly WO1s from Harry's unit and an aerial field artillery unit that was forming up to also join the 101st. Harry walked up behind one of these pilots he had been in flight school with. As he leaned on his right shoulder to tell him a joke, the guy threw a half-full schooner of beer in his face. He didn't stop the follow-through, and the schooner bounced off Harry's forehead. Harry was stunned and asked what the hell that was for. He said he though Harry was going to pour a beer on his head. The blow split the skin on Harry's forehead, and they went into the men's room to try to stop it. Didn't work. Harry wound up going to Reynolds Army Hospital Emergency to have it treated. No stiches, but several bandages worked. The doctor asked how it happened. Harry didn't want to use the old door ruse, so he said he'd hit it on a door closer. The doctor didn't believe him, but that's what went into the record.

The newly formed 293rd Aviation Company was changed to C Company, 159th Aviation Battalion, 101st Airborne Division, on 24 July 1968. The training continued along with field tests and with support from the artillery school. The initial C models had beefed up transmissions to carry the load of a newer Lycoming engine. However, the engines were not yet in production, so they had a C- aircraft.

The pilots were asked what they wanted their call sign to be on the radio while they were still the 293rd Aviation Company. Being rather irreverent, they came up with Playtex. This was the era of "the living bra." They were told it would be changed when the unit went to Vietnam, but it wasn't.

All during this time, the unit was preparing for deployment to Vietnam. They were fortunate to have a CW2 named Gehling. They called him Papa Pickle because years before, when forming up with the 1st Cavalry Division, he dropped—"pickled"—a blivit of gasoline into a fish farm. Not good for the fish. Nor for the army who had to pay for the fish and the cleanup.

The unit was allocated eighty-four steel boxes called conex containers. The army version is a steel shipping container capable of carrying nine thousand pounds. It is eight feet six inches long by six feet three inches wide by six feet ten inches high. That's just over 363 cubic feet of storage/shipping space. Papa Pickle was a great scrounger. He wound up getting everything the unit would need in Vietnam and then some. He even scrounged up some flush toilets. Never used them for their original purpose but did use one at a party. Papa Pickle was very familiar with the army supply system. He got a penciled requisition approved for four sheets of plywood. Only he had the written description as four sheets but the part number of a skid (pallet). When he got to the supply point they checked the number. When questioned about the discrepancy, he told them someone had made a mistake, erased the written "sheet" and replaced it with "skid." They magically had four pallets of half-inch plywood for Vietnam. Harry was told the unit left Fort Sill with more conex containers than any other unit bound for Vietnam.

On 15 October there was a command maintenance management inspection, a CMMI. This was a really big deal for the unit. The company scored the highest of any unit en route to Vietnam ever tested at Fort Sill. They were ready!

One of the final actions by Playtex at Fort Sill was a graded field exercise. The men were sent to a field north of Fort Sill and set up operations in tents. The aircraft were lined up along a row of trees. Daily missions were assigned to see that the company could operate under combat conditions.

One morning Harry was observing some aircraft preparing to take off for the missions. Eric "Rick" Van Opstal was in one of the aircraft. As he was hovering to his left to get clear of the trees and other aircraft, a huge pink cloud came out of the back of the aircraft. As hydraulic fluid is pink, Harry knew immediately that they had a major malfunction of one of the hydraulic flight controls. Rick hovered the aircraft back to its parking slot. Just as he got the aft gear on the ground, another huge pink cloud appeared. The other flight hydraulic system had failed! He reduced power and successfully got the aircraft on the ground without further incident. Excellent testimonial against flying a Chinook on one flight hydraulic system!

# On to California

O n 8 November the unit's aircraft departed Fort Sill. An advance aircraft was sent on the seventh, and the other fifteen left the next day.
When the company aircraft left Fort Sill, the CO, Major Adamcik, had
fifteen in formation of five Vs of three and did a low pass over Fort Sill.
Quite impressive, and it rattled a lot of windows!

Harry was flying with Gene Pissed Off Collings. The unit refueled at
Lubbock, Texas, and then flew on to El Paso for the night. When they
landed for refueling at Lubbock, Texas, a hydraulic line ruptured on
start-up. A replacement hose was flown in from Fort Sill the next morning. The aircraft was repaired, but now they were a day behind the main
flight. During the flights, two other aircraft developed mechanical problems that had to be addressed. They waited for Harry to catch up, and
the three proceeded to Bakersfield, California, to meet up with the rest
of the aircraft on 10 November 1969.

The second day, the flight went on to Phoenix while Rat and Pissed
Off were trying to catch up with them. During this stretch Mike Maloy's
aircraft showed a chip detector light. This is a sensor that finds metal
chips in the transmission oil. Not a good thing. He did an emergence
landing to check it out. All was well with the transmissions it was only
small metal filings. However, he had landed in an open area just south
of the border – with Mexico. Yup, WO1 Mike Maloy and crew invaded
Mexico on 9 November 1969! The flight went from there to Bakersfield,
California.

Harry was leading the flight of three into the last ridgeline before the coast. They were cruising at about one hundred knots when a single-engine, fixed-wing aircraft came up and started slowly circling the flight. The two people on board seemed to be showing off. This pissed off the rotor jocks. As they headed up the last valley, Harry had the flight increase speed and get above the fixed-wing. By then the valley was fairly narrow, and the fixed-wing must have had a fun time trying to get turned around under them before running into the ridge. Smart ass!

As they crossed the ridgeline, the ground disappeared. Smog! Thick stuff you couldn't see through. They could just make out the outlines of buildings directly below them. Harry had the flight circle while he called Bakersfield tower for assistance. The tower said that it was a good day. Visibility was three-quarters of a mile. Harry told him they were flying helicopters in from Oklahoma where on a bad day you could see forty miles! He laughed and told Harry to go due west to the big highway and turn north. He gave him the distance to the airfield and said it was on the west boundary of the highway. Harry took the flight over to the highway, then north. They could see the border fence for the airfield and the approach end of the runway. They all landed without further ado.

Harry and his flight of three had landed at Bakersfield just a few hours after the main body. On the eleventh, after waiting for the weather to clear at about 1330 (1:30 p.m.), they all proceeded on the last leg of thirty miles or so to Sharpe Army Depot. There they left the aircraft and the twenty-four men who would remain with the aircraft to get them ready for shipment to Vietnam. Harry and the rest of the pilots and crews took a bus to San Francisco International Airport for the flight back to Oklahoma.

All this took place within about seven months. Very busy time. Highly educational and mostly enjoyable. Harry and the Chinook got along just fine.

# PHU BAI AND CAMP EAGLE

The C Company Playtex area was on the southern edge of Camp Eagle, home base for the 101st Airborne Division (Airmobile). This was about eleven kilometers (seven miles) southeast of Hue, the old Imperial capital of Vietnam. Hue is only twenty-eight kilometers (seventeen miles) southeast of the DMZ (demilitarized zone, or border with North Vietnam). It was located in Thau Thein Province in I Corps, the northern area of the Republic of Vietnam. The helipad was still under construction/expansion, and the company area was still being built. Seabees were constructing barracks (hooches), a mess hall, and administrative buildings. The hooches were not completed, but they moved in anyway. The men assembled cots, opened their sleeping bags, and tried to settle in for the night.

The following day the men got to have a look around. Not much. The company area was being built. The Seabees were doing a great job. Some of the guys who had some construction experience helped them put the galvanized metal sheets on the rafters for a roof. Many of them just wandered around, trying to stay out of the way.

Some of the men went over to take a look at the helipad. It had evidently been used by the 1st Air Cavalry Division when they were in the area. There was a half-collapsed bunker near the corner closest to the company area. The helipad was being renovated to accommodate the Chinooks and an AH-1 Cobra gunship company. The aircraft had been flown by the company pilots to Stockton, California, in early November for processing at Sharpe Army Depot. The aircraft had the blades removed and wrapped in a protective cocoon for loading on the flight deck of a US Navy aircraft carrier. Upon arrival at Da Nang Harbor, they were unwrapped. The blades were restored, the aircraft was readied, and they were ferried to Phu Bai by advance party personnel who went with the aircraft. All sixteen Chinooks of the company were now on the helipad. C Company had gotten all its aircraft directly from the Boeing Vertol plant in Pennsylvania. They were sequentially numbered from 67–18499 through 67–18515, sixteen aircraft in all. As each aircraft was readied, a crew was sent from Fort Sill and ferried the Chinook back. Harry was not selected to go on any of those trips.

At Phu Bai it was the monsoon (rainy) season. There was a low overcast of solid cloud cover leaving everything looking pretty much gray. There did not seem to be much aerial activity going on.

The pilots were told that they would be sent to A and B Companies to receive their in-country orientation. While waiting for that to happen, there was a company party one evening. Six or eight Korean tech-reps (technical representatives) for Ford Motor Company wanted a ride to Da Nang. This would be much safer than a road convoy down Highway 1, known as the Street without Joy. The 84.5-kilometer (52.5-mile) trip was very dangerous. Especially as over half of the trip was along the cliffs of the mountains where they went to the South China Sea. In exchange for the ride, they barbecued a potbellied pig. Don't know where the pig came from or who paid for it, but the Koreans set it up on a spit over a fire in the afternoon to cook it. By the time it was near ready it had gotten dark. Captain Cooper, the company operations officer approached Harry and asked if he'd had anything to drink that evening. Harry held up a can of Coke and said, "Not yet." Cooper asked if he'd like to fly right seat (pilot) to Da Nang to take the Koreans down there. Of course Harry jumped at the opportunity to fly.

Harry and the AC (aircraft commander) preflighted the Chinook and got the Koreans on board. They took off and headed south. The AC called for any artillery warnings, and all was clear. Every flight required clearance from artillery warning. They would provide the pilots with grid coordinates for the origination of the fire and grid coordinates for the impact location. One did not want to fly through any of this artillery fire! When they got to altitude, the AC gave Harry the controls and called Da Nang radar for clearance and routing. It was night and cloudy, monsoon season. They were flying in and out of clouds but were on radar. As they neared Da Nang, they popped out of yet another cloud, and huge tracers came across the nose of the aircraft from right to left.

Now tracer rounds going by will definitely get your attention. In the daylight an AK (7.62 millimeter) tracer looks about the size of a pencil, at night the size of a baseball. A .51-caliber round in the day is about the size of your thumb; at night it's a softball. This stuff was forty millimeter! It looked like meteors coming at them! Harry bottomed the pitch and pulled the nose up to stop from going into the tracer stream. He turned the stick right and pushed right pedal to turn around 180 degrees. Then he pulled pitch back in, rolled over the nose, and ducked back into the cloud. This was NOT a maneuver taught in flight school or transition! Just then the radar controller called and asked them to state the type of aircraft they were. The AC told him, "Charlie Hotel four seven." Radar came back and said, "OK, I wondered how you turned around that fast." The AC told him what happened and asked if he knew what was going on. Radar said the there was a "duster" (twin 40 mm cannons mounted on a Sherman tank frame) that fired out onto the AU peninsula (the only part of Vietnam that extended into that map grid zone), and it was not big enough to warrant an artillery warning. The AC told him that when you were up here, and it came across your path, it was plenty big enough to warrant a warning!

They continued the flight to Da Nang and returned to Liftmaster Pad. Two interesting things. One, somehow this flight never got into Harry's flight records. Two, his first flight in Vietnam being at night was a portent of things to follow. Harry wound up being the high nighttime pilot in the battalion. Not something one wants to do. Flying at night in the mountains of I Corps with virtually no navigational aids is not conducive to longevity.

# Pachyderm and the Rat

Harry was sent over to B Company (Varsity) for his in-country orientation. They were located on the side of a hill in Camp Eagle. There was no helipad, just separate landing sites with revetments large enough for a single Chinook. The revetments were two sets of two banks of steel planking filled with sandbags. The aircraft would land between these to give them some protection from shrapnel from mortar or rocket attacks. The hillside lent itself to them having a nice outdoor amphitheater for movies and shows. The officers' hooches were two parallel buildings with a common walkway that contained separate two-man rooms. This was basically four walls, a ceiling, and a door. The rooms were about twelve feet wide and sixteen feet deep. The wall had been removed from two of these rooms near the center of one building and made into an O Club (officers' club). There was a bar of about eight feet in length by the left wall and a couple of refrigerators. There was a mishmash of tables and chairs. The hooch rooms were two air force cots with mattresses and whatever additional furniture and comforts that could be scrounged or bought at the PX (post exchange—like a department store).

Harry flew with two IPs (instructor pilots) for the orientation. Due largely to the weather and the 101st just getting into the area, there was not a lot of real estate to see. All of the supported FSBs (fire support bases) were along the coast and Highway 1. There were only two inland. One was an old marine FSB named Vehgel. The other nearby was named Zon (pronounced zahn) by the 101st from their World War II experiences in Europe (seen in the movie *A Bridge Too Far*). Harry noted that there were at least two marine and one 1st Cav helicopter wrecks on the perimeter of FSB Vehgel.

With the solid overcast, you couldn't get back into the valleys leading to the A Shau Valley or the Khe Sahn plateau. The ceiling was between two hundred and three hundred feet, so you were constantly fairly close to the ground and subject to ground fire. Fortunately, no hits were taken during the orientation flights. Most of the sorties were taking 105 mm artillery ammo, small-arms ammo, C rations (canned meals), and sundries to the FSBs. Harry enjoyed the flying and learning the new area. It was very different than flying in the States.

One evening, while in the O Club, Harry heard an explosion. He knew it was incoming, so he crouched down and headed for the door. At the lower end of the hooches there was a bunker, and all the pilots were heading for it. It had an L entry to the left so an explosion outside would not send shrapnel inside. Once inside, there were benches along each side wall, and it was soon fairly full. About the time Harry hit the bunker, the warning siren went off, telling everyone there was an attack. Harry and the others had figured that out from the rocket explosions. After they'd been in the bunker about ten minutes and long after the last rocket hit, they heard a shuffling coming in the entrance. Then a thud and some cussing. A few of them got up to see what was going on. There in the entry was Harold. The Harold. The doofus who should have never made it through flight school. He was wearing his underwear and flip-flops, a flack vest, and a steel pot (helmet). He was carrying an M-16 and a bandolier of ammo. What he thought he was going to do with that during a rocket attack is anyone's guess. But that was Harold! He had tripped over his flip-flops and landed on the steel plating that was the floor of the bunker.

Harry met Harold in primary flight school at Fort Wolters, Texas. They were in the same company but different platoons. The company was split in two by type of trainer flown, and then each of those groups split alphabetically, forming four platoons. One platoon would be in class while the other was at the flight line. The second half of the day they would switch. There were two guys who were real foul-ups, Albert and Harold. One had to wonder how they even made it past the preflight portion of the training. Albert bunked a couple of rooms down from Harry. The company had a chance at a weekend pass if they could pass inspection on Saturday morning. They knew that Albert could not make it, so several of the men went into his room to help him get his gear in order. After an hour or so of working on Albert's gear, Harry went down and got Cokes for himself and the five other guys working on his room.

On the way back, Harry walked past the day room and saw Albert playing pool. Here they were, trying to help this guy out, and he's shooting stick in the day room! Harry went back to Albert's room and had the others follow him back to the day room. He pointed at Albert and said that he was done. He would not help him out again. As it turned out, neither did anyone else. He lasted about another two weeks before he washed out.

Now Harold proved himself to be a certified idiot. He was training in the Bell H-13 Sioux. This was one of the Korean War-era bubble helicopters. It had a three-man bench seat across the cockpit with controls at the center and left stations. To keep the CG (center of gravity) within limits so the aircraft could fly, there were three locations in the open grid tail boom to place the battery as a counterweight to the pilots. The more men in front the farther back the battery was placed to keep the aircraft near level. One day Harold was assigned to fly solo. As he was preflighting it, he noticed the battery was in the rear position. He figured that was wrong and called one of the civilian mechanics over to move the battery to the forward station. The mechanic told him that it was OK where it was. After a brief discussion, Harold told the mechanic that he'd show him it wouldn't fly with the battery where it was. He started up the aircraft and lifted it off the ground. With the CG out of limits, the aircraft began moving backward, and full front stick would not correct it. Harold moved backward about forty feet before he put it on the ground, sliding backward. He was fortunate that he did not run into anything or catch the rear cap on the skids and tip over. He knew the aircraft wouldn't fly and flew it anyway. Now that's stupid. Rumor had it that his father was the last flying NCO (non-commissioned officer) pilot in the U S Navy. He had to have something going for him. It certainly wasn't him. Rumor also had it that he did not receive his aircraft commander orders in Vietnam until after he was grounded to rotate back to the States.

Oh, and to top it off, Harold received a Purple Heart for stubbing his toe going into the bunker!

Harry flew three days—9, 11, and 12 January—with Varsity, getting his in-country orientation and a check ride in the B model Chinook. He passed and was returned to Playtex. As he was already qualified in the A and C models, he was now qualified to fly any of the Chinook models. He flew the remainder of the month with Playtex doing resupply missions to the FSBs along the coast and Highway 1, Camp Sally, Camp Evans, FSBs Roy and Tomahawk, and inland to FSBs Zon and Vehgel, about twenty-three clicks (kilometers) southwest of Hue. At the time, the 101st had a fairly small AO. Pretty much a triangle of sixty-five kilometers (forty miles), going inland at one point about forty kilometers from the South China Sea (twenty-five miles). This was about thirteen hundred square kilometers, or five hundred square miles. It would increase to over four times that area, six if you included the area in which he supported the marines. Other that the lousy weather and low-hanging clouds, it was uneventful. The clouds would force the helicopters to fly at two hundred to three hundred feet, well within small-arms fire. Nothing happened, but it kept him nervous. He only flew 12.6 hours during January. Lousy weather!

On 1 February 1969 there was a major shuffle in the battalion. The powers that be did not want all the newbies together, nor did they want an entire unit with the same DROS (date rotated overseas) and all going home together. So they moved Harry along with CPT Dickey, 1LT Cuda, CW2s Parrish and Gehling, and WO1s Andrews, Belmont, Hines, Powers, Sheff, Such, and Weatherly to A Company, Pachyderm. At the same time they moved 1LT Ailes, and CW2s Bolt, Eckert, Herrick, and Murkland from B Company Varsity. That was seventeen new pilots into Pachyderm although five of them had been in-country for a while with Varsity. A full complement in a Chinook Company is thirty-two pilots. This transfer was over half the pilots in the company. Given that several were in administrative roles (i.e., CO, operations and maintenance officers), rather than flying positions, it made well over half of the pilots new to the company and almost half newbies!

# PACHYDERM BEACH

**A** Company, Pachyderm, was located on the northeast corner of the marine base at Phu Bai airfield. The area was the edge of the coastal plain and all sand. The company area was referred to as Pachyderm Beach, or simply The Beach, although there was no waterfront. There was a saltwater channel seven kilometers (just over four miles) east, and the South China Sea was 11.5 kilometers (seven miles) from the beach. The helicopter landing pad was just inside the perimeter wire with the parking revetments just beyond. The revetments were PSP (pierced steel planking—metal planking with holes in it) with sandbags placed in between. There were two walls, and the pilots would taxi the helicopters from the landing pad to between the revetments before shutting down the aircraft.

Beyond the parking area on the right was the maintenance area and the enlisted men's quarters beyond that. Straight ahead was the company area with headquarters, operations, supply, and so forth. The mess hall (meals) was between these buildings and the enlisted area. The officers' quarters were to the left front of the parking ramp. There were two hooches parallel to each other, about twelve feet apart and three feet off the ground. Two concrete sidewalks accommodated the buildings and the steps leading to each room. The pilots' rooms were about twelve feet wide by sixteen feet deep and had two air force beds—with mattresses! *Wow!* During Harry's first tour, a good night was one with a sleeping bag and a cot! At the end of each hooch closest to the company area and flight line were two rooms that were larger. These were to accommodate the field grade officers (majors and above). They were another four feet wider, were for single occupancy, and shared a small lavatory room along the front wall. No toilet, but a wash basin and a shelf. As all the pilots' rooms were full, and there were only three field grade officers in the company, Harry was assigned the second room in the left-hand hooch, closest to the landing pad.

Because the room was larger, they put three pilots in it, so Harry had Lowell Powers and John Such as hooch mates. They were all from Playtex and knew one another pretty well. Powers was a funny guy. He was always making others laugh at something. He had been an announcer at a race track in Phoenix before the army and had a lot of funny stories from that. He had been a Huey crewman first tour, and that provided more for his tales. Good guy. Such was fairly quiet and soft-spoken. He was married, and his wife, Nancy was a real joy as well. Intelligent, attractive, and loved to laugh. John had a good sense of humor but wasn't loud with it. Another good guy. Harry felt fortunate to have these two as roommates.

So now Harry was a Pachyderm, flying C model Chinooks out of Pachyderm Beach and rooming with a couple of excellent roommates. Harry was still a "Peter Pilot," not an aircraft commander. This meant he was not in charge of the aircraft and usually flew in the right seat. They had all turned in their one-piece overall-type flight suits when they left Fort Sill. This left them flying in their jungle fatigues: lightweight cotton pants with cargo pockets on the sides, a below-the-waist jacket with bellows pockets in front, and cargo pockets at the lower front. They wore their jungle boots, nylon and leather. Had any of them been involved in a fire, everything they wore would burn nicely.

February is into the monsoon season. Overcast, low clouds, and lots and lots of rain. There was one period of several days when no one flew. It rained so hard that you couldn't see the other hooch building when your door was open. It didn't do any good to run anywhere. You couldn't get any wetter than you would in the first few steps. The army poncho is designed to keep the rain off your head, shoulders, and torso. However, when it's raining like that, it carries all the water to your lower legs, and then it runs down in a torrent into your boots. One of the guys told Harry that it had rained fifty inches in four days. That's a bit over a foot of water a day! Harry did not find that at all hard to believe.

Right away there was a nice feature at the Beach. We had our own mailman. Larry Lurch Hines would get the mail for the officers every day.

Lurch had been an infantryman during his first tour. The mail seemed very important to him. It was probably quite erratic when he was a grunt, so he made up for that at the beach. He would get the mail in the afternoon if he wasn't flying, and if he was, he'd get it as soon as he landed. He'd bring it to the officers' hooches and put it inside their door. It was really nice. Harry never went to the mail room except to mail packages.

Lurch was given the nickname by Lowell Powers. He was built a lot like the Lurch on TV. Big, square-shouldered, and fairly soft-spoken. Lurch was another of the good guys. It was good to have him in the unit. Harry was glad he'd been transferred from A Company with the group who came over.

Harry learned that one of his former classmates from flight school had been killed. When Harry was platoon leader at Fort Rucker, he had some interesting characters in his platoon. One of these was a guy called Floyd—a certified screw-up. Harry didn't understand how he had made it this far with all the filters built into the system. Harry was trying to impress upon these young men that they needed to pay close attention to what was going on around them. On an almost daily basis Harry told Floyd, "Floyd, if you don't get your head out of your ass you won't make it two weeks in Vietnam." They graduated on 9 April 1968. Everyone got a thirty-day leave. This took Floyd to 9 May. Then Floyd would have gone to Vietnam through Travis Air Force Base, California. He'd have spent a day or two at Travis and lost a day at the International Date Line. This puts him in Vietnam about 12 June. Another two or three days in a replacement depot, probably at Bien Hoa, and then on to his unit, which

47

was B/7/17 Cav, 1st Cavalry Division. By the time he started flying, it was probably 18 June. He was killed on 24 June 1968. This is about twelve days in-country and no more than ten days in his unit. It seemed Floyd had not taken his head out of his ass.

# FLYING IN I CORPS

The 3rd Marine Division, based out of Vandergrift Combat Base, started Operation Dewey Canyon on 19 January. This would become very important to Pachyderm. They were moving south and west to interdict the supply lines of the NVA (North Vietnamese Army) into the north end of the A Shau Valley and then on to Hue/Phu Bai and Da Nang. The marines had observed work being done on Route 548 in the A Shau Valley and Route 922, its extension, into Laos. They had also seen as many as one thousand trucks a day on those roads. The marines knew that the first thing the enemy needed to do was move all the things of war. All their materials from the sanctuaries of North Vietnam needed to be brought down the Ho Chi Minh Trail and stockpiled before they could engage the forces of South Vietnam, including the marines and the 101st. They would pre-position their materials, then rush in troops to pick up the supplies and launch an attack. The marines wanted to stop this from happening.

Harry was happy, as he was back to flying, albeit not very much because of the weather. The first eleven days he had only five days of flying for a total of 10.6 hours. That changed on the fourteenth when he got 9.1 hours, including an hour of nighttime. Harry thought fighting fires at night at Fort Sill was dark. Nothing compared to Vietnam. If nothing else, you always had the light from the fire to see a bit by. In Vietnam, with overcast skies, it's like being in a closet—in a basement—with no windows—on a dark night. It is simply *black*. There is nothing outside the cockpit but *black*. When you are flying in the mountains, this can get really interesting.

As the marines were moving south to the north end of the A Shau Valley, the 101st was moving west to the northern area of the valley. They were rebuilding a road from Phu Bai through the mountains and into the valley. To do this they placed additional FSBs west of Veghel and Zon to protect the road and the men working on it. These also provided cover for the infantry units sweeping west to clear the area of NVA. First was FSB Cannon, about five kilometers southwest of Veghel, which was also on the road. FSB Cannon was located on a hill on the far side of a narrow valley. Beyond it was a higher ridgeline, then the A Shau. On the higher ridgeline was placed Eagles Nest, at 1487 meters, or 4879 feet, north of the road with FSB Berchtesgaden on the south side.

# FSB Vehgel and Rotorwash

Harry was flying a load into FSB Veghel one morning when the cloud cover was higher. He was able to have some altitude to avoid ground fire. At the time, Veghel was the edge of the army-controlled territory. Beyond it was Indian country. Harry had seen that there were at least two marine and one army helicopter wrecks on the edge of the perimeter. Harry wanted to stay as close to the FSB as possible as he descended to drop off the load. So he maintained his altitude until over the FSB and began what's called a "high overhead approach." That is where the aircraft corkscrews down in a tight circle. Harry began his descent, and on the second revolution, he flew into his own rotor wash! That was a shock. A lot of turbulence and a rapid drop in altitude. Harry quickly moved the stick, side-slipped out of the turbulence, recovered the aircraft, and put the load down on the smoke marker. Good lesson learned. He wouldn't do that again!

# AILES'S CIRCUIT BREAKERS

Harry had noticed something strange in the cockpit. At the back, upper end, of the overhead console there are circuit breakers for different electrical systems. Two of these were for the "beep" trim on the engines. On the thrust lever, operated by the left hand to change the pitch in the blades, are two rocker switches. One is #1 and #2; the other is #2. They control minor adjustments in the output of the engines and are controlled by AC (alternating current) power. Should they malfunction there are two toggle switches on the center console that are #1 and #2 beep trim and are DC (direct current) power. These change the engine power far quicker than the AC-powered switches. So, if the convenient switches on the thrust lever malfunction, you can use the DC-powered switches. However, when they are released, the AC switches will take over again. The cure is to pull the circuit breakers on the overhead console. What was strange was that the aircraft had about four inches of safety wire hanging from these circuit breakers with a washer on the end. Hmm. Wonder why they did that. It makes them a lot easier to get ahold of, but why had he never seen it before at Fort Sill, at Playtex, or at Varsity? Well, the first time he flew with Bill Ailes he learned why. Bill was short. Where he positioned his seat he could not reach the circuit breakers without releasing his seatbelt. Not a good thing. Harry thought it was actually a very good idea just for its practicality. It made the circuit breakers easier to find and easier to pull.

# Maloy Crashed

In February Mike Maloy crashed Chinook 67–18501. They were on final approach into FSB Cunningham when they experienced beep failure. The aircraft was bleeding off rotor rpm. Mike tried to release the load with the emergency switch on the overhead panel. This allows the air pressure that holds the cargo hook closed to bleed off, and the hook will fall open—eventually. Maloy didn't know it at the time, but if the switch were moved back to its off position, the bleeding of the air charge would stop.

The load pulled the aircraft into the FSB, and they crashed. Maloy suffered from spinal compression and was evacuated to the hospital ship *Repose*, which was on station off the coast.

Maloy was in Harry's flight school class and one of the original Playtex. He was another of the good guys, and Harry considered him a good friend.

Now, Maloy was a little guy. He seemed about five feet two inches tall, less than 150 pounds, and looked like he was twelve. Oh, yes. His dad was a general in the US Air Force. Maloy was also young. He was taken to Japan and then back to the States for further treatment and recovery. Upon release to return to duty, Maloy requested and was granted duty with Playtex. Because of his size, he had acquired the nickname Flea. When he got back to Playtex it was changed to Super Flea for having survived the crash and being able to return to flight status. Maloy was then on his second combat tour in Vietnam and still under twenty-one years old.

# TAC-E TO FSB CANNON

I t had been long day. Harry had been flying to the FSBs built to protect the road construction for the A Shau Valley road for over eight hours. They finished the day's missions just in time to refuel and get back to the Beach for a hot meal. Harry was really looking forward to a cold beer—until he found that he was on Tac-E standby. Each night one Chinook and crew would be placed on standby for any tactical emergency that might arise. These missions were deemed more important than the aircraft or crew. That meant that they were supposed to be reserved for situations of dire need. The operative word being "supposed." That did not always happen.

Harry proceeded out to the aircraft to meet the crew and preflight the Chinook so it was ready to go if something should come up. The full crew was there checking everything over for themselves when Harry arrived. He went through the pilot's preflight with the FE (flight engineer, the enlisted man responsible for the aircraft's maintenance). Everything checked out, so Harry climbed into the cockpit and performed the checklist there as well. He started the APU to make sure the flight controls were working well. Everything checked out, so he shut it down and thanked the crew. He told them he hoped to not see them that evening. They agreed.

Harry then went to the O Club to have a cold soda and talk with the other pilots. Around 2000 (8:00 p.m.) the field phone rang in the club that connected to operations. A Tac-E had been called. Harry and the AC (aircraft commander), who was also drinking soda in the bar, left to go to operations and get the details. They were to go to the resupply pad at the southwest edge of Camp Eagle, pick up a load of 105 mm (millimeter) ammunition, and take it to FSB Cannon, installed to protect the road the 101st was building to the A Shau Valley.

Harry and the AC looked at their tactical maps to confirm the best way to get to FSB Cannon in the dark. While they had both been there before, they still wanted to see the map, as things are very different in the dark. FSB Cannon was beyond the road construction area and would fire to the east to protect the engineers building the road. They knew it was in the mountains and found it on the map as being about halfway through the mountains where they are narrow at the western edge of a large coastal valley. The valley started out quite wide with a large old Buddhist cemetery at the head. This cemetery had obviously been used by the wealthy from the old imperial capital of Hue. There were some huge monuments there, mostly of Buddha. There was one that they referred to as the "Sleeping Buddha," as the monument was of a prone Buddha and quite large. It was very easy to spot when flying over the graveyard. The Buddhist graves had a small circular wall of about three feet in height and an opening to walk into the site. Outside the opening was another wall that was straight and in front of the opening, so one would have to step around it to get to the entrance. This was to deny the "bad spirits," which had to travel in straight lines to access the grave.

Beyond the cemetery were FSBs Bastogne and Vehgel, left over from the marines and the 1ˢᵗ Air Cavalry with three crashed helicopters in the perimeter, and Zon. FSB Bastogne was about seventeen kilometers (10.5 miles) southwest of Camp Eagle and fairly centrally located in the valley. FSB Zon was about thirty-seven kilometers (twenty-three miles) southwest of Phu Bai and thirty kilometers (eighteen and a half miles) south southwest of Camp Eagle. FSB Vehgel was another four kilometers (2.5 miles) south of there. FSB Cannon was another seven kilometers (4.34 miles) beyond FSBs Zon and Vehgel. This was not really very far for a mission. However, the mountains started at FSBs Zon and Vehgel so FSB Cannon was in them a ways. The valley was fairly narrow by the time it got to FSBs Zon and Vehgel and was only a riverbed a couple of kilometers east of FSB Cannon. *Any* distance into the mountains was a long way!

They discussed the best way to get from Camp Eagle to FSB Cannon. They quickly agreed the best way was to go south from Camp Eagle and head for the middle of the valley. From there they'd turn west and head for the FSB. Harry suggested they have the pathfinder launch flares, so they could find it in the dark. They both knew it was going to be pitch-black out there. It was overcast, and there were no light sources out there. The AC agreed. They had a basic plan and went out to the aircraft, started it up, and took off for the short seven-kilometer (four-and-a-half-mile) trip west to the resupply pad. En route they called for any artillery warnings and found that no one was firing at that time. They hooked up the load and headed south, then west. As they entered the valley, Harry called the pathfinder and asked if they had mortar and hand-launched flares. He confirmed that they did. Harry told him to have a mortar tube pointed straight up, ready to send up a flare upon their request.

When they figured they were halfway up the valley, Harry called for a flare. There it was, straight ahead. Harry thanked the pathfinder and asked if they had any wind. He said it was all but dead calm there. Harry and the AC thought it best to approach straight in from the east, and after dropping the load go straight up, do a 180-degree pedal turn, and head back east, out of the mountains. Harry told the pathfinder their plan. He also asked that they get three red-lens flashlights to make a triangle marking where they wanted the load. The pathfinder confirmed that they would be ready.

The flare hit the ground and went out. They flew on for another five minutes, and Harry called for another flare. It again popped straight ahead. So far everything was going as planned. Just so it kept up that way. When that flare went out they again waited for five minutes, and Harry called for a hand-launched flare. Harry thanked the pathfinder and told him there was to be *no white light* at the FSB. It would ruin the pilot's night vision. The pathfinder confirmed they would use only red-lens flashlights. One more hand-launched flare, and they were there.

Harry told the pathfinder to have the flashlights turned and pointed at the aircraft. They spotted the flashlights. Three red spots directly ahead and below. The AC had already begun his descent into the narrow valley where the road was being built. He continued down and put the load in the middle of the three flashlights. Then he pulled in a bunch of pitch, and the aircraft went straight up rapidly. He did the pedal turn and lowered the nose slightly. They gained a bit of airspeed and a lot of altitude.

As they got back into the valley a ways, they could make out a bit of light from the Phu Bai airfield in front of them and Camp Eagle off to their left. They went back to Camp Eagle to refuel. This was also dark. The Chinook had two landing lights. They were normally stored flush with the bottom pointing straight down. When activated with a switch, they can be run out and rotated by use of a "Chinese hat" on the top of the joy stick. They both ran out their lights and turned them on. The AC set his light straight ahead as a landing light, while Harry used his as a searchlight, locating the refuel area and keeping the light on it as the AC maneuvered in for a landing. They left the lights on to provide some light for the crew to refuel the aircraft.

Refueling complete, they took off for the short flight to Phu Bai. They had turned on their navigation lights when they left the valley, but for added safety from other aircraft, they left the landing lights on as well. When they got to Pachyderm Beach they used their lights in the same manner to locate and land at their home helipad.

They landed and taxied into a revetment. Once parked, they shut down the aircraft and filled out the log book. It would have been really good about then to have a cold beer, but they were still on standby so had to settle for soda.

Even though Harry did not fly the mission, it was still nerve-racking to be out there in the pitch blackness, wondering if one of those mountains was going to reach out and slap you out of the sky. The second consideration was that Harry had not been in-country even two months, and this was his second night mission. He hoped it was not a portent for the future. Unfortunately, it was.

# ANOTHER TAC-E

Following a long day of flying, Harry was called out of Pachyderm Beach for another Tac-E (tactical emergency—the mission is more important than the aircraft and crew) night mission. The pilots and crew had performed a thorough preflight inspection while it was still light out. Operations had all the information on the mission. What they were to pick up and where, where to take it, and the radio frequencies and call signs for the contacts on the ground. They went from operations to the flight line and to the aircraft, checked with the FE that all was still OK, and strapped in. After going through the cockpit checks and getting the engines started, they went up to Camp Evans to pick up a sling load of 105 mm howitzer ammo for FSB Berchtesgaden. The resupply point informed them that they had time to "depalletize" the ammo. This meant they took it off the pallets and out of the wooden boxes, and it was loose ammo. The rigger told them that as the load was lighter, he added a fifth pallet to the normal load of four. So they had five pallets of ammo without any wood. The fifth pallet of ammo weighed more than all the wood, so the load was actually heavier, not lighter. Thank you very much! Now they are flying at night, in the *dark*, in the *mountains*, with a *heavier load*. Life was just about perfect!

There was no way to know where they were going in the dark, so they climbed to about six thousand feet to be over the mountains and headed southwest for the area they needed to be in. Harry radioed to the pathfinder at Berchtesgaden and asked if they had mortar and hand-launched aerial flares. The pathfinder confirmed that they had both. Harry told him to launch a mortar flare every ten minutes until told to stop and switch to hand-launched. The pathfinder said fine and that the first one was on its way. Both pilots scanned the sky in the direction of FSB Berchtesgaden. They couldn't see it. Nothing out there but *black*! After another ten minutes they spotted a glow almost directly in front of them. They'd made a good guess at where to go. The flares became bigger and brighter in the blackness as they neared the FSB. As all the higher ground was on the east side of the FSB, they went out over the A Shau and made a turn back in to the FSB. When they completed the turn and began descending, Harry told the pathfinder to stop the mortar-launched flares and go to hand-launched flares. Harry told him to get three red-lens flashlights to point up and mark where they wanted the load. They would place the load in the center of the three lights. In that darkness, the red would show up very nicely but not interfere with night-vision capabilities. The last thing they wanted was white light in the cockpit that close to the ground. The pathfinder said fine, but they would have to put it down on top of another load of ammo, as there was no other place to put it. Now isn't this just wonderful! There they are, on a *Tac-E*, at *night*, in the *dark*, in the *mountains*, with a *heavy load*, and the FSB has so much ammo they have to place this load on top of another. Just who the hell is in charge of this clusterfuck?

They found the three flashlights and placed the load between them, on top of the ammo already there; released it; and lifted off. On the way back, Harry called the pathfinder again and asked if they had any contact (with the enemy) missions. No. Did they have any contact (at the FSB)? No. Do you have your basic load of ammo? Yes, and then some. "Then why the hell did you call a Tac-E?"

He replied, "Don't know, sir. I did not do it or know you were coming." Wonderful, just fucking wonderful. As they headed back to the Beach, another Pachyderm who had been sent out as backup called. They told them it was a Chinese fire drill and to take the load back. They were all done playing in the dark.

Harry felt he was getting waaay too much night flying in those mountains!

# ARVN into Kerkle and Lurch's Aft Rotor

The guys who transferred into Pachyderm had been flying with their new outfit for only a couple of weeks. All were assigned to fly with different experienced ACs (aircraft commanders). They were to become familiar with the aircraft and its capabilities before they in turn would be named as AC. One day Lurch was assigned to fly with a CWO AC named Kerkle. One of their missions was to take a contingent of ARVN (Army of the Republic of Vietnam) out and drop them off on a ridgeline in the mountains. Not far into the mountains, just a little way. Harry did not think there were any "bad guys" in the area.

After going through the process of getting the aircraft started, they went over to the pickup point and loaded the ARVN troops into the main cabin. They had the FE tell the ARVNs to exit the aircraft to the sides and go downslope. The ARVNs were not to go to the rear of the aircraft.

They took the troops out to the designated drop-off point west of Hue and landed on a ridgeline. The only place to land was a saddle with an upslope to the front and rear. They told the FE to go behind the exit ramp and direct the ARVNs to the sides of the aircraft. This worked for all but one of the troops. This guy ran right past the FE, who tried to stop him from running up the slope behind the aircraft, but it did not work. The soldier ran straight back and up into the aft rotors. The first blade came by and took off his helmet. The second blade came by and took off his head. By the time the third blade passed, there was nothing left to hit.

The ARVN was of course dead. They loaded him into a body bag to return to the pickup point. Two of the blades were damaged, and the set of three had to be replaced.

# Building a Box at FSB Tomahawk

SB Tomahawk was the southernmost of the FSBs of the 101st. It was located on a small peninsula on the east side of Highway 1. In this area the mountains went right to the South China Sea. There was no coastal plain from just north of Tomahawk down to Da Nang. With the small number of FSBs that were open, there wasn't a lot of work for the Chinooks.

Harry felt fortunate that he drew a mission to resupply FSB Tomahawk. He went through the preflight with the AC. They started the aircraft and went over to Camp Eagle to pick up their first load for Tomahawk. It was four pallets of 105 mm cannon ammo. Off they went to Highway 1 and followed it down past Phu Bai to Tomahawk. Harry was flying, and as he'd not been there before, he gave it a good look on his way in. There was an access road from Highway 1. It actually only went through the perimeter wire, as the concertina extended nearly to the highway. Just inside the perimeter on the northwest was the resupply area. The cannons were on the east side, and the administrative area (sleeping, eating, headquarters, and so forth) was on the southwest side.

The AC had called the pathfinder and gotten the winds at the FSB. Harry could land to the southeast. Harry spotted the smoke grenade on the pad, and the AC confirmed the color with the pathfinder. He went in and dropped the load on the smoke. All went well.

So back to Camp Eagle for another load. Same routine. This time he had the smoke just past and to the right of the load they had just dropped off. Hmm. Why did he do that instead of starting at the far corner? Oh well, Harry dropped the load in just past the first load with no problem. Load two done.

Back for another load. Same routine, same route. This time the pathfinder put the smoke on the near side of the first load. Harry put the load on the smoke. Now there were three loads of four pallets each neatly lined up in an inverted U.

The next load was placed just outside the open end of the U. What he had done, in a convoluted manner, was build a box of loads of ammo. Harry had to wonder about two things: How bored was this guy to come up with this plan, and what was he going to do with the next load, which was his last? Another hmm. So what's next? He now had four loads of four pallets each. Probably a week's supply for the artillery there.

Harry had a hunch that turned out to be accurate. When they came back with the last load, the smoke was in the center of the box. He wanted the load stuffed in the middle of the other four loads already there. That's what Harry did. It really was not difficult for him to plant the load in the center of the box. As they again departed to the southeast, Harry went out a bit farther over the water and turned to see the finished product. There was a very nice, neat box of ammo on the resupply pad, with smoke coming out of the center—not colored marking smoke, but burning nylon and wood smoke. The smoke grenade for the last load started a fire at the bottom of the load. The pathfinder and several others were scrambling over the ammo trying to get at the fire before it got to any of the ammo. Maybe the cute plan wasn't such a good idea.

## At the Beach
## Nomex Flight Suits

Sometime in March the Pachyderm pilots and flight crew members received the new Nomex flight suits. In the States Harry had flown in cotton coverall flight suits. They were chemically treated, one-piece flight suits with a lot of pockets for easy access in a cockpit. When Harry got to Vietnam, they were flying in jungle fatigues and boots. The lightweight uniform and the nylon-topped boots were highly flammable; should a flight member be involved in a crash involving a fire, there was no protection. Nomex changed this. The Nomex two-piece flight suit had several unique characteristics. First, and most important, it was highly flame resistant. It had a lot of pockets. One on each calf, a double pocket on each thigh with a zipper on either side to access the two pockets. Front and back pants pockets. Two front pockets on the shirt with an additional pocket on the left sleeve with pen slots. The second thing about them was that when it was hot and no breeze, they were *hot*. For some reason they seemed to trap the hot air inside and magnify it. However, if it were cool and there was a breeze, it went right through them, and one would freeze. Finally, when one sweated in them, whether from the temperature or what was going on, they stank. They had a unique and foul odor that would come on quickly with any type of sweat. The flame resistance made the other items of little concern.

# Mess Hall

The food in the mess hall wasn't bad, just consistent and boring. Breakfasts were good, as Harry really didn't expect a lot of variety. However, the dinners and suppers all seemed to be some version of roast beef. Now there are a lot of things that can be done with roast beef, but it's still roast beef. It does get old eating many variations of the same thing. One day they had mutton. Harry was glad that only happened once! No wonder the Aussies were tough. Eating that stuff regularly would certainly do something to you. Another day they had liver. It was like trying to eat boot sole and about as tasty. Maybe that was done to make the roast beef look better.

The cooks were a good bunch and did the best with what they were provided for rations. Harry still liked C rations and was glad to have them as a change from *roast beef.*

# Fifty Inches in Four Days

It was early in the height of the monsoon season, or at least the rain from it. It was rumored that there were two typhoons out in the South China Sea stirring up a lot of precipitation. It rained every day. Sometime more than others. When it got to its maximum, Harry was told by one of the other pilots it had rained fifty inches in four days. He believed it! It was coming down by the bucketfuls. It had been raining so hard that Harry could just barely make out the hooch directly across the twenty-foot-wide courtyard area. It was coming down so fast that guys were taking showers in it. It wasn't hard rinsing off; it was hard to get the soap on in the first place!

For rain gear the army has this wonderful thing called a poncho. It is about a six-food square of rubberized material with a hood and drawstring, snaps along two sides to fold it over and snap together, and a short drawstring at the front to tighten it around your waist. This device is excellent at keeping the rain off your head and torso. It is also excellent for gathering the water and shedding it on your lower legs so it runs into your boots. Additionally, it is so airtight that it holds in your body heat very well, and your torso gets wet from the inside out with sweat. Wonderful piece of equipment. One can snap two together and have a decent pup tent. Or you can tie a poncho liner in it, snap the two sides together, and have a really decent sleeping bag. As a rain protector—not so good.

It was raining so hard that it did no good to run anyplace. You'd be soaked in the first four or five steps. The poncho would keep you fairly dry up top if you weren't going far, but your boots would be soaked, and there was no way to dry them out.

Of course there was not much flying being done at this time. Harry wondered if the rain would drown the engines. Probably. No one tried it.

One afternoon, when Harry returned from flying in the shitty weather, CPT Cooper was waiting at the edge of the landing pad. He asked how the missions had gone. Harry said, "Sir, I have a note from my mother saying that I don't have to go out and play in the rain." Cooper laughed, and they discussed the day's flight.

It finally let up a bit, and they could go back to flying the missions.

# ARROWS IN THE DARTBOARD

Harry was sitting at the bar in the O Club one evening, as usual. Several of the guys were playing cards at a table in the corner. Looking from the bar, they were in the right-rear corner with a dartboard on the left wall near the corner. They were all drinking and having a good time.

One of the other guys came in, went behind the bar, and made himself a drink. He finished that one in short order and made another. After one swallow, he went over to the other corner of the wall where the dartboard was located. There he picked up a bow and some target arrows that Pachyderm had acquired somewhere and returned to behind the bar. After a couple of more swallows of his drink he picked up the bow, nocked an arrow, drew it back, hollered, "Duck!" and let fly into the dartboard. The guys at the table playing cards had the sense to hit the floor with the warning. They picked themselves up and went back to the card game.

Several minutes later, another "Duck!" and another arrow went into the dartboard. Guys on the floor, then back up to their card game. This went on for a couple of hours. The card players would not move their table, although there was plenty of room to move it out of the line of fire, and the *archer* did not stop shooting arrows into the dartboard. Harry wasn't sure who was crazier, the *archer* or the card players!

# HARRY BUILDS A CLOSET

Papa Pickle was truly a great scrounger. He could come up with the goods, time after time. Harry had no idea how he did it, but he managed to scrounge a pallet of quarter-inch plywood. It was the Philippine mahogany wood that had a rough surface. Harry and his roommate, Such, liberated some to build a closet with a hot box in their room.

They had already scrounged some wood and built raised platforms for their beds. The extra elevation allowed for better storage space underneath.

In that very humid climate about the only way to get your clothes dry or keep them dry was in a hot box. The concept is simple. You put an incandescent lightbulb in the bottom of a closet, locker, or wardrobe. The heat generated by the lightbulb will dry out the air in the enclosed space and keep the contents dry.

Harry designed the closet to be built into the angle behind the lavatory room. It had two doors, each with a drawer below. The drawers were shallower than the cabinet to accommodate two light fixtures mounted to the floor at the rear of the closet. Harry tapped into the power to the room and ran a hot line to the closet. He got a couple of porcelain light fixtures and mounted them to the floor. To install them he had to unscrew a porcelain piece around the light base. This left the sharp edge of the brass female piece exposed. As Harry was finishing the mounting of the second light base, Such came into the room and walked over to take a look. As Harry was putting in the last screw, Such observed, "That looks awfully sharp. Be careful." Harry looked up at him and said, "No sweat,

I'm almost do...oh, shit!" His hand had slipped. He looked down at a large gash just above the first knuckle of his right index finger showing exposed bone before it filled with blood. After getting the blood to slow down and putting a bandage on it, he finished tightening the last screw.

They finished the construction of the closet. The light fixtures always had electricity, so all they had to do was have a bulb in them to keep their clothes dry. Nice!

Harry went to the company medic and had a stich put in to hold the wound together. The next day he tore it out while flying. Not such a good idea. From then on he just let it heal with Band-Aids.

There was some wood left over from the closet, so they made a nice wall-mounted desk in the right front of the hooch. It was large enough to accommodate both of them and their personal stuff.

# CRUDDY AND THE .45

One of the Playtex pilots had *acquired* a three-quarter-ton army truck. This vehicle is like a pickup truck with a bench seat in front and a truck bed in back. This one had the side rails, which also held fold-down bench seats. There was room for three in front and easily eight in back. He had gone to Pachyderm to see if any of the guys wanted to go over to Playtex and have a party. Several of the guys who didn't have to fly the next day thought it would be fun to see some of the old crew. Harry was one of these.

They all piled into the truck and headed for Camp Eagle and Playtex. When they got to the gate, the MPs had the traffic backed up and were checking papers. These guys had none. Not only was their having the truck unauthorized, their being outside the camp was also unauthorized. One of the guys hollered to the driver, "Go around and holler 'perimeter defense' as you pass the gate." So he did—and it worked!

When they got to Playtex, they went into the Playtex Living Bar. This was a small space at the end of one of the hooches. Having a battalion next door with an O Club that they wanted the pilots to patronize prevented them from having a nice bar. When Harry walked in, Pissed Off was standing at the bar. They chatted for a while, then Pissed Off asked Harry if he wanted a drink. He said he did, and Pissed Off asked Harry if he wanted to get drunk. Why not? So Pissed Off suggested Polish boilermakers. This was shots of Drambuie liqueur with beer chasers. They stood there at the bar drinking and talking with each other as well as the others in the bar.

By the time they were halfway through the bottle, they were both still sober. Pissed Off suggested they go to rusty nails instead of just Drambuie. A rusty nail was just a fifty-fifty mix of Drambuie and scotch. Harry thought this sounded good, so they started drinking this mixture with their beers.

By midnight they were pretty well plastered and went outside for some fresh air, if there was such a thing in Vietnam. As they were standing there talking, the flashing red lights of a tall ASA (Army Security Agency) antenna caught Harry's attention. He pulled out his .45 semiautomatic pistol, pointed it at the antenna, and said, "Bang! Bang! Bang!"

Just then, Cruddy walked up. He stated that he was the duty officer. Are you guys causing trouble?" He was being sarcastic.

Harry told him, "I'm just shooting out the red lights."

Cruddy reached out and pushed the slide of the pistol back a bit, rendering it inoperable. He said, "Go ahead and try it now."

So Harry jerked the pistol back and to the side and pulled the trigger. Cruddy ducked at the explosion. Harry wasn't sure who or how many there were, but he was tackled. Then the lights went out.

When he awoke in the morning, he found himself tied in a sleeping bag and could barely move. He certainly couldn't get out. He hollered until someone came in. They told him they had tied him up to protect him and them. He asked to be released to go the piss tube. He was, he did, and all was well.

## MARINES
### FLYING SUPPORT FOR THE CORPS

At the same time the marines had gotten into trouble. They had moved into FSBs south and southwest of Combat Base Vandergrift (Vandy), trying to clear the Song Da Krong Valley. The upper part of the valley is sixty-two kilometers (38.5 miles) west of Hue and forty-eight kilometers (thirty miles) southwest of Quang Tri City. It is remote, near the Laotian border, and accessible only by helicopter. The border runs south, then squiggles east, and curves back around to the southeast. There was a stretch about eight kilometers south of FSB Erskine where it runs close to east-west for about ten kilometers (six miles), then turns southeast for another thirteen kilometers (eight miles) before turning south at the west side of the A Shau Valley. At this last turn is Co An Nang Mountain, elevation 1,228 meters, or 4,029 feet, better known as Tiger Mountain. Nearby is what would become Hamburger Hill. They had re-opened FSB Henderson, ten kilometers (just over six miles) southwest of Vandy; then FSBs Shiloh, twenty kilometers (12.5 miles) south; and Tun Tavern, twenty-four kilometers (fifteen miles) south. On 24 January they opened FSB Cunningham on a ridge thirty-seven kilometers (twenty-three miles) south southeast of Vandy and followed with FSB Erskine, 41 kilometers (25.5 miles) south of Vandy and two kilometers (1.25 miles) south southwest of Cunningham. Then the weather closed back in. Some days it was solid overcast in the mountains. On others it was overcast with openings in the clouds called "sucker holes," as a pilot had to be a sucker to go down through one because it may well close back up. The marines were having a hard time resupplying these last two FSBs and asked the army for help. Harry couldn't tell if the problem was because RLOs (real live officers—commissioned officers) were flying the marine helicopters or because they relied too heavily on their sophisticated navigational aids. More on that later.

Harry was flying a lot with CPT Bill Ailes. Harry thought Ailes was a good pilot. He knew how to fly the aircraft and was a good AC in teaching Harry the tricks of the trade. Harry learned a tremendous amount about flying the Chinook in combat from Ailes and while flying with him. It seemed to Harry that a lot of RLOs were not very good pilots. He didn't know if this was because they thought they outranked the warrants who were trying to teach them and didn't listen well, or there was some other cause. Whatever the reason, it worked out that the best pilots were the warrant officers. Ailes was an exception. Ailes and Harry were taking a lot of loads of ammo and other materials to FSBs Cunningham and Erskine. During this time Harry realized he wasn't getting directions from the FE when hooking up loads. He would hover over the load, pretty much spear the doughnut with the cargo hook and bring the slings taut. As he was lifting the load off, the FE would call out, "Five feet, ten feet, twenty-five feet, cleared for flight."

The Chinook hovers with its nose high. This places the cargo hook about five feet below and twenty-five feet behind the pilots. The pilots cannot see the hook, they need to just know where it is. Also, the rear of the aircraft is much lower than the hook. So if a pilot hovers too far forward, the pilot will strike the load with the belly of the aircraft. Not good.

FSB Cunningham and FSB Erskine bear special notice. Harry learned a lot flying resupply into these two marine FSBs. A lot of avoidance flying, how to do really stupid things like fly down through sucker holes, and a lot about how to get sling loads hooked up and delivered.

FSB Cunningham was the larger of the two FSBs. It held two artillery batteries and was located on a ridgeline. FSB Erskine was located on a small hill.

FSB Cunningham's artillery was aimed to the west. FSB Erskine was much smaller in size, had a smaller log (logistics or supply) pad, and had fewer guns than Cunningham. It was also more exposed to enemy activity.

Harry's first experiences with FSBs Erskine and Cunningham came one morning when Ailes informed him that on that day they were flying up to a marine base and hauling resupplies out to a couple of the FSBs. Harry hadn't heard of Combat Base Vandergrift until that day. He knew the Third Marine Division was up on the DMZ. He did not know that they were based out of Vandergrift.

They took off from Pachyderm Beach early and headed up Highway 1. The weather was marginal with slightly broken overcast at a few hundred feet. They went north past Camp Sally and Camp Evans, the farthest north Harry had been until that day. They continued farther up to Quang Tri and ten kilometers (six miles) beyond. There they turned to the west and followed a river and a road out to just north of Vandergrift. Once at Vandergrift, they set the aircraft down and went to *ground* with the engines while Ailes got out and talked to some marines, obviously getting mission information from them.

Upon his return they returned the engines to *flight* and went over to the marine resupply area to pick up a load of four pallets of 105 mm ammo. Ailes turned the aircraft to the southeast past Vandergrift and started following a river valley. Harry watched the ground out his window to see if anyone was shooting at them. They were below the clouds and in a valley. This put them near the ground in three directions. Not a real good place to be.

Ailes went over a saddle in the mountains and followed another river valley farther south. Another saddle and another river. Yet another saddle and another river. All this while they were headed generally in a southerly direction. Finally there it was! FSB Cunningham off on their right side and above them. While FSB Cunningham is thirty kilometers south of Vandergrift they probably traveled over forty kilometers to get there. Ailes quickly slowed the aircraft, turned left, and called the path-finder. He was making a 270-degree left turn to gain a bit of altitude and give the pathfinder time to get a smoke out. As they started the turn, all that Harry could see of the FSB was the empty shell casings that had been tossed over the edge of the FSB and down the steep slope into the valley.

Ailes got the rotors into the clouds, Harry called the smoke, and Ailes proceeded with a very shallow approach to the resupply pad. He sat the load down on the smoke, released the cargo hook, and turned left, toward his side, maintaining his altitude. Just then Harry saw several marines scrambling for bunkers. He told Ailes what he saw. Ailes asked the pathfinder what was going on. He told him that they had a mortar that was zeroed in on the pad. When they saw a helicopter, they fired off a round. It would have been nice to know this *before* they approached the pad. The pathfinder informed them that it took four to four and a half seconds from appearing above the ridgeline until the impact of the mortar round. Harry thought *great*! It's like pulling the pin on a hand grenade every time you appear. Fortunately, the east side of the ridge dropped steeply into a fairly deep valley that you could hide in until you popped up to drop the load.

For the return trip, Ailes found a sucker hole in the clouds and climbed up above the cloud layer. They looked around and saw that there were a number of good-size holes in the clouds in the area. There did not appear to be any wind moving the clouds around, and they thought this might be a better way of getting the materials to the marines. They returned to Vandergrift above the clouds and found another sucker hole in the valley near Vandergrift. Ailes dropped down through it and turned the aircraft over to Harry. He proceeded to the log pad and picked up another four pallets of 105 mm ammo.

As they lifted off, Harry spotted a hole and asked Ailes if it was a good one. He approved, and Harry went through it and above the cloud layer. He then headed south.

# Pachyderm and the Rat

The army did not have any sophisticated navigational instruments in their helicopters. In fact, the only thing that worked for them was a non-directional beacon locater, a homing beacon, if you will. The marines had a system that would tell them exactly where they were. Must be nice!

Harry figured Bill had him flying to let him try to navigate by looking at the terrain through the holes in the clouds. It worked. He spotted a hole and told Harry to go down through it. Harry thought he recognized the patterns from their last trip. The holes did not seem to be moving much. This was a good thing.

Harry dropped down through the hole Ailes had designated and found they were again east of the FSB. Ailes had called the pathfinder, and there was a smoke that he identified. Harry told Ailes he was going to try going in below the ridgeline and pop up to drop the load. This would keep them concealed as long as possible. He told him OK but to watch the power carefully.

Harry pulled in the power to near the red line, keeping some power in reserve. At the same time, he turned toward the ridge where the FSB was located and dropped the nose to stay below the ridgeline. Ailes called the pathfinder for a smoke. One was popped, identified, and confirmed. They were fairly close to the ridge when Harry started the turn, so there was not a lot of acceleration before he brought the nose up and traded airspeed for altitude. As soon as he thought the load was above the ridgeline, Harry decreased the power, lifted the nose, and let the load swing forward and pull the aircraft down. Just before the load landed on the pad, Harry leveled the aircraft and added more power. The load did indeed pull itself and the aircraft to the pad. Harry could feel when the load touched down as the aircraft continued to settle in. He released the cargo hook and the FE immediately called, "Load clear!" He then added a lot more power and headed for the clouds. They did not see the mortar round explode on the pad, but the pathfinder confirmed that it had. When Harry broke through the clouds, he turned north to get another load.

Ailes and Harry spent the remainder of the morning repeating the procedure. They were joined by another Pachyderm. There were no marine helicopters to be seen. Ailes told the other AC what was going on and how they were getting around the weather and the enemy mortar. For safety purposes they agreed that they would not go up through a sucker hole, only down. That way there wouldn't be two helicopters trying to use the same hole to get through. They also agreed that when on top of the clouds, they would maintain at least two hundred feet above them so that someone coming up through the clouds wouldn't run into someone on top. When coming up through the clouds, they would immediately level off just above them and search for any other aircraft in the area. These safety procedures worked out very well for them. Not that dropping down through sucker holes or climbing up though clouds was all that safe. However, there were no accidents and no near misses using these methods. The ingenuity of army helicopter pilots to get the mission accomplished!

In the early afternoon, they were given a mission to take ammo to FSB Erskine. They found the coordinates on their tactical maps and saw that the terrain to the southeast of it had a fairly wide valley. They figured that if they could find a sucker hole over that valley, they could get into FSB Erskine. To aid with this effort, Mother Nature had seen fit to have the cloud cover raise some and for more holes to appear.

Ailes picked up the load and headed for the area of FSB Cunningham, as they were familiar with the holes in the clouds in the immediate area. Knowing that FSB Erskine was just a bit over a mile away made this the best course of action to locate a hole near the location of FSB Erskine, drop down through it, and find the FSB from under the clouds.

As luck would have it, there was a nice-size sucker hole just to the south of where they thought FSB Erskine was located and over the middle of the valley. They could see the stream in the middle of the valley. Ailes dropped down through the hole as Harry called the pathfinder, notified him of their approach, and called for a smoke. The pathfinder acknowledged and popped a smoke grenade. Harry called the color, and it was confirmed. Ailes continued his approach to the log pad. Just as the load touched down there was a puff of what looked much like smoke off their right front. The pathfinder called, "We're taking mail!" Meaning that the bad guys were sending in rounds, mortar rounds. Bill quickly pulled back up into the clouds. Fortunately, as FSB Erskine was much smaller than FSB Cunningham, they did not get as many loads of resupply. However, you could all but guarantee that when a load touched down there would be a mortar round landing, welcoming the aircraft and them in a not-too-friendly fashion.

There they were, flying supplies into two marine FSBs. One had a "Deadeye Dick" that never missed, but they had four to four and a half seconds from appearance to explosion. The other had a gunner with impeccable timing, but he can't hit the pad. Were they having fun yet?

The following morning Harry got up, took a shower, and was combing his hair when he noticed two gray hairs at his part line. He named them Cunningham and Erskine.

Pachyderm spent the next several weeks resupplying the marines. By now everyone had the information on the two FSBs and the rules of flying in and around the clouds. One morning Harry was flying with a different AC, following Ailes and a Peter Pilot down the valley to FSB Cunningham. Ailes turned right and approached the ridgeline. All of a sudden there was a wall of tracer rounds in front of his aircraft. Ailes pulled the nose up abruptly, stopping forward flight, kicked in pedal to turn 180 degrees, lowered the nose, and got away from there as quickly as possible.

Ailes had used the same maneuver that Harry had on that night trip to Da Nang so long ago. During the night, the NVA had moved some .51-caliber machine guns into the valley at the base of the ridge below FSB Cunningham. They had them pointed near straight up and waited for a Chinook to fall into their trap. Had they waited just a bit to start firing, it might well have worked. As it was, the marines were pretty pissed. They got to the edge of the ridge and fired their rifles down into the NVA. Seemed that the NVA should have known that would have happened. It was a suicide mission for those soldiers. Harry guessed that they thought bagging a Chinook was worth it.

As the monsoon season neared its end the clouds rose and thinned. The holes got bigger, and they finally saw marine helicopters in the area. The marine infantry out of FSB Cunningham must have located the mortars and eliminated them as threats to either of the FSBs.

# Distinguished Flying Cross—DFC

Harry flew daily from 20 February through 15 March, missing only 23, 24, and 27 February and 12 March. He had flown fourteen days in February with the lousy weather for 67.5 hours. For March it was twenty-one days for 90.6 hours. The army did not want the pilots flying more than one hundred hours in any thirty-day period.

28 February 1969. A normal day in northern I Corps. "Normal" at that time of year means marginal weather. Cloud cover from broken to solid overcast. Flying conditions were questionable.

The 159th ASHB of the 101st Airborne Division was assigned support for the marines of Operation Dewy Canyon. The marines had moved west from Dong Ha to the area of Combat Base Vandergrift. This operation took them south to the northern edge of the A Shau Valley and west to Laos. They moved past the closed base at Khe Shan, the scene of so much activity the previous year. They moved southeast toward the upper end of the A Shau. Just northwest of the head of the valley they set up two fire support bases, FSBs Cunningham and Erskine. Both bases were there to provide interdiction and support for activity along the Laotian border.

The border in this area runs generally from the northwest to the southeast. South of the two FSBs it turns to the east before continuing its southeast meander. Cunningham and Erskine were continually firing to the west and southwest. The marines sent a raiding party. They were to cut Charlie's supply line into the north end of the A Shau Valley along Route 922. This route paralleled the Laotian border on the Laos side until crossing into Vietnam below Tiger Mountain directly into the A Shau. Harry didn't know Route 922 existed on the morning of the twenty-eighth.

Captain William (Bill) Ailes, Aircraft Commander, and WO1 Harry (Rat) Nevling of A Company, 159th ASHB, Pachyderm, were assigned to fly support in this area—again. Although an RLO, Ailes was a great pilot and a real good guy. While Harry had a fair amount of flight time while forming up at Fort Sill with what became C Company, he still had a lot to learn. Ailes was a terrific teacher. Ailes and Harry had been flying a lot together, most of it in support of the marines.

Early that morning they had preflighted their CH-47C Chinook (actually a C minus) at Pachyderm Beach, their home at Phu Bai. They had aircraft 67-18523 with Peter Paden as FE, Mark Sweeney as CE and Andy Huerra as Gunner, an excelent crew. After flying up to Camp Evans to pick up their first load of the day, they found the resupply pad was not ready. They decided to put the delay time to good use and make a weather check out over the mountains to the area of Cunningham.

The weather over the coastal plain was broken clouds. However, both experience and visual inspection told another story. Flying over the first ridgeline showed a mass of cloud cover extending far back into the mountains. They continued on to see if there were any holes they could use to drop down through rather than trying to fly out of the valleys. This choice was common at that time. The marines were way out there in Indian country, and the only possible way to them was helicopter. The choice was to go out under the cloud cover by flying the valleys or to go on top and try to find a sucker hole that looked good. The sucker holes were preferable because you could get the sorties accomplished faster, and Chuck couldn't shoot at you from the valley sides like he did if you were under the clouds.

This morning they found a large hole just to the east of Cunningham—and it looked like a keeper. This was going to be there for a while. They radioed back to tell the other aircraft to get a load and come out, they could get in from above the clouds. They radioed the pathfinder at

Cunningham and told him what was going on. He asked them if they had a load, and they told him no, there hadn't been any ready, and they were empty. He asked if they could help out by picking up some wounded marines and taking them back to Charlie med, the Marine Evacuation Hospital at Vandergrift. They said they would be right down. He told them they were not at his location. There were a pair of marine gunships that would take them to the wounded marines' location. They asked for the location of the wounded and again were told the guns would take them. He gave them the gunships' call sign and told them they were on his push (frequency). They contacted the marine guns and again asked for the location of the wounded marines. They were told they were south of Cunningham, and they'd come and get them and lead them in. They again asked for the location as they headed south. Once again they were told the guns would lead them.

By this time they probably should have been a bit suspicious. However, they had a great deal of respect for the marine gunship pilots. They would do just about anything to help the grunts. They spotted each other and fell in behind one of the ships with the other following. He led them around several cloud formations in what became an obvious circuitous route. They discussed on the intercom whether he didn't know where he was going, unlikely, or if he were trying to get them lost, likely. Harry got out his map to try to find a landmark, but with the cloud cover, this was impossible. So they followed the gunship, not knowing where they were or where they were going, but convinced they were lost intentionally.

Soon the gun pilot called and pointed out a small sucker hole off to their right front. He said he'd drop down through and go west along a road. Harry and Bill were to follow. Both of them knew there were no roads south of Cunningham.

They followed the gunship down through the hole and were right over the road. They contacted the ground commander on the FM radio and hovered under the low, really low, cloud cover to a small hill just north of the road. There was a small clearing with red smoke. The marines liked to use red smoke, while the army used it as a "do not land" warning. They called the smoke, and it was confirmed. Harry was flying, and they proceeded up to the clearing from the southeast but couldn't fit in the opening to land. He hovered around the hill to see if there were a different access. They went around the hill counterclockwise and had gotten southwest of the opening when the ground told them not to go north or west of the hill because that's where Charlie was. *Oops*, too late! They had taken no fire and could only credit this to the two marine gunships with them.

Harry finally found an access from the south, eased into the small clearing, and set the aircraft down. While the marines were getting their wounded on board, a major appeared under the right front, Harry's chin bubble, with his hands up and together as if in prayer or begging and pointed to four body bags right under the chin bubble. Harry told Ailes what was going on. Ailes told the FE (flight engineer) and said they really wanted to take them out. If any of the body bags leaked, he and Harry would help clean the ship. The FE went out and got the marines to bring the dead on board with the wounded. They had picked up four dead and about a dozen wounded.

The FE pulled up the ramp and cleared them to leave. Harry pulled up and backed off the hill. A right pedal turn headed them back down the road and then up through the hole. They were off and headed for Charlie med.

The marine guns called and asked where they were. Ailes told them they'd picked up the wounded and were getting them to Charlie med as fast as they could. They said there were more. When asked where, they told them back on the same road but about a half click (kilometer) to the east. They headed back with Ailes now flying. After dropping down through the same hole they hovered up the road to the east, calling the marines on FM radio again.

They had just come around a curve to the right in the road. There was a burned-out enemy truck on the left side of the road. They were approaching the truck when a whole bunch of things happened at once.

The guns called and asked where they were. Harry told them on the road headed east. They replied to come back up and let them escort. They were about to turn when an NVA soldier with an AK-47 holding a thirty round banana magazine jumped up from behind the truck and started firing at them. This guy was so close, Harry could tell he needed a shave. Harry grabbed for his .38 to shoot through Ailes's chin bubble but thought better of it. This was not the time for loud noises in the cockpit. They were scared enough. Harry then called on the intercom. "Gunner, shoot that son of a bitch! Shoot him!" No outgoing rounds were heard. Ailes wisely pulled pitch, and they disappeared into the clouds. They knew the cloud cover was only about a hundred feet thick and fairly even above them

As they came up through the clouds, Harry asked why the gunner hadn't fired. The response was his gun wouldn't traverse back that far. Harry asked what he was talking about; the guy was just off the left front. The gunner responded he was trying to shoot at the .51-caliber machine gun firing from the ridge behind them. He hadn't seen the man with the AK-47.

They contacted the gunships and related where they had taken fire and what type. They asked if they'd be willing to go back down with them as escort and try for the other wounded. Now there's a decision for you. You've got a helicopter the size of a boxcar that makes enough noise to wake the dead and is armed with only two 7.62 mm (.308 caliber) machine guns. You know there's at least one man with an AK-47 right in the middle of where they had to go and a .51-caliber machine gun with an open field of fire for their route. They had wounded marines on board and a crew of five. Yeah, they were stupid. They said, "Sure, lead on."

They followed the gunship down through the hole with his wingman following. Ailes hovered up the road without incident and found the marine element. After they picked up another eight or so wounded they headed back toward the hole to get back to Charlie med. The marine pathfinder thanked them and asked if they had any food or water. He said they hadn't been resupplied in three days. The FE said there were four cases of C rations on board. They asked the pathfinder if they dropped them on the road if the pathfinder could get them. Harry and Ailes did not want to expose any of those on the aircraft any more than necessary. He said affirmative, and they dropped them near the truck. As they were pulling up through the hole, they said they'd get the resupply people at Vandergrift to get them food and water. Their only other request was for small arms ammo and grenades.

Bill had been in-country over six months, Harry about two. Neither had ever heard a marine ask for anything but ammo. Three days out there without resupply, or medevac, is a very long time.

They called the gunships and told them they were headed for Charlie med. They thanked them profusely and wished them well. Harry thanked them for their cover that made the difference. (They did not know who those marine gunship pilots were, but they'd like to buy them a beer!) Harry called FSB Cunningham and told them they had the wounded and were on their way in. They also told them the guys in the bush needed food and water along with small arms ammo. Then Harry called Charlie med and advised them they were coming in with wounded. They also notified resupply at Vandergrift of the requests for food, water, and small arms ammo.

They radioed ahead to the evacuation hospital to let them know they were inbound with a load of wounded. Ailes landed at Charlie med, and the walking wounded left the aircraft while medical personnel got the more seriously wounded and dead off the aircraft.

It's interesting to note that the food and water weren't delivered until about sixteen hundred (4:00 p.m.). It was delivered by an army Chinook, commanded by CWO Harold ("Weird Harold") Eckert, who had landed at Vandergrift and physically threatened the resupply people if they didn't get a load together for their marine grunts.

It's also interesting to note that it wasn't until their flight back to the evac hospital that they had time to look at the map and find where they had been. By then it wasn't much of a surprise to find that the reason they didn't know that road was there was because it was in Laos, not South Vietnam!

Most amazing was that when they shut down the aircraft to check for damage there were no bullet holes! The guy with the AK-47 had missed them completely. He was close enough that had he thrown his weapon up in the air he surely would have gotten a rotor blade. So with the fire from both the AK and the .51 caliber, they didn't even have a bullet hole to show for it! In reflection, that's OK. Had the man with the AK been a better shot he would have hosed the cockpit. Had the .51 caliber hit them it would have been in #1 engine or the aft transmission. It was really OK that they both missed!

As no good deed shall go unpunished, Harry and Ailes, as a direct result of this mission, were sent into northern Laos in March to assist with relocation of Hmong natives from the edge of the Plain of Jars. But that's a later story.

CPT Bill Ailes was awarded the Silver Star, and Harry was awarded the Distinguished Flying Cross for their actions that day.

# QUANG TRI

The weather got even worse. There were days when you couldn't even take off from Pachyderm Beach or the Liftmaster Pad. So the powers that be decided to relocate some aircraft to increase the chances for getting out to the marines. Two aircraft were positioned at Vandergrift, two at Camp Sally, and two at Quang Tri with an army reserve unit (there were NO National Guard units in Vietnam.) It was interesting that in civilian life the CO of this tank retriever unit worked for a company owned by the first sergeant of the unit. Ailes and Harry were sent to Quang Tri. The days were long regardless of how many hours they flew. They were up early to be available to take off at first light and available until late afternoon. During this twenty-one-day stretch, Harry flew seventeen days and logged 90.8 hours of flight time, including 3.3 hours of weather instrument time—this is time in the clouds, flying by instruments only. Most of the flights were to Cunningham and Erskine, but they also went to other marine bases including FSB Fuller up near the DMZ.

One day they had to land on Fuller for something. Fuller was a small FSB on the top of a mountain about four kilometers south of the DMZ. Harry thought its primary purpose was to interdict infiltration from the north through the DMZ.

Harry was sitting in the right seat watching a marine in a small bunker to the right front. He had a pair of huge ship's binoculars. Harry couldn't even guess how powerful they were. Certainly bigger than any he had ever used. The marine was scanning to the north of the FSB toward the DMZ. He sat the binoculars on the sandbag wall and moved over to a .50-caliber machine gun—with a scope on it! He jockeyed the gun, looked through the scope, nudged a few times, and then stood up and pressed the butterfly trigger. He had it set to single shot, and that's what it did. He then picked up a pack of Lucky Strike cigarettes and a book of GI matches. It took two tries, as our rotor wash blew out the first one. The marine took a drag off the cigarette and then picked up the binoculars. After a couple of seconds he again sat the binoculars down, picked up a piece of chalk, and added another line to his score on an overhead timber. What amazed Harry was the time between the shot and the confirmation. Harry didn't know how far away it was, but it took a long time for the .50-caliber slug to get to its target. Harry could imagine how unnerving it would be for a couple of NVA soldiers infiltrating down through the DMZ. They stop for a rice ball snack in a shell crater and are having a chat when one of their heads explodes! Man, he thought, that would send the other one back north in a hurry.

Later in the spring the NVA climbed up the cliff face to FSB Fuller and released nerve gas. It killed nearly all the marines there. Harry was not involved, but Andrews took a flight of bodies back to Vandergrift. Wonder why that never made the papers.

Harry and Bill remained at Quang Tri for several days—long days—flying support for the marines. Even when the weather did not allow a lot of flying time, the days were still long. The waiting may have been more tiring that the flying. They were quartered in tents. On two of the nights they were gassed. The first time, it was tear gas sent in through the perimeter wire by the NVA. A real nuisance, as both Harry and Bill had left their gas masks back at the Beach. The cure was to stick their heads in their sleeping bags and use them as filters. It worked pretty well.

The next night there was another gas attack. This time it was much, much worse. That stuff got to them even with their heads stuck in their sleeping bags. They found out the next morning that the soldiers had seen some NVA coming through the wire and released CS gas. Then the breeze shifted, and it came back into the camp. That was some nasty stuff!

One morning Harry and Bill were waiting near the resuppply pad and a convoy came by. For protection there was a quad .50 caliber mountd in the back of a duece-and –a-half truck. On the front shield was painted "Here Comes De Judge", a line from a popular comedy show on TV. Right behind it was an eight inch SP howitzer. On it was painted "De Judge". This gun carried fleschette rounds that would really make a mess of anyone firing on the convoy!

The weather got even worse, so some genius thought it would be effective if they were to take a load on a reverse GCA (ground-controlled approach) up through the clouds. Once clear on top of the clouds, they could get a vector from the plane that did the radar approaches for the B-52. "Stratofortress" bombing missions. The initial reaction of the pilots was that someone was nuts! You do not want to fly into clouds unless it is absolutely necessary. You do not want to fly into clouds with an external sling load— *period. Ever.* If the load becomes unstable and starts to swing, things will get real bad real fast. If the oscillations cause vertigo you're cooked!

The pilots talked it over and said they would give it a try. They had to get the supplies to the marines out there somehow. They told the powers that be if anything went wrong, the first thing they'd do was pickle (drop) the sling load. They had enough sense to see this was the correct thing to do. The procedure was to pick up a sling load of supplies, usually 105 mm howitzer ammo, at the Camp Evans resupply pad. Then they would hover out over the perimeter fence and around to line up with the runway. Back across the fence and slowly down the runway. A Chinook transitions from a hover to flight at about fourteen knots. They wanted to be above this speed but not much, so twenty knots was their limit. If the GCA radar picked them up, they would increase speed and climb into the clouds, which were at the rotor head height or slightly above. If the GCA didn't get them, they'd slow down and hover around the camp and back to the starting point.

Once in the clouds, it was all about the instruments in the cockpit. Pitch, power, roll, and trim. Airspeed and rate of climb. Stay on the glide slope for the GCA—backward.

Watch all the other instruments. Don't bother looking up. There's nothing to see but the gray of the clouds.

The glide slope went directly into a mountain about three kilometers south of Camp Evans. This necessitated a ninety-degree right turn while in the clouds. After a climb through the clouds of three hundred to five hundred feet, they would break out on top. A call to Crown 6 to see if they could get them on their radar. Crown 6 was the call sign for the airborne radar aircraft. If successful, they would give them a heading to fly and tell them when they were directly over Cunningham. Time to look for a sucker hole, drop down through it, and deliver the load. And watch out for the mortar rounds hitting the pad at Cunningham. Then a slow climb back up through the clouds. The pilots determined that when on top they would stay at least one hundred feet above the clouds. That way the aircraft coming up through the clouds—slowly—could spot anyone above them. They did not want to run into one another. Another thing not conducive to longevity.

On Harry's first trip, all had gone well. GCA picked him up on the first try, and he went into the clouds, made the turn, and climbed out on tip of the clouds with no problems other than sweating and concentration on the instruments. Was relieved when the airborne radar picked him up and gave him the heading to FSB Cunningham. Harry turned to the new course. After a couple of minutes, the radar control radioed, "Two degrees port." *Two degrees? Port?* Harry radioed back. I'm army, not marines, not navy. I don't know which way *port* is! Besides which, you've got to be kidding about two degrees. My compass is bouncing more than that with the vibrations!" Harry learned later that if you got off course by more than about three degrees, their precision radar would lose you. It was a real bitch trying to get back on their scope once it dropped you. Harry managed to guess what his compass should be doing and stayed on the radar vector to FSB Cunningham.

More days of the same thing. Flying up through the clouds or sucker holes, dodging other clouds dodging mortar rounds, and keeping the marines supplied with ammo, water, and food. Sometime during this stretch the NVA moved a cannon into position in Laos to be able to hit FSB Cunningham. Fortunately, there was still the delay between the appearance of the Chinook and the artillery shell landing. If the NVA had put their spotter to the east of FSB Cunningham instead of the west it would have given them the extra time to get the shell and the helicopter on the pad at the same time. Harry was extremely glad they did not think of that.

## "Weird" and the Smoke Grenade

Late one morning Harry and Ailes landed near the Pachyderm Operations shack at Vandergrift. Bill went in to talk to CPT Cooper, the operations officer. As Harry was waiting, another Chinook came in, landed nearby, and shut down. Weird Harold got out and walked into the operations shack. A couple of minutes later, Andy Belmont came down the ramp and walked in Harry's direction. He was trying to light a cigarette with matches, but his hands were shaking so badly the match went out. On the third try he finally got it lit. As he neared, Harry asked, "What's up, Andy?" He mumbled something about Weird trying to kill them. When pressed, he told Harry that they were out trying to get a load of ammo into FSB Razorback. It was socked in with the clouds just below the ridgeline. They couldn't get in from above, so Weird found a sucker hole and tried hovering up the side of the ridge. However, with the clearance required by the sling load, he lost sight of the trees and had to turn and climb above the clouds. Weird called the pathfinder and asked what color the sky was overhead. He responded, "Gray." Weird pressed for more info and found out that the pathfinder had a light-gray cloud overhead. He requested the pathfinder pop a smoke grenade. Weird circled overhead until the smoke came up through the clouds. He then hovered down the smoke trail until the load touched down. He released the load and went back up through the clouds and returned to Vandergrift. Andy was stunned and amazed. Stunned that Weird would try something that crazy and amazed that it actually worked! He was still shaking when he finished the story and the cigarette. Weird returned, they got back in their aircraft, and took off. Andy was still shaking his head as he disappeared up the ramp.

# HITCHING A RIDE

Harry had flown fifteen of the previous sixteen days for a total of 57.9 hours. Even on the short flying days he was up early and to bed late. Add to this the stress of flying under, over, and through the clouds, not to mention the enemy activities, and it makes for a very tiring time. Even though he did not feel tired, a relief pilot was sent to replace Harry. He needed to hitch a ride back to Pachyderm Beach. So being really tired and not thinking straight, he bummed a ride with CW2 Kerkle and WO1 Tom Andrews. Andrews was a good friend from the beginning at Fort Sill. A soft-spoken Texan. Harry couldn't recall Tom ever being angry. Harry asked if he could get a ride back to Pachyderm Beach with them, as that was where they were based for this effort. They said sure, he could have a ride. Then Harry did the dumb thing. Instead of waiting for the day to be done and just riding back with them, he decided to ride with them the entire day. Stupid. Well, at least damned foolish. Why would you put yourself in harm's way as the third pilot in a two-pilot aircraft? To spend the day in an uncomfortable jump seat watching the action and activities—and catching whatever comes the aircraft's way—like bullets, mortar rounds, and other objects that may well ruin your day.

Kerkle and Andrews got into the cockpit seats and started the pre-flight procedure as Harry pulled up the jump seat and prepared it for use. Everything went smoothly, and off they went. Andrews was doing most of the flying, and Kerkle was taking pictures with a small 35 mm camera. On final approach to a marine FSB located on a ridgeline, Kerkle was taking pictures of the marines and their camp. If something bad is going to happen, this is when it is likely to occur. Kerkle's head (eyes) are out of the cockpit when they should have been inside monitoring the instruments. Sure enough, something happened to the "beep" trim on both engines. Rotor rpm began to bleed off, and Andrews could not get it back with the AC-powered rocker switches on the thrust lever. On the center console there are two beep trim switches that are powered by DC (direct current). They can override the AC (alternating current) switches and work much faster. Harry leaned forward and shoved both switches forward to get the rotor rpm back in the green. About this time, Kerkle realized there was a problem, put his camera down, and started paying attention to the aircraft.

Understand that the speed at which the rotor blades are turning puts a tremendous amount of centrifugal force on them. Normal rotor rpm on a Chinook is 233 rpm. Should that drop below about 180 rpm the blades lose enough strength from reduced centrifugal force to literally fold up. The aircraft falls out of the sky. This is yet another of those things that is not conducive to longevity.

Harry was convinced that he saved them from at least a nasty crash into the marine base. He also promised himself to *never* hitch a ride into a hot area just for the ride!

They went back to Pachyderm Beach about 1600 (4:00 p.m.). Harry went to the mess hall for supper then back to his hooch. He went to the shower building and took a shower. Then back to the hooch and bed. He woke up about 1600 the following day and went through the previous afternoon's routine. He woke up at noon the following day. He had been so tired he didn't know he was tired. Sending him back to the Beach was a very good idea.

# LIAISON OFFICER

Pachyderm had a liaison officer stationed at Combat Base Vandergrift. Harry thought this was a request from the marines because of all the Chinooks that were flying support for them. The three-day duty was rotated among the Pachyderm pilots. Harry had talked to a couple of the guys who had done the liaison officer duty and learned they did not do much. When his turn came, he took a couple of books along. He went to headquarters and was briefed by a marine major. He told Harry to be at headquarters at 0800 for the morning briefing, where the officers' mess was, and where he was to bunk. Harry thanked him and took his gear to the building specified. It was a wooden-framed tent that the army called WEBTOC. Harry didn't know what the acronym meant, but he was right at home. This was the same quarters Harry had when he was in the 4th Infantry Division's base camp his first tour. This one had wooden half-walls with a screen above. They had used the wood for something else at the one he was in at the 4th, so all he had was a wood floor and canvas. One other notable exception. When Harry opened the door, all there was inside was one cot and a sleeping bag. He had the whole building all to himself. The building was located not far from the 3rd Marine Division Headquarters on the slope of the ridge on the south side of the base. The only thing that happened occurred that afternoon. Harry was sitting on his cot reading a book when he heard the sound of an incoming rocket followed immediately by the explosion. He jumped off the cot in a low crouch and headed for the door. As he opened the door, he realized he had no idea where any bunkers were located. He looked up at the ridge the rockets were coming over and realized the rockets could not clear that ridge and land anywhere near where the hooch was located. He went back to the cot and his book.

During his time at Vandergrift as liaison officer he did not liaise at all. He attended the morning briefings, ate his meals, and read books. What a monumental waste of time!

# Personal Weapons

As the area of the 101st operations expanded, the additional area supporting the marines meant a lot of missions into the mountains—Indian country. This made Harry a bit nervous. The army had issued all the pilots in his unit a .38 special caliber revolver with a four-inch barrel and a shoulder holster. Not much for defense if one went down in the mountains. So Harry started carrying extra loads of ammo for the six-shooter. Something still seemed to be lacking. He acquired an M-16 rifle, then extra magazines, then a bandolier of extra ammo. He got a box of ammo for the .38. Still didn't seem like enough, so he got a couple of hand grenades and a smoke grenade. The army had also issued a hand-held strobe flasher for identification and a "blood chit" that stated in a variety of languages the holder was a US Army soldier and there would be a large reward if he were returned to US forces. Harry put most of the extra items in an ammo can and carried the rifle and bandolier out to the aircraft for each flight. He felt a bit better with the extra armament.

Then came 20 March. Oh shit! Harry and Such were ambushed at FSB Whip, and he wasn't able to fire a shot. After that incident he thought back to the situation in Laos with Ailes. He had a shot but couldn't take it. It occurred to him that all this stuff he was carrying wasn't going to do any good. From then on he carried the revolver and left the rest of it in his hooch.

When he got to the "Muleskinners," they issued him a .45 semiautomatic but no holster. Harry cleaned and oiled it, wrapped it up in a cloth, and stuck it on a shelf in his hooch. He never carried a weapon with Muleskinners and was never shot at.

# HAMBURGER HILL

A lot of people have heard of Hamburger Hill. Harry heard about it when it was going on but didn't know where it was. It is fourteen kilometers (8.5 miles) north of the village of A Shau in the A Shau Valley. It is only two kilometers (a mile and a quarter) from Laos on one of the Ho Chi Minh trails, the main one into the valley. The road through the valley is Route 548. It runs north and south through the A Shau Valley. At the northern end it turns northwest to the Laotian border. There Route 922 goes into Laos and parallels the border for several kilometers. When the border turns north, it continues on west and links to the main Ho Chi Minh Trail.

The battle was from 10 to 20 May. Hamburger Hill was Ap Bia Mountain or Hill 937 (937 meters, or 3,074 feet elevation). It is a very rugged mountain with steep slopes and double and triple canopy jungle. The undergrowth was a further problem with tall elephant grass concealing the enemy and his positions. The mountain was the headquarters for the NVA 29th PAVN (People's Army of Vietnam) Regiment, nicknamed the "Pride of Ho Chi Minh," and a veteran of the 1968 Tet Offensive assault on Hue. As the regimental headquarters, it was a major communications hub. It had extensive defensive positions and underground facilities that were impervious to air attacks and artillery fire.

The NVA had had controlled the A Shau Valley since the 1965 Battle of A Shau, when they captured the Special Forces camp there. Since that time they had pretty much had free run of the valley. This allowed the transport of men and materials into the valley for use along the coast from Quang Tri through Hue to Da Nang. The 101st initiated Operation Apache Snow to change that. Things culminated at Hamburger Hill.

By the end of the battle, the American forces suffered 72 KIA (killed in action) and 372 WIA (wounded in action). Several helicopters were shot down during the battle as well. Of course the media and the politicians had a field day with the casualties. With their misinformation, intentional obscuration, and totally neglecting the estimated casualties of the 7th and 8th Battalions of the 29th NVA Regiment, including 630 dead (discovered on and around the battlefield); including many found in makeshift mortuaries within the tunnel complex tey reversed the success of the operation. No one could count the NVA running off the mountain, those killed by artillery and air strikes, the wounded and dead carried into Laos, or the dead buried in collapsed bunkers and tunnels. Nor did they pay any attention to the captured eighty-nine individual weapons and twenty-two crew served weapons.

Harry had picked up a load of bunker materials at Supply Point Birmingham. The net contained rolls of concertina wire and timbers. This type of load was unstable, and at around fifty knots, it would start flying itself. Not a good thing. The oscillations of the load could swing it into the belly of the aircraft. As they couldn't fly the load fast, they flew it high. Harry went up to about five thousand feet and over the mountains to the A Shau Valley.

They had the grid coordinates for the location, the radio frequency, and call sign for the unit. As they crossed the valley Harry started his descent to the target. When they got to the far side of the Valley they called the unit on the ground for smoke. The ground unit returned the call with, "Smoke out!" They confirmed the color and proceeded to a small opening in the jungle at the top of the mountain. They saw only a few troops on the ground and no artillery. It was definitely not an FSB.

As they departed, the ground unit called and asked, "What is this crap?" They replied that it was the load that Birmingham had told them to deliver. The ground then asked, "Do you know where you are?" They told him that they just had the grid coordinates and contact information. He replied "Well, this is Hamburger Hill, and we sure as hell don't need this crap!" They apologized and told him they'd pass the information back to Birmingham. The units that had taken the hill weren't planning to stay long, and they had plenty of defenses that they had captured from the NVA. They certainly did not need to build any. Another higher-up fuck-up.

# BACK TO THE BEACH
## BUILDING THE OFFICERS' CLUB

They were fortunate to have Papa Pickle transferred with them to Pachyderm Beach. He had been a scrounger extraordinaire at Fort Sill. He was just as good in Vietnam. Many of the things he got made things more comfortable at the beach. One of these many things involved some kind of deal with the Seabees so if they had cement left over from a job they would bring it over to the beach. They had a lot of concrete in their area. They expanded their O Club with a slightly larger building attached to the old one, which they then turned into a game room. They added a huge patio on the other side of the original O Club, now a game room, and turned it into a roofed and screened patio. An Aussie with one of the USO troupes who stayed with them painted a mural across the far wall of the screened patio. They added another large patio outside this, and John Michael Weatherly, JM, built a large and beautiful stone barbecue pit on it. Harry had no idea where the stone came from, but it was probably from another of Papa Pickle's deals. All of this was connected to the hooch area by sidewalk. They built a new shower building with cement floor and a drying-off room. They also put a sidewalk in to these showers, which were behind the far end of the right-side hooches. They put in another to the officers' latrines past the left-side hooch, which made it convenient to the O club.

The Seabees would call that they had concrete for them and any officers who were not flying would scramble to get forms ready. One day they had a job that fell through, so they got several mixer trucks of concrete. Harry was not flying that day so he was part of the scramble to make the new outdoor patio. He was also there the day that JM made the barbecue.

Harry flew only once with Papa Pickle. That was enough. It was what they called a milk run to Da Nang for parts. Instead of just flying down Highway 1, the shortest route, he insisted on going about a half mile out to sea and flying off the coast. He figured no one could shoot at you out there. He never went into the A Shau. However, for all the good that he did and the comforts he provided, all the guys gave him a lot of slack. Papa Pickle was one of the good guys.

He had a sort of assistant scrounger. An RLO we'll call Paul. Harry had worked with RLO Paul at Fort Sill and really didn't think much of him. The reverse also seemed true, but Harry just thought it was because he wouldn't buy into Paul's bullshit.

Harry had learned first tour that certain items were invaluable in Vietnam. Simple things like a saw, hammer, and drill. He had these items shipped over by family, and his toolbox included a quarter-inch electric drill with a variety of bits. Harry was helping build the new O Club. His drill came in very handy. One day he was scheduled to fly and kept the drill in his hooch. As he was going to the flight line, Paul approached him and requested the drill. Not quite an order, but not a request. Harry told him no, it was too valuable to let out of his hands. Paul then ordered Harry to give him the drill. Harry told him in no uncertain terms that the drill was personal property, and Paul had no authority over it. Paul changed his tone and method, and Harry finally agreed to let him borrow the drill. He told Paul that he was responsible for the drill, no one else. If it started to rain again, he was to put it inside the door to Harry's hooch. He agreed. When Harry got back from his missions, it was raining lightly and had been for some time. He looked in his hooch and no drill. He went to the new O Club building and found the drill laying out in the rain. It was an inexpensive metal drill and had already started to rust. Harry took it back to his hooch, scrubbed off the rust, and oiled it. When he next saw Paul, he chewed him out for not taking care of the drill as promised and told him to not even bother asking for it again. Harry didn't know if this is what caused Paul to do some things later, but it might have been. More about Paul later.

# Ground Crazy

In order to do the job they had to do, and do it properly, the pilots had to believe they were invincible. Most of them did. It led to crazy stunts like this to let off steam.

# KILLER FRISBEE

Some days funny things happened. The guys would find interesting, and sometimes dangerous, ways to entertain themselves when not flying. One of these entertainments was "killer Frisbee." They had some regular Frisbees that they'd play catch with, but someone decided this was not entertaining enough. So they started playing with several guys and two or three Frisbees. One never knew where they would come from. Keeping an eye on them was a real challenge. Perhaps it was good practice for their flying needs.

When they got bored with this they went to killer Frisbee. The "hooch maids," Vietnamese women who came in for the day to clean their rooms and do laundry, had large aluminum wash basins. They were bowls about two feet wide and six inches or so deep. One of the guys decided these would make for a better game of Frisbee, so he picked one up, turned it over, and found it flew just like a Frisbee. If you were on the other end of the toss you wanted to be very careful how you caught it! Someone came up with an even better idea. Get three or more of the pilots together, and use two of the wash basins. Now that got very interesting! You had to know where both bowls were at all times. Of course this activity dented the bowls. The hooch maids did not like this one bit and raised quite a fuss, so the guys stopped playing killer Frisbee.

# BUNKER ROOF

One night the pilots in the O Club heard some explosions. They went outside to see what was going on and saw rockets exploding about a half mile away in a different compound. As the attack continued, some of the guys, a long way from sober, climbed up on the roof of the bunker to get a better view of the attack. Harry was not that crazy—or maybe not that drunk. Major Butler came up and was not happy. He called the men down off the bunker and told them that even if they didn't care about getting hurt, the army had a very large investment in them and didn't want the men throwing away the investment. All of us, rather sheepishly, went inside the bunker where we should have been until the all clear was sounded.

# The Archers

One day, Harry was walking past the hooches toward operations and the mess hall when he saw a group of guys standing in the sand between the hooches and the landing pad. (The guilty shall go unnamed.) As he looked closer he saw they had a bow and some target arrows. One guy would take the bow and draw an arrow. He'd then, while looking straight ahead, point to where he thought straight up was and let go. The arrow would go up—and then down. It was a strange game of chicken. They would stand there and look at one another until the arrow landed, then pass to bow to the next guy. Killer Frisbee was one thing, but this was way past nuts. This was really no crazier than what they did each day they flew. The risks with this game were no worse, just unnecessary.

# Weird Harold and His Shirt

Another evening in the old O Club, Harry was having a drink when the CO came in. The major was not a stranger to the bar, but he didn't live in there like a lot of the pilots. Harry struck up a conversation with him, and the two were enjoying their drinks and conversation when Weird Harold came in. Weird was barefoot, wearing shorts, a T-shirt, and his dog tags. He was carrying a pack of Winston cigarettes and a Zippo lighter. He said good evening to the major, who turned to him and acknowledged the greeting. He then asked Weird, "Mr. Eckert, you know the club rules. Please get into appropriate attire." Now there weren't a whole lot of rules, but number two was "You must wear a shirt and shoes in the club." Weird looked over at the rules and read number two out loud. He turned to the major, said "Yes, sir," and left. About ten minutes later he returned to the club and went behind the bar. He asked if the major wanted another drink, and as he said yes, Weird made the drink and put it on the bar in front of him. He then moved over in front of Harry and asked to bum a cigarette. Harry was puzzled, as he'd seen Weird with his cigarettes and lighter on his first entrance. As he gave Weird the cigarette he looked down and saw why he was bumming a smoke from Harry. Weird a T-shirt—period. He had even taken off his dog tags! Weird gave Harry a little shake of his head to not say anything. The rule said shirt and shoes. That's what he had on. He stood behind the bar like that and chatted with them for at least another hour before the major left. Harry and Weird got a good laugh out of that one. And it wasn't even dangerous.

Weird Harold came by his nickname honestly. He was a bit strange around the edges. When he was in B Company his hooch mate was known as "Strange Stride." He and his hooch mate at Pachyderm got some flat black paint and painted the interior of their room with it. Even with the light on it was dark in there.

They put a trap door in the floor of their hooch and hauled sandbags under the hooch to build a bunker down there. If something happened, all they had to do was open the trap door and drop in.

As with any group of people, Pachyderm had some unique characters, like Lurch, Weird Harold, and Papa Pickle. Some were good, some just different, and some not so good. One of the "just different" ones was Roy.

## ROY'S RICE

Harry opened his door one morning, and as he stepped out, he saw Roy working a small patch of sand next to the steps to his hooch. Roy was one of three civilian tech reps (technical representatives) who lived at Pachyderm Beach. Roy and another guy, Stan, worked for Lycoming, the company that built the engines for the Chinook. The third was Joe who worked for Boeing Vertol, the manufacturer of the aircraft.

Harry walked over and asked Roy what he was doing. He said he was tending to his rice. He told Harry that he had planted some rice there in front of his hooch.

"All right," Harry said, "where did you get the rice?"

Roy replied that he had gotten it from the mess hall.

Harry wondered how that was going to work. The rice in the mess hall was processed and couldn't possibly grow. Thinking that something else might be going on, he asked if he got it from the mess sergeant.

"No, I took it off my food tray," Roy informed him.

"You mean that you planted processed, cooked rice and expect it to grow?" Harry asked.

"Sure, why not?" "Well, Roy," Harry told him, "processed rice won't grow. Cooked rice won't grow. You have a double impossibility of getting anything to grow there."

Roy continued to tend to his garden for another couple of months before he gave up on it.

When Roy was not tending his rice garden, he was doing reports on the engines to send back to Lycoming headquarters for analysis. Not sure what this involved, but Roy had a thirty-day leave and went back home. When he returned it took him less than four hours to catch up on his paperwork. Nice job if you can get it. No wonder he had time to try to grow cooked rice!

The tech reps were a good bunch of guys. They fit in well with the pilots, and they enjoyed one another's company. Joe had submitted Harry to Boeing Vertol for a Rescue Citation for pulling the wounded marines out of Laos. Joe presented the certificate, a wallet card, and a nice lapel pin of a Chinook one evening in the O Club. Harry was quite surprised and thanked Joe for doing this.

So, Joe was the Boeing Vertol tech rep, and Roy was the Lycoming tech rep. The third tech rep, Stan, also worked for Lycoming, but no one seemed to know just what he did. No matter.

# Tech Rep's Colossal Hangover

One night a bunch of the pilots were in the club drinking. Those who had to fly the next day, not so much. The others drank a lot. Stan was drinking with them that evening, as was Joe, his hooch mate. Stan was drinking black Russians. For those who may not know, this is officially one and three-quarters ounces of vodka and three-quarters of an ounce of Kahlua coffee liqueur. It goes down easy and is very potent. After Stan had finished off five or six of these, he was pretty drunk. By the next one he fell off his barstool. When a couple of the guys finished their drinks, they picked Stan up, put him on his stool, and gave him another drink. This happened two or three times. Stan was *very* drunk. On the next drink, Stan raised the glass to his mouth, tipped back, and drank it all down. Only he kept going backward. He and the stool hit the floor together. They thought that was probably enough for him and let him lie on the floor till Joe decided it was time for him to go. A couple of the guys helped him get Stan off the floor and back to his hooch.

The next day Harry was able to get back to the beach for lunch. After eating, he went to the O Club for a cold Coke to take with him. When he entered the barroom, there was Stan, sitting in a cushioned chair with his right foot up on the cushion. His right arm was on his right knee, holding a half cup of coffee. Stan was wearing dark sunglasses. As there were no windows in the building, it was pretty dark to begin with. As he walked by, Harry said hi to him but got no response. He went behind the bar and signed a chit for the Coke. As he left he asked Stan if he was all right. Again no response.

Harry got done with his missions around 1600 (4:00 p.m.), and he was back at the beach for supper. Again, after supper, he went down to the O Club. There was Stan, sitting in the same chair and holding what appeared to be the same half cup of coffee from noon. Harry greeted him again with no response. He went to the bar and got a beer before asking those present if Stan was OK. None of the guys there had seen him move in the half hour or so they had been there. Harry went over to check on him. He still could not get a verbal response, so he raised Stan's sunglasses. His eyes were open and unfocused but did not look dead. Harry put the sunglasses back and felt his right wrist for a pulse. He told the guys, "His heart is still beating, but I don't know if he's actually alive."

The next evening Stan was back among the living but still with one hell of a hangover. Some of the pain was probably from his head hitting the floor on his final topple. He swore off drinking that night. It lasted about two months.

# HERRICK'S PRIVATE POOL

Then there was Jack Herrick. One afternoon Harry had gotten done with his missions early. As he walked to his hooch, he saw a strange sight. In the small grass area between the sidewalks along the hooches was Jack Herrick, one of the company's IPs (instructor pilot) laying in a large Styrofoam box filled with water. Harry walked over and asked Herrick what it was. He said, "It's my private pool."

"Great, Jack, but what is it?" Harry asked again.

"Oh, it's a bomb box."

"A what?"

Jack explained that it was a shipping box for sending bombs to Vietnam. It was just the right size for one person to lie in and get some "rays." Any afternoon that Herrick wasn't flying, you could find him enjoying his private pool. GIs can be rather creative with what they can find to make life more comfortable.

# Booze in the Toilet

Harry had no idea why Playtex took a couple of flush toilets to Vietnam. He knew that Papa Pickle had scrounged a couple, and they were in one of the conex containers shipped with the unit's other gear. You need two things to make a flush toilet work: water coming in and someplace for it to go out to. The input is not a huge problem. Even without running water you can use gravity feed to operate them. Heck, most showers in Vietnam were gravity fed. The problem was where would it go? There were very few septic systems in Vietnam. Most liquid waste went into what were called "piss tubes," which were simply a metal tube angled into the ground. Solid waste went into halved fifty-five gallon drums, mixed with diesel fuel, and burned. So why take them?

Well, give a GI something, and he will figure how to use it.

Battalion had a big party one evening. Everyone was invited to attend. Sitting on a table was one of the porcelain thrones. Yup, one of the flush toilets was center ring at the party. After a very thorough cleaning, they had plugged the outflow and sealed it with paraffin wax. Then they filled the tank with a bottle of just about everything, flushed it into the bowl, and floated a block of ice in it. The concoction was cold, strong, and tasted terrible. However, after the first cup no one cared!

Harry was standing near the table when a major he didn't know came up. He couldn't get any of the booze out of the toilet, as the level was pretty low. Harry stepped up and said, "Not to worry, sir," and tripped the flush handle. The tank was full of the concoction as well, and it flushed into and refilled the bowl. The major was appreciative and had another cup.

# BALLISTIC FLIGHT HELMET

About this time the US Army decided to issue new flight helmets. Harry was still using his original flight helmet issued at Ft. Wolters and worn all through flight school, his transition and training at Ft. Sill and his time thus far in Vietnam. The flight helmet was an APH-4. It was not terribly comfortable as your head was surrounded by pads to customize the fit of the helmet. There was no 'breathing' room so it was hot. Also the ear protection was not very good. As the noise level in the cockpit of a chinook was around 100 decibels this was not a good thing. It weighed in at 3.5 pounds which was fairly heavy to have on your head all day.

The Army issued a newer model flight helmet that was to provide better air circulation and hearing protection – and improved ballistic protection. This was a something -7. (It is not listed in the official history of US Army flight helmets. Perhaps because it was in the field for such a short time.) This helmet was cooler as it used straps to fit the helmet to one's head and provided better heating protection. It also had much improved ballistic protection from bullets. However, it weighed around seven pounds, twice the weight of the heavy APH-4. After four or five hours of wearing this helmet one had such a headache it was hard to see the instruments and the terrain.

This monster was not around long and was replaced by the SPH-4B. This was a nice helmet. It weighed a half pound less that the old APH-4 and had the improved suspension system and hearing protection. It also had an improved microphone so it was easier for others to hear you on the intercom and radios. This helmet had bulges around the ears to accommodate the improved hearing protection and immediately labeled the *Mickey Mouse* helmet. The SPH was a great helmet. A significant improvement over the APH and miles better that the ballistic model.

# OH SHIT!—AMBUSH AT FSB WHIP

Harry had a few days off and enjoyed some downtime at Pachyderm Beach. It seemed to be a good time to be there. On 17 March, Chinooks 67–18520, 67–18531, and 67–18540 all were shot up. Bill Cristobol was the AC on 540. They were taking a Marine battery into a new place west of Vandergrift. There was a daisy chain of Chinooks carrying 105 mm howitzers on an artillery raid. They would take the guns into the location where the crews would set them up immediately for a fire mission. Cristobol was the second aircraft in the formation. On final approach, the NVA popped up out of "spider holes" and started shooting at the aircraft. At least two of these were twin .30-caliber machine guns. Cristobol and 67–18540 got the worst of it. None of the aircraft put their loads in. Everyone got out of the area as fast as they could, but 540 lost its SAS (stability augmentation system), its intercom, and radios. No one was hurt as they headed back to Vandergrift. With the SAS gone, the aircraft was wallowing, and the *cargo hook open* warning light was lit. Cristobol did not know this was from another bullet. In fact, the hook was closed, and the 105 was still below the aircraft. As he approached Vandergrift, he decided to make a running landing rather than try to hover without the SAS working. The FE figured out what he was doing as they were on short final approach. Without the intercom, he couldn't tell Cristobol the gun was still on the hook. He headed for the cockpit but too late. Cristobol set the aircraft down on the cannon. Big hole in the belly. He picked the aircraft up, the FE released the load, and he set down beside it; 540 was sent to Red Beach at Da Nang for repairs.

The following day, 18 March, both 527 and 535 were shot up; 527 was hit twice that day.

On 20 March, 67–18540 was back on flying status. Harry and his roommate, John Such, were assigned that aircraft for the day's missions. Harry was assigned as first pilot. They were flying loads out of a new resupply area about nineteen kilometers west of Phu Bai called Supply Base Birmingham or just Birmingham, or even B'ham. This was located in a large valley that went from the mountains to the coast. It allowed the 101st to get the supplies there by truck and kept the resupply and refueling area away from all the helicopter traffic at Camp Eagle and Phu Bai.

Harry and Such were taking the supplies to FSBs along the west side of the A Shau Valley. Places named Whip (about sixteen kilometers, or ten miles west southwest of Birmingham) and Thor (about eighteen kilometers, or eleven miles south of Birmingham). Harry flew all morning. He enjoyed the flying, while Such preferred handling the radios and performing other duties. They had decided that they would fly at least one mission a day without the SAS so if something happened to it, as happened to Cristobol, they would be more comfortable with the way the aircraft handled. As they developed these skills, it got so they could fly a complete mission without the SAS and without any input from the FE to hook up the load, get it to a FSB, and return. It's a real trick to spear the doughnut on the slings of a load when the cargo hook is five feet below you and twenty-five feet behind you with no way of seeing either one. To overcome the lack of SAS and the inherent instability of the dual rotor system they would make constant minute control inputs to keep the aircraft doing what they wanted it to do and not what it naturally wanted to do. At a hover, this was mainly done with the toe pedals. In flight they had to use pedals and stick to keep the aft rotor from trying to pass the forward rotor. Nice trick once they got the hang of it. A lot of sweat to get that "hang of it."

It was a beautiful day. Good visibility with some haze, normal for Vietnam. Light winds and no clouds. No enemy activity, no shots fired at them. They wer just "fat, dumb, and happy" as the pilots called days like this. No one and nothing trying to kill them. Not the weather, not the terrain, not other aircraft, and not the enemy. A beautiful day.

A little after 1100 (11:00 a.m.) Such said, "I'll take this load, then we'll have some lunch." Harry had just hooked up the load and gave Such some crap for having Harry hook it up before he took over. On days like this the crew would often put cans of C rations near the aft transmission to heat them up. They had their own built-in oven for hot food. Such took over the load of 105 mm cannon ammo and headed for FSB Whip. As they approached, Harry contacted the pathfinder to request wind information and to have him pop a smoke grenade where he wanted the load placed. Harry noticed three Hueys off to the left and informed Such. The Hueys called the pathfinder and told him they had troops and mail to drop off. It appeared that all four aircraft would get to FSB Whip at the same time. Harry told the Hueys to go ahead and for Such to make an orbit to let them in. The Hueys thanked them and went into FSB Whip. Two landed on the main pad and the third on an admin pad on the shoulder of the mountain. They were indeed in and out, so as Such completed the orbit, he started his approach into the main pad. A smoke grenade marked the spot, and Such headed for it. Just as Such brought the nose up at the end of his approach all hell broke loose. The inside of the cockpit looked like a blizzard, and they could hear the pop-pop-pop of rounds going through the skin of the aircraft. The blizzard was from pieces of aircraft skin, Plexiglas, fiberglass, and insulation shreds. At that point there is nothing you can safely do but set the load down. Such did that. As Such was flying, Harry started check-ing all the instruments and warning lights to see what damage was done. After a quick scan, he used the selector switch to check each of the five transmissions. Everything looked good. As he scanned back to the flight instruments, he saw the artificial horizon showing a slow forward roll. The white dot at the bottom of the ball had just come into view. This meant that they were heading into a forward roll and about to become inverted. Harry could see the aircraft tipping over and going down the far side of the mountain, crashing into the trees. Time to bend over and kiss your ass good-bye!

Harry looked up to see where they were going to crash. Much to his relief, the actual horizon was just where it should be. One of the bullets had severed the connection from the gyroscope in the avionics closet behind Such to the instrument on the dashboard just as Such rolled the nose over after dropping the load. The instrument was just following its last instruction and continued the slow roll.

Harry told Such that everything appeared OK. He checked with the crew to see if anyone was injured. They all reported that they were OK. He asked the FE if everything was OK. He said he was still checking, but everything seemed OK. Such had turned and was headed for Birmingham. Harry checked all the gauges, warning lights, and instruments again. With the exception of the rolling artificial horizon, everything looked good. All the gauges were in the green, and there were no warning or caution lights. Whew! That was a close one.

Harry looked around the cockpit. He could see a bullet hole in the bottom of his escape door and another just to the right of the overhead console. He couldn't figure how a bullet had gone through that way without going through his right leg. He checked. Nope, no holes. Good thing. He continued looking and saw three spent AK-47 rounds laying on the floor below Such's seat. He picked them up, and Such asked what he was doing. He showed the bent up slugs to Such, who became noticeably whiter. "Where did you get those?" he asked. "From under your seat, Such!" Harry replied. Harry gave one of the slugs to Such and kept the other two.

They made it back to Birmingham and Such landed. This was the nearest friendly area where they could shut down the aircraft and not be in someone's way. As they were shutting down, the FE told them not to shut down #1 engine or start the APU. The #2 engine was already shut down. The FE told them that there appeared to be a bullet hole in the APU. Such stayed on the controls, and Harry got up to check the aircraft with the FE.

They first looked at the APU. There was a bullet hole into the insulation on the lower right of it, but they could not tell if it was damaged. They thought it best not to try to start it. The CE went up on top, carefully avoiding the turning rotor, He did not find any damage up there. Harry and the FE checked the lower portion of the aircraft. They could not find any serious damage, but there were a lot of bullet holes. They figured out that the bullet that went in through Harry's door actually went through his right toe pedal and out the nose of the aircraft. The one that he saw beside the overhead console had entered through the right open door where the CE was manning the machine gun. It went through the closet behind Harry's seat, into the cockpit just above Harry's head, and out beside the console. Had Harry been flying the aircraft, the bullet that came in through his door would have gone through his right calf. Bit of good luck there. Thanks, Such!

On the way to Birmingham, they had informed Pachyderm Operations what was going on. After restarting #2 engine and taking off for the beach, they called again and requested a maintenance officer be there to check the APU before they shut down the aircraft. Upon landing, maintenance checked and told them to go ahead and shut down the aircraft. It turned out that there was no damage to the APU, just a bullet hole in the insulation around it. Harry had been shot at with artillery, mortars, and small arms prior but hadn't taken hits like this. There were days he'd be flying along and see muzzle flashes and may or may not take a hit or two. At times there would just be the telltale *pop* of a round going through the aircraft. This incident was a lot of *pops*!

Throughout the event, Harry was calm and did his job as the pilot not on the controls. All was well. The inspection at Birmingham was fine also. It wasn't until they landed and shut down the aircraft at Pachyderm Beach that the effect hit Harry. He got the shakes. He was shaking almost as badly as he had seen Belmont at Vandy. He had a Zippo, so he could get a cigarette lit. After several hours he got back to normal and was ready to go out again.

On the same day 527 took a bunch of hits, 533 took hits, and both 537 and 538 took hits with one of the crew in each wounded. Overall, not a good day—but it could have been a lot worse!

# LAOS II—NO GOOD DEED...

It was a fine spring day at the end of March 1969 in wonderful downtown Phu Bai.

Captain William "Wild Bill" Ailes and WO Harry Rat Nevling were on their way from A/159th Assault Support Helicopter Battalion, 101st Airborne Division (affectionately known as Pachyderm Beach) to XXIV Corps Headquarters.

They had been summoned for a briefing on a special operations mission.

Ailes and Harry had been flying together frequently. Ailes was the aircraft commander and Harry the pilot on a rather interesting mission earlier that spring. They had wound up in Laos on a medevac mission for the marines. Harry was certain the old adage, "No good deed shall go unpunished" was in play. He was sure their reward for that good deed was this call.

Upon arrival at the headquarters, Ailes and Harry were taken into a briefing room. They were told a Chinook was needed in northern Laos. There was a US-backed effort to relocate Hmong tribe members from the Plain of Jars area to a more secure area farther south.

The Chinook was needed to move some construction equipment for Pacific Architects & Engineers (PA&E), a subsidiary of the CIA (Central Intelligence Agency).

The operation would stage out of Luang Prabang, site of the Laotian Imperial Summer Palace. This was about 217 kilometers (135 miles) northeast of Vientiane, about 402 kilometers (250 miles) west-southwest of Hanoi, and 177 kilometers (110 miles) west-southwest of Dien Bien Phu.

The mission was to move the equipment from an existing stronghold and haven for civilians to a new area, farther from harm's way. The Pathet Lao, the North Vietnamese, and the Chinese were putting increasing pressure on the area at the edge of the Plain of Jars.

An airstrip was required at the new area. This necessitated the relocation of construction equipment to build a new runway to support up to C-123 Provider aircraft.

The mission would require them to fly the Hook from Da Nang, across the panhandle of Laos to Ubon, Thailand, about 370 kilometers (230 miles) west-southwest of Da Nang, receive additional briefing information, and then go on to Luang Prabang, another 590 kilometers (365 miles) to the northwest.

From there, they would make daily missions to a pickup zone, to be identified later, to pick up the equipment for transport to the drop-off zone, also to be identified later.

They were shown the intelligence map displaying the antiaircraft weaponry along the Ho Chi Minh Trail and its branches that would be crossed. There was an impressive array of colored pins showing the various calibers of weapons, ranging from quadruple .51-caliber machine guns up to 122 mm cannons.

The weapons on the Trail were there to shoot at tactical air bombers, all jets. There they were, considering going across this antiaircraft arsenal in a Hook that has a top speed of around 175 miles per hour and a ceiling of 13,500 feet pressure altitude. They had to be nuts!

They were offered the additional comfort of knowing they'd be escorted by two US Army OV-1 Mohawks. Yeah, that's right, *unarmed* observation aircraft—no guns!

They were given the location of a safe zone on an escarpment in Laos. If something went wrong and they could make it there, they'd be OK. Yeah, like when it hits the fan, you've got a lot of choices where that flying brick is going to go down! Well, they were nuts. They said they'd do it.

They would have a CH-54 Tarhe, better known as the Sky Crane or Flying Crane, accompany them to relocate equipment too heavy for the Hook. Harry thought they were being rewarded for the good deed of rescuing the marines from Laos the previous month. He wondered what good deed the Crane crew was being rewarded for.

Bright and early the next day, 28 March, they left Pachyderm Beach for Da Nang. After topping off the fuel tanks, they headed west on the two-and-a-half-hour flight to Ubon. They rendezvoused with the Crane outside Da Nang and the Mohawks over the southern end of the A Shau Valley. They all continued into Laos.

Looking down at the tracks of bomb craters that clearly marked the main route and branches of the Trail, they couldn't help thinking how slow the Hook was traveling. Even the Mohawks couldn't go that slowly. They were flying slow circles around the lumbering helicopters.

They were sitting ducks for anyone who wanted to take a potshot at them. Fortunately, the briefing officer appeared to be correct when he said, "Don't worry. All the gunners will be asleep, so they can defend the Trail at night." Charlie must have been asleep. No tracers, flak bursts, or other nasties were sent up to greet them.

Their arrival in Ubon was a relief. The security of a Royal Thai air base with US Air Force personnel seemed a very safe haven.

They were taken to a briefing room where they were greeted by men dressed in civilian clothes. They were asked why they had insignia and patches on their flight suits. The response was no one had told them any different.

The aircraft also had "US ARMY" stenciled on its sides. When asked if they had any civilian clothes with them, they responded no. Again, no one had said anything about that, either.

They told them they could cut the identification off the uniforms and, if they had any OD paint, they'd cover up the markings on the aircraft. After some discussion among themselves they decided that would not be necessary.

The bad news was that without civilian clothes they wouldn't be able to take the helicopter crews into Vientiane. So they stayed in their Nomex flight suits with the insignia and patches. The formal briefing began.

They were given more details of the mission.

They would fly directly to Luang Prabang and were given the frequency for an NDB (nondirectional beacon) at that location. There was an airstrip in the town used by Air America (CIA) for resupplying the Loyalist forces in northern Laos led by General Vang Pao. They would be staying there with Air America personnel in their compound.

The pickup area was located at Muong Soui, a village with an airstrip about 135 kilometers (eighty-five miles) southeast of Luang Prabang and 290 kilometers (180 miles) north of Vientiane. The drop-off was in the area of Muong Kasi on the Nam Lik River about 89 to 111 kilometers (55–69 miles) west of Muong Soui, 96 kilometers (60 miles) south of Luang Prabang, and 240 kilometers (150 miles) north of Vientiane.

They were provided with the names and grid coordinates for the pickup and drop-off zones, radio frequencies, call signs, and maps of the pickup and drop-off locations. Secure areas, enemy activity, and defense forces also were described.

They were told that if they went down in an unsecured area, the aircraft would have to be destroyed, and they'd try to get them out. They were not to take any type of photographic equipment with them. Overall, it was fairly dismal information.

The briefing also contained information regarding the Hmong tribesmen. These are the aboriginal people indigenous to the area. The Hmong had actually migrated south from China several centuries earlier and inhabited the mountainous regions of what is now Laos, much like the Montagnards of South Vietnam. This was now their homeland. They were very interested in protecting it. They are cousins to the Montagnards of Vietnam.

During World War II, the Hmong had fought the Japanese invaders with flintlock rifles. Some were still using these weapons against the Pathet Lao and North Vietnamese. Unusual looking, they had no stock. The handle was like the head of a golf club and was held in the hand rather than against the shoulder. The Hmong were deadly with the use of this antique weapon.

They are very family- and tribal-oriented. Their loyalties are to their tribal family and its leader. This was General Vang Pao. The general was not only the chief of the Hmong, he was also the leader of the loyalist forces in Laos.

The Hmong are quite industrious people. They were told to watch for their trails en route. When they wanted to go someplace, they simply took the straightest line. Most of these straight lines involved significant vertical changes. Straight up the side of a ridgeline, and straight down the other.

After the briefing, Ailes and Harry went to the aircraft. They were informed by the flight crew that the fuel control unit for No. 2 engine was leaking. Ailes made arrangements for another unit to be flown in by Mohawk.

They had lunch and waited for the replacement part to arrive. When the unit finally arrived, they found that the Mohawk that brought it over wasn't as fortunate as they had been. The aircraft had taken several hits flying over the Trail. Charlie must have been awake!

The crew quickly installed the fuel control unit, so they could be on their way to Luang Prabang. The flight was uneventful, which was wonderful. The scenery was spectacular. The mountains in the area were quite rugged. Many of the ridgelines were nearly vertical, much like the mountains south of Hue.

Here was the evidence of the Hmong trails. As they had been told, they were straight lines, even if that straight line happened to go over a two-thousand-foot-high ridge, they went straight up the ridge and straight down the other side.

There was not the obvious evidence of the conflict in this area. No large bomb craters, no defoliation, and no roads. Just the trails going from village to village.

The vegetation was much like that around the A Shau Valley and Khe Sahn. Deep jungle with open areas the Hmong had cleared for their slash-and-burn agriculture. Spectacular scenery in an almost pristine area.

But, back to reality. Coming over yet one more ridgeline Luang Prabang appeared below. The summer palace of the Lao royal family was nestled into the ridge on the west side of the town.

To the east, another ridge, more like a cliff. The small valley in between also held an airstrip—right in the middle of the town.

The road, the first they'd seen since leaving Ubon, came up the valley and crossed the middle of the airstrip. Next to this crossing was an observation tower for control of the traffic on the road and the airstrip.

The control method was simple: When the observer, an American, spotted an approaching aircraft, he would fire his .30-caliber carbine into the air. The ground traffic cleared the strip, and the aircraft landed.

The signal for departure was the revving of an aircraft engine or, in their case, picking up to a hover. The movie *Air America* used this airfield as its model for the film.

After landing, they were directed to a parking/loading area. The larger aircraft, like C-123 Providers, seemed to be in-and-out traffic, not actually based there. Their Chinook and the Crane took up a significant part of the parking area.

They were taken to the Air America compound, actually a house in the town with a fence and a gate. After stowing their gear, they had a beer with the other pilots at home there. They provided them with more information about the AO they were heading into.

More dismal information. If they were to go down for some reason and the Hmong were to get to them first, they'd be OK. The alternative was not pleasant.

During their chat with these men another man in civvies came in. They could tell by the reaction of the others that: a) he wasn't a pilot, and b) he was someone important.

He informed the army pilots that they were to have dinner with GEN Vang Pao that evening. He told them that this was quite an honor. The murmurs of the others in the room confirmed this. It appeared none of the regular pilots had been invited to dinner with the general.

They talked with the other pilots more and then got ready for the evening. This meant a shower and a clean Nomex flight suit—with patches and insignia.

About 1830 hours (6:30 p.m.) they were picked up by the man who had informed them of the dinner and taken someplace in or near the summer palace compound.

Upon entering the dining room, they were introduced to several Laotian officers by their escort.

The room was very pleasant, quite comfortable, and ornate. The table, with seating for sixteen to twenty, was set with linen, china, and real silverware. For a couple of GIs from 'Nam this was impressive!

GEN Vang Pao entered the room, and all were called to attention. They didn't speak any Lao but didn't need to for an understanding of this command.

They were introduced to the general by their escort. The general, through an interpreter, welcomed them to Laos and thanked them for their assistance. He then called for an aide with a small box. The box contained rings.

Their escort displayed a look of surprise at seeing the box and its contents. The general removed a ring from the box and gave it to Ailes. He repeated this with Harry.

He then said that these were symbols of appreciation he and his people had for what they were doing for them. He understood that this was a voluntary mission, and they did not have to be there to help his people with this problem.

They thanked the general for his gift and said they were glad they could be of some assistance.

Their escort went on to explain that these rings were Hmong tribal rings. In effect, the general had adopted them into the Hmong tribe. These rings were a tribal symbol, made of almost pure silver, with a wound silver frame on the front, forming four rows of triangles. Each of these triangles was filled with a colored substance that looked like enamel.

Very simple, very beautiful. He said they should be impressed. They were.

Harry was probably more impressed than Ailes. On his first tour Harry had been a grunt with the 4th Infantry Division. He'd been adopted by a Montagnard tribe outside Pleiku. A bit different process, but that's another story.

They all sat down to a thoroughly enjoyable meal. One local custom is that the only glasses on the table are for whiskey. The silverware included a large spoon at each place. This was used to dip liquid from the vegetable bowl and sip from the spoon. The whiskey was served straight and at room temperature.

After dinner and a bit more conversation, they gave their thanks and farewell and were taken back to the compound for a night's rest.

The next morning they joined their flight crew at the aircraft. They performed a very thorough preflight check for the day's mission and departed for Muong Soui.

Another beautiful flight over spectacular mountain scenery. Muong Soui turned out to be a small dirt airstrip at about 4,200 feet altitude for C-123 Provider and Aero Porter traffic. This wasn't as nasty as the dirt strip in *Air America*, but there was a definite slope to it.

The strip had a small loading area beside it near the middle. This contained fuel bladders and fifty-five-gallon drums of fuel. Just above this, on a small hill, was a compound. The strip was outside any defensive perimeter for the compound.

They had been talking to Special Forces by radio before seeing the airstrip or compound. After landing and shutting down the aircraft they were greeted by a sergeant first class (E-7) and taken up the hill to the Special Forces headquarters in the compound.

As they went into the compound they noticed a wide array of weaponry that the Hmong had, including many Uzis. At the headquarters they were introduced to a Special Forces captain, the officer in charge of the compound, and the senior adviser for the AO.

They had a nice conversation with this officer. While he was pleasant, he had very hard eyes. He looked as if he'd had nails for breakfast—hold the milk and sugar!

He said that the fuel in the bladders was contaminated. He suspected sabotage. What this meant to them was hand pump refueling from fifty-five-gallon drums. A Chinook burns about two thousand pounds of fuel an hour. As JP-4 weighs about 6.8 pounds per gallon, they burn about five and a third drums per hour. Boy, were they ever glad they'd topped off their tanks at Luang Prabang.

They listened intently to the briefing by the Special Forces captain on local operations and activity. This included the story of his complaint about not having any mobile artillery, as large weapons were restricted to 4.2 inch mounted mortars. So the sergeant went out with a patrol and took a tank away from the North Vietnamese/Pathet Lao. Now the captain had his mobile artillery. However, the sergeant told him he was on his own for any additional ammo he needed.

He also told them the officer in charge of the airfield had been killed a few nights before. Someone had penetrated the compound and tossed a frag (grenade) into the bunker where he was sleeping.

They went back down to the ship and helped the crew pump fuel. After getting a full load on, they talked to the PA&E people about the loads they were to transport.

The first item was a small grader. While they had hauled "baby bulls" and later D-7 bulldozers into the A Shau Valley in 'Nam for making landing zones and fire support bases in the mountains, as well as a variety of other construction equipment, this was the first grader either of them had hauled.

The second item was a rubber-wheeled packer. This piece of equipment used dirt for ballast and was lightened significantly by the removal of this ballast material. This was the Crane's first load.

They had a second load of a large generator. They checked the rigging on both of their items, as these were their only flights scheduled for the morning.

They cranked up the Hook, picked up the load, and headed off for Nam Lik, about 110 kilometers (sixty-nine miles) away. They departed to the south along a beautiful valley of rice paddies. The west side was a low ridge about one hundred feet above the valley floor. The east side was a cliff of more than two hundred feet.

About a half mile from the airstrip the valley abruptly ended with the hill to the west becoming a ridge turning sharply to join the cliff on the east. Beyond this ridge the land dropped away sharply in a series of ridgelines of lower and lower elevations. This would become very important later.

They were able to make a fairly straight line to their destination. Radio contact was established with the drop-off point. A smoke grenade was popped, the color confirmed, and they put the grader on it. Whew! One down and no one shooting at them. What a relief!

They were a bit, just a bit, relaxed as they returned to Muong Soui and talked about the spectacular scenery and the immense difficulty of trying to transport equipment through this rugged terrain.

They had moved supplies, equipment, and troops for the building of the road from Phu Bai to the A Shau Valley, as well as inserting the fire support bases for their protection. That terrain certainly had its challenges, but it was nothing compared to this.

They made another run with the generator. This trip was also uneventful, other than getting to see more of the spectacular scenery of northern Laos.

Upon their return to Muong Soui, they shut down for lunch.

They talked to the PA&E people about how many loads they had for the afternoon. They only wanted to move two more loads that day. Both were cargo net loads of miscellaneous equipment.

They thought that was great! An easy day, and more importantly, they had plenty of fuel to take both loads and get back to Luang Prabang without having to hand pump any more fuel!

The fun began when they cranked up after lunch. When they took the engines from flight idle (about 37 percent power) to flight (about 92 percent power), the number two engine went up to 42 percent and hung there. Cycling the engine control lever had no effect. They couldn't get more than 42 percent out of number two.

After trying everything they could think of, with no effect, they shut down to check the engine.

The flight engineer opened the number two engine nacelle and went over the engine, especially the fuel control unit. This is a highly complex piece of equipment that receives the demand asked of the engine, measures the pressure altitude, and meters the appropriate amount of fuel into the engine.

Close examination of this piece of equipment revealed the fuel drain had clogged. This prevented the fuel from draining upon shut down. The relatively cool fuel in the engine from flight was trapped upon shutdown. The expansion resulting from the heat increase blew out an internal O-ring seal. This prevented the fuel control unit from performing its essential function.

They talked with the local cadre about getting a part flown in. They informed them if their aircraft sat on that loading area overnight it probably would be destroyed by morning. Not an acceptable situation.

They cranked up the ship to see if they could get it to hover at that altitude and temperature. They were unsuccessful. They shut down again to make arrangements for any excess weight they could shed. An Air America pilot told them he'd take their crew and equipment to Luang Prabang for them after he dropped off his load. They shut down the aircraft and made the decision to switch out the fuel control unit back to the leaky unit. Again, they couldn't leave the aircraft on the strip overnight.

They took out the guns and ammo along with the toolboxes and anything else they could get by without. This was going with their crew chief and gunner on the Air America plane.

While they were waiting, they witnessed an interesting accident. Another Air America pilot, flying an Aero Porter, was chafing at the bit to get out but was told to wait for an incoming C-123 Provider. This seemed to upset him.

He stomped around for a bit, then got in and started up his plane. He taxied into the parking area facing toward the strip. As the loaded C-123 landed, he gunned it and pulled onto the strip immediately behind the C-123s tail with the throttle to the firewall.

The turbulence got him. His hurry put him up on one wing and then into the strip. Oops! Not going very far now!

The pilot jumped out of his aircraft hollering about the turbulence and that the accident wasn't his fault. But it was!

Ailes and Harry tried real hard to ignore him.

Ailes, Harry, and the flight engineer cranked up again for the flight. They pulled another hover check, and with the increased temperature, they couldn't get a hover, but they could feel it was light on the landing gear. Both engines were running, but number two was at flight idle.

They discussed a running takeoff. If they left the ship there it would be destroyed so it was worth the try.

They taxied to the far eastern end of the strip. They couldn't take off to the east, which was open plain and slightly downhill, as they had been told that if they tried to go in that direction they would be headed into Russian .51-caliber machine guns. They wanted to avoid that problem.

So they headed west, which was uphill and toward a ridgeline. Ailes had practiced this running takeoff procedure at Da Nang on several occasions. (This maneuver was taught in transition.) He eased the stick forward, and they moved up the strip. He got the aircraft up on the main (front) gear and increased airspeed as they moved along the strip.

All the instruments looked real good. They were moving along at about forty knots when Ailes eased the nose off the ground. They came up slowly and settled back in, although they were well above what should have been flying speed. One bounce, and they were near the end of the runway. They were in a slow climb, rotor rpm was steady, and airspeed was increasing. All right! This was going to work!

Well, almost. They cleared the end of the strip, and everything went to hell. The rotor rpm started bleeding off along with their rate of climb and airspeed.

Ailes told the flight engineer to get buckled in quick. They looked out at the ridge at the end of the valley. It was approaching fast. The extra 150 feet of altitude needed to clear that ridge was nowhere to be found.

Ailes was trying to get them back to the airstrip. He headed to the left, and the ground dropped away below them. Then he eased back on the stick, but she still wouldn't climb.

Harry said, "Let me try this," and flipped number two engine to its flight position. The engine picked up to about 42 percent, as it had before, and hung there. The good news was this seemed to lessen the drag on the system enough for them to start regaining their rotor rpm.

Ailes had been bleeding off airspeed, as they didn't want to crash at that speed. He had been trading air speed to maintain the low rotor rpm and altitude.

Ailes eased back on the stick again, and they began a shallow climb. As they approached the ridge he found a break in the trees at the far end. He pulled back more on the stick, and they slid over the top. As he dropped into the next valley he traded the altitude for rotor rpm and got it back into the green along with additional airspeed. This he again traded to get them over the next ridgeline.

Upon their arrival they were taken back to the Air America compound. As they got out of the vehicle they witnessed a very strange occurrence. At the entrance to the compound a group of Laotians had assembled. This was not unusual, as helicopters and their pilots often attracted groups of the curious.

What was strange was one of the men had a camera and was taking pictures of them. They had never experienced a local taking pictures of GIs. It was always the GIs taking the pictures.

When they got inside the building they mentioned this to the Air America men. They all jumped up, asked them what the photographer looked like and how he was dressed, grabbed their weapons, and ran out looking for the man. When they couldn't find him they returned to tell Ailes and the others if they ever saw someone taking their picture they should shoot him. It seems the photographer was probably a spy for the Pathet Lao, and their pictures were for their wanted posters of "American agents in Laos." Oops!

They checked the situation with the PA&E people. They determined they had moved the essential equipment. The remaining equipment could be transported by the Crane and an Air America Huey. They were released from the mission.

The flight engineer made some unauthorized repairs and rebuilt the leaky unit with parts from the disabled unit. This was depot-level repair, not field repair!

The flight engineer replaced the fuel control unit, and they were ready to try again. This time things worked. The leaky unit no longer leaked, number two engine worked fine, and the aircraft was ready to go.

They got their gear together and headed south to Udorn, Thailand. The fuel control unit worked fine. They made an uneventful flight south and landed at Udorn airport. This was a joint military-civilian airport used by the US Air Force, the Royal Thai Air Force, and Royal Thai Airways, a commercial carrier.

After landing and hovering to a taxiway, a "Follow Me" truck escorted them to a parking ramp and handed them off to a ground handler. He guided them into a parking slot—and a light pole. Yup, he guided them right into a steel pole holding lights for the parking ramp.

The flight engineer was yelling, "They're too close!" They thought he was talking about the edge of the ramp, and they were about to go off the concrete onto the grass. Wrong!

The rear blades took down the pole with little effort. They shut down and examined all three of the aft blades.

One was damaged with a large dent in the leading edge. All three had tears in the lower side. Hook blades come in sets of three, they are very heavy, and the aft rotor head is about twenty-five feet off the ground. They have to be replaced in sets, even if only one is damaged.

For the really important things doing so well, the disabling small things were getting really old.

To top off the situation the air force came over and told them they couldn't leave the aircraft on that ramp overnight. They had to move it to the far end of the airfield.

They went into flight operations and contacted their headquarters with the bad news. They would make arrangements to get them a new set of blades and a means to get the old blades off and the new ones hung on the aft rotor head.

They next made arrangements with the air force for billets for their crew and themselves. They wound up putting them up in Udorn at the Hotel Sharon. This was nice. A real hotel with real restaurants.

They were expecting Quonset huts with cots at the air base. This made the accident seem almost worthwhile.

They had another nice dinner. This one at a rooftop restaurant at the hotel. Harry thought the real tomato soup was wonderful! Ah, what a wonderful evening.

The only thing that spoiled it was that peculiar odor of Nomex. They were still wearing flight suits. These were the only clothes they had.

The running water in the hotel was not potable, but all they had to do was open their door and a steward would come to see to their needs, including drinking water. The *hot, running* water in the shower sure felt good!

The following morning brought more bad news. Harry had developed a major case of gastroenteritis. Sweat, chills, and stomach cramps.

At the airbase the flight surgeon made the diagnosis and provided the appropriate medications. It took a long six to eight hours to overcome the symptoms. (Wonder if it was the tomato soup.)

Ailes and Harry had lost their caps. They had tossed them on the seats in the back of the aircraft when they were filling out the logbook after the mishap with the light pole. They couldn't check the blades until they wound down and stopped. They went outside the ship with the flight crew and checked the blade damage. Upon their return to recover their caps to leave the flight line, they discovered the caps were gone. Nice disappearing act on the part of the caps. After making arrangements for the replacement blades and billets, they went looking for a BX (base exchange, air force version of army post exchange) to get new headgear.

As they were walking along, an air force colonel was walking along the other side of the street. He called Ailes over and read him the riot act for being outside without headgear. Ailes wasn't given the opportunity to explain the situation.

They found the BX and removed any further opportunity of ass-chewing with new air force caps.

The replacement blades finally arrived. With the help of the air force, the old blades were removed, and the new ones were slung on the aft rotor head. They tracked the blades and got the ship ready for the return flight to Vietnam.

With a new set of aft blades, a full load of fuel, and a flight plan filed with the air force, they cranked up and headed for home.

Another extremely apprehensive flight across the Ho Chi Minh Trail, this time without an escort. They thought they'd be as safe or safer without an unarmed escort. They felt removing three additional targets might further dissuade any interest from the gunners along the Trail.

This flight was a bit different, as they went directly to Phu Bai instead of Da Nang.

The scenery was strangely familiar. The main track of bomb craters clearly showed where the trail went.

They were very glad to pass the eastern edge of the A Shau Valley and have the sight of Hue and Phu Bai in the distance.

They descended out of their nose-bleed altitude and made a long approach to Birmingham Supply Point to refuel, then on to Pachyderm Beach.

It was great to be *home*!

# MARCH WAS A TOUGH MONTH

**M**arch was when the expansion of the AO and the addition of marine support caught up with Pachyderm. The NVA (North Vietnamese Army) were not happy with the incursions into "their" territory. The US forces were inflicting a lot of damage to their troops and finding a lot of their weapons caches. If fact, the largest cache to date had been discovered. Chinooks of the 101st, especially Pachyderm, spent an entire day pulling one load after another of captured weapons and supplies out of one cache discovered.

The location was the side of a ridge. The trees had been cut away to allow access by the Chinooks. However the trees on the sides of the cleared area still fell over the landing area. The triple canopy jungle in the area had trees up to 150 feet tall. The Pachyderms would hover in under the top canopy, hook up a load, then back out, pulling the load off the ridge. When the load slid free of the ground, it was an abrupt change in the weight, and the swing would tend to throw the aircraft forward. They had to be very careful and anticipate when this would happen, so they could counteract it with the controls. Once the load was clear, they could back away, turn parallel to the ridge, and take off for Camp Eagle, where the cache was being reassembled.

Needless to say, this pissed off the NVA some. They took to setting up ambushes for the Chinooks. The .51-caliber machine guns at FSB Cunningham seemed to be the first concentrated attempt to specifically shoot down a Chinook. The ambush of the artillery raid 3 March was another. The ambush of Harry and Such on 20 March was nearly successful. Another ambush, specifically set up for a Chinook on 18 May, they got right and took out Chinook 67–18536, killing CW2 Harold (Weird Harold) Eckert, AC ( CW2 Davis, pilot; F. E. Nevel, C. E. Combs, and G. Shellum. More on this incident later.

Overall, March was a bad month. The following aircraft were hit and damaged:

| DATE | AIRCRAFT | RESULTS |
| --- | --- | --- |
| 3/17 | 520 | Hit |
| 3/17 | 540 | Hit |
| 3/17 | 541 | Hit |
| 3/18 | 527 | Hit—Twice |
| 3/18 | 535 | Hit |
| 3/20 | 527 | Hit—Many times |
| 3/20 | 537 | Hit-1 injured |
| 3/20 | 538 | Hit |
| 3/20 | 540 | Hit—Many times |

The only good thing was that no one was killed in any of these attacks, and only one crewman was injured.

Following the Chinook-specific ambushes and all the activity of March, it struck Harry that they were all alone out there. If something happened, help was not immediately available. It would take some time to get help if one were able to call for it. Any time out there on the ground alone was too long. While Harry did not dwell on this and the pilots never talked about it, it had to be in the back of their minds every day.

Harry had flown twenty-one of the thirty-one days in March. He logged a total of 90.6 flying hours.

# LOWELL POWERS

April started off bad. While Harry was gone to northern Laos, the Pachyderms lost another aircraft and a pilot. On 2 April 1969, Lowell Powers was flying with Major Burns, the company commander. They were assigned a mission to take ARVN troops on an insertion for a sweep to try to locate NVA soldiers. Just before touchdown, they lost power in one of their engines. The aircraft touched down on the side of a ravine and rolled to the bottom, winding up on its left side. The aircraft exploded, probably because of fuel from a ruptured fuel cell hitting the hot engine. Powers assisted the CO to get out of the aircraft but apparently was unable to get himself out. Powers was killed in the accident.

Twenty-three of the ARVN soldiers were killed and twenty-six others injured in the crash.

Because helicopters burn extremely hot, they were unable to identify Powers's body. Records listed him as MIA (missing in action) for several years.

Harry and Such both missed Powers. He was a fun guy to have around. The other guys from the original Playtex group also missed his positive attitude and great sense of humor. They missed Powers's many stories and jokes. He had taught Harry how to play pinochle. The two of them played many games in the O club. Harry has not played pinochle since Powers's death. Lowell Powers was definitely a loss to Pachyderm.

# Chief Warrant Officer 2 (CW2)

On 9 April 1969, Harry and Belmont, along with Paul Clement, another original Playtex, were sent to battalion headquarters. There, in a brief ceremony, they, along with Beauchene from Varsity were promoted to Chief Warrant Officer 2. They were now officially Chief. Following the ceremony they congratulated each other and the three returned to Pachyderm Beach for a beer.

# Such and the Rockets

One night Harry awoke to the sound of an exploding rocket. It was not real close but close enough. Harry had learned that close resulted in a *bang!* Really close resulted in a *ba-bang!* When you heard both parts of the explosion, the explosion and the implosion, it was really close.

Harry rolled out of his bed onto the floor and under the bed. Above there was a metal roof that would explode the rocket if it hit. Then there was a one-inch sheet of plywood. Added to this was the mattress over his head. He figured he was fairly safe from a direct hit. A near miss would have to send shrapnel through the one-inch plywood exterior wall. Again, Harry felt fairly safe from this. Not as good as a bunker but he was already there and did not have to go outside to get to a bunker. During his first tour Harry was in a mortar attack. Several guys jumped out of a trailer and ran for a bunker. A mortar round landed by them and injured several, one severly. Harry had jumped out and gone back under the trailer. He was uninjured.

As soon as he got under his bed he called to his hooch mate, "Hey, Such." He had not heard any sounds from his side of the room and got no response to his query. "Hey, Such!" Harry called out louder. Still no response. "Such, you OK?" Again no response. Harry listened for a while and did not hear any more rockets after the three that exploded nearby. He turned on the light switch by the door. He turned back, and there was Such, sitting on the edge of his bed wearing his steel pot (helmet) and his flak jacket. Harry had not head a sound, but he had managed to get that far. Harry again asked if he was OK. Such replied that he was fine.

They chatted for a few minutes, then turned off the lights and went back to bed. Just another day in the paradise of Southeast Asia.

## Beer for Cannon

One morning Ailes and Harry were taking a load of ammo to FSB Cunningham and flew past FSB Shiloh. They were east of the FSB but within easy sight of it. The pathfinder called over the radio, "Hey, Pachyderm." Harry was flying, so Ailes responded. The pathfinder stated that they had a bet that a Chinook could not pick up a 155 mm howitzer. As one might guess, a 155 mm was larger and heavier than a 105 mm howitzer, significantly heavier. They had a gun they needed to relocate and would give them a case of beer if they could do it. Ailes informed him that they'd just refueled and didn't want to try it. He told the pathfinder to get the gun ready. They'd be back in a couple of hours and move it. The pathfinder replied that they'd be ready.

Ailes and Harry took some more loads from Vandergrift to various FSBs in the area. When the fuel got to where they needed to refuel, Ailes called the pathfinder on FSB Shiloh and told him they were inbound. The pathfinder told them they were all set and popped a smoke grenade. Harry identified the color, and it was confirmed. Ailes flew up to the cannon, hovered over the gun, and picked it up. Being low on fuel (light), they moved it to the smoke in the new gun pit on the other side of the FSB. For the marines to manhandle that gun across the top of that mountain would have been a real pain in the ass! When they set the gun down, a marine got up on it and passed a case of beer up through the cargo hook hole to the FE. The marines thanked them, and Harry told them anytime.

After departing the FSB, Ailes asked the FE if they had any ice in the Igloo water cooler. Many of the FEs had a water cooler strapped to the airframe beside the avionics closet behind the AC's seat. The FE told him that they had put a good-size chunk in the insulated container that morning. Ailes asked if it would be OK to put the beer in the Igloo to get it cold, then place it in a sandbag to take back to the marines. The FE agreed. He thought that was a good idea and would be a real treat for the marines. The marines had no ice on those FSBs and no cold beer.

That afternoon when they had taken their last load out, they called the pathfinder and asked him to get on the gun they had moved. As they approached the FSB, they saw him on the gun and hovered up to him so the FE could pass the sandbag of cold beer down to him. The transfer was a success. As they left the area, the pathfinder called and thanked them profusely for the return gift of *cold beer*!

# SP Packs to Burtchesgaten

**M**any of the pilots tried to look out for the flight crews. These were the guys who took care of the aircraft and therefore the pilots. Sometimes there were things the pilots could do for the crew.

One morning Ailes and Harry picked up a load at Supply Point Birmingham that was headed out to one of the FSBs along the A Shau Valley. As he hovered over the load, he looked to see what it was. It was real obvious it was not the usual 105 mm cannon ammo. It was cases of something. C rations? Nope. As he got closer, he could see the printing on the boxes. They were SP (Supplemental Packs) packs. These were supplemental personal items. Everything from stationery, pens, and envelopes to cigarettes, candy bars, and chewing gum. Obviously they were highly valued. Harry told Ailes, "This is a load of SP packs. I don't see anything else in there." As they lifted off, Bill confirmed with the FE that indeed it was a sling load of SP packs. It looked like there were enough in there for one pack for each two guys on the FSB. They were designed to cover far more than two soldiers!

Well, wasn't that nice. *A lot* of SP packs. Surely they wouldn't miss a few out of this entire load! Ailes asked the FE—if they set down somewhere—could he drop through the cargo hook hatch and grab some of the SP packs? He replied that he sure could. So they picked a spot on the road the 101st was building to the A Shau to sit down on. It was level, it was clear of any obstructions, and the dust they would kick up would prevent anyone from seeing what they were doing.

Harry set up a quick approach. It was a fairly light load, and he had plenty of power to spare. As the load touched down, the dust cloud appeared. Harry kept his visual reference through the chin bubble, the only place he could see the ground. He dropped as close to the load as he could but still allow room for the FE to drop down to the cargo net. The FE dropped down and passed SP packs up to the CE. The FE crawled back into the aircraft, and Harry pulled pitch. They took the remainder of the load to the FSB and dropped it off.

On the way back to Birmingham, Ailes asked the FE how many SP packs he'd gotten. The FE told him they had four. Ailes said, "How about you guys take three and we'll take one to put in the O Club?" The FE said that was fine. They'd keep one for their platoon, give one to the other flight platoon, and pass the third on to the maintenance platoon. A good deal for everyone.

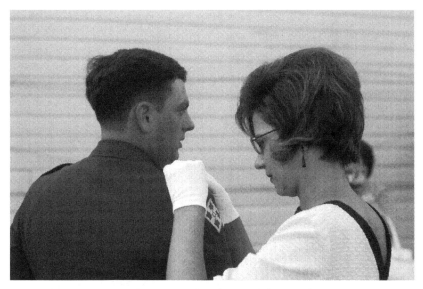

Harry getting his WO bars

TH-55

TH-55 instrument panel

UH-1D instrument panel

UH-1D center console

CH-47 instrument panel

CH-47 overhead console

Chinook at Ft. Sill

Chinook in Vietnam

A load of 105mm ammo

Pachyderm Beach

Packy Sunday brunch, O club in background

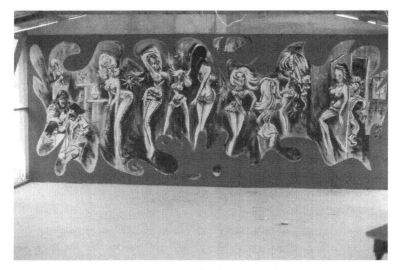

Mural on O club patio wall

Harry's bunk at Pachyderm

Marine Combat Base Vandergrift

FSB Cunningham

Road to Khe Sahn

Airstrip at Luang Prabang

Road to A Shau Valley

Exit wounds FSB Lash

CW2 Nevling Harry
Muleskinners, Cu Chi, Vietnam
August 1969

CW2 Nevling

# MARINE CHICKEN SHITS

Harry wondered why the marines needed so much support from the army. Two incidents gave him a real clue as to why. One morning Ailes and he departed Camp Evans with a load of ammo for FSB Cunningham. They were behind a flight of four CH-46 Sea Knights. These were a much smaller version of the Chinook. They could carry about ten marines or one pallet of 105 mm ammo. Each of these had the single pallet of ammo.

As they crossed the first ridgeline, one of the flight called the leader. He had some very minor problem with the aircraft that actually sounded like an excuse to Harry. He told the leader that he was returning to base to have the problem checked out. Then his wingman called and told the leader that he was returning with his wingman. The leader told him that was OK. They never went anyplace without a wingman. Harry never went anyplace with one! There were two pallets of ammo not delivered because of a rather lame excuse. As they followed the other two CH-46s to FSB Cunningham, they overheard the two talking about where they were by using their TACAN (Tactical Air Navigation System). The TACAN showed them where they were in relation to where the transmitting station was located and haw far from that station they were. When you put the two together things together, they could tell where they were. (This is like modern GPS.) They would know the radial from the beacon and distance from the station to where the FSB was. When they got to the correct radial and the right distance they would look down.

They got directly over FSB Cunningham and looked down. Of course it was socked in. However, about half a click away was a large sucker hole. Flight lead called his wingman and announced they had arrived, and he could not see the FSB. Both of these CH-46s turned around and went back. Ailes and Harry dropped down through the sucker hole, flew back to FSB Cunningham, and dropped off their load. That was four marine pallets of ammo that were not delivered and four army pallets that were. No wonder they required so much army support!

# TIGER MOUNTAIN

The marines moved even farther south and occupied the top of Co An Nang Mountain sometime around the beginning of March. The marines and pilots just called it Tiger Mountain. It was mentioned before it had an elevation of 1,228 meters, or 4,029 feet. It sloped to the west and dropped off very sharply to the east and south. Along the south side of the mountain was the road that branched from the main north-south road in the A Shau Valley, paralleled the Laos-Vietnam border for a distance, then connected it to the main Ho Chi Minh Trail. This is the route that the marines had crossed the border to intercept in February. It was a major supply route for the NVA.

The marines had at least one battery of 105 mm howitzers on top. Ailes and Harry were taking loads of ammunition and other supplies up there for the marines. The NVA didn't think much of the marines being up there and tried to push them off. When that failed, they managed to get a 122 mm gun emplaced to the west in Laos. So, like FSB Cunningham, when you went in there with a load, an observer would spot the helicopter, and a round would be fired. Fortunately, as with FSB Cunningham, they had about four seconds to get themselves gone.

They would fly from Vandergrift down the valleys or out from one of the 101st resupply areas and across the A Shau Valley. They would stay at or below the top of the mountain to swing the load up and drop it, and be gone in a hurry. *Boom!* A round would hit close enough that if you were on that pad you'd be in serious trouble. Again, for some reason they never had an observer on the east side who could warn them in advance that you were coming. The near vertical terrain on the east side also pretty much prevented them emplacing a .51-caliber ambush on that side. Tiger Mountain was not one of the pilots' favorite destinations! All of the FSBs out there were dangerous. Tiger Mountain, with that cannon, was a bit worse!

The marines were up there less than a month when the FSB was evacuated and closed. Pachyderm was instrumental in getting the marines and their equipment off the mountain. Following the relocation of the marines, their guns, and equipment, the FSB was bombed. This accomplished two things. When an FSB was closed, the NVA would rush in to see what they could recover from anything left by American forces. Blowing up the FSB would usually catch some of them. It also served to destroy anything that was left behind.

# Moving Bulldozers into the A Shau Valley

As the engineers from the 101st Airborne Division continued to re-build and upgrade Route 547 from Highway 1 to the A Shau Valley, someone had the bright idea to take equipment into the A Shau and build/upgrade to the east and join up with the westbound crews. Harry thought that the 101st engineers had help from other engineer outfits as airborne units do not have heavy equipment, such as D-8 and D-9 bull-dozers, so there must have been other units involved. Now a D-9 weighs in at 108,000 pounds, and a D-8 is eighty thousand pounds. Neither of these is within the cargo capacity of twenty thousand pounds for the Chinook's cargo hook. However, they also had some D-7 bulldozers that weighed a mere 31,800 pounds. (They also had "baby bulls" that were relatively tiny and could easily be carried to the mountain top FSB for clearing and grading.) Still way beyond the Hook's cargo hook capacity, but where there's a will there's a way. Someone—must have been a heli-copter pilot—figured out if you disconnected the blade and the tracks, the body of the bulldozer would be below the twenty-thousand-pound limit of the Chinook. So was the blade, so were the tracks.

So here's how it worked. Two Chinooks were assigned to move each dozer. Because of the labor involved there were only two, as they couldn't prepare fast enough for two bulldozers coming in together. Harry went in and picked up the body of a bulldozer. They had disconnected the tracks and the blade from the body so Harry picked up just the bulldozer body. He headed for the A Shau Valley—slowly. Then another Chinook came in and picked up the cargo net the dozer had been parked on, taking the two sets of tracks. The blade had been disconnected on a cargo net forward of the dozer. That Chinook went as fast as it could out into the valley and set the net down where the engineers marked with smoke. A large group of men then manhandled the tracks into the proper width and distance so the body could be set into the tracks it had just been removed from. The helicopter that had brought out the tracks would have already gone back for the blade. Harry then went in with the body and carefully lined up with the tracks and blade. There were tether lines on the body to turn it to align with the tracks. After a bit of careful maneuvering, Harry set the body down on the tracks successfully. As he departed the drop-off area, he saw the group of men on the ground getting the tracks up on the drive and idler wheels to connect them again. Then the first aircraft would return with the blade. This was set down just in front of the dozer so that once the tracks were attached properly the dozer could just move forward and be in position to reattach the blade. Now the engineers could work on the road from two directions and get the mission accomplished that much sooner. Harry wondered why put all this effort into a road when the 101st was an airborne division. He learned firsthand later that it was because the army wanted the 11th ACR (Armored Cavalry Regiment) to have access to the A Shau to try to sweep the valley of NVA with its tanks and armored personnel vehicles.

# KHE SAHN

One of the many days that Ailes and Harry were hauling loads out of Combat Base Vandergrift they were given a load to take out to Khe Sahn, where the marines had had such a tough go of it the year before. Harry wondered if they were going to try to occupy it again. As it turned out, they weren't. It was more a raiding party than anything else.

To get there under the clouds, the best thing to do was leave Vandergrift to the north-northwest and intercept route QL4. They would then follow that south to a Y in the river and go west-southwest to the Khe Sahn plateau. QL 4 ended at the river, but there was another road, a two-wheel track really, that continued on beside the river to the plateau where there was a waterfall on the river. In a straight line, the distance was eighteen kilometers (eleven miles). The route they had to take because the weather was about double that.

Ailes was flying as he usually did when going to a new area. As he was following the road, then the track, Harry was watching the ground out his window to see if anyone was shooting at them. They were below the clouds and in a valley. This put them near the ground in three directions. Not a real good place to be. As they went along, Harry noticed the fairly recent work on the road and what looked like new construction after they got to the river. He was counting the number of small bridges that were on the road and blown up. There were twenty-one of them by the time they reached the Khe Sahn plateau. How were they to protect that many bridges and culverts over thirty kilometers of road? Not to mention that much of the road was on the side of a valley between the river and the steep sides of a canyon. It would have been easy to blow the road in any number of places. The marines had tried to resupply Khe Sahn by road. That road? If so, someone in planning really had his head up his ass.

# NEW TO AREA A/C ON TAC-E

Late one afternoon Harry checked the flight board for the following day to see if and where he'd be flying the next day or if he were on standby that night for Tac-E. Now the assignments could always change, especially if CPT Paul came by to duck out of his missions. There it was, Harry had standby for Tac-E that night. Yet another night. By now he had a bit more nighttime flying in the mountains and pretty well knew what to do to not get himself killed. He checked, and the A/C was a pilot transferred up from down south (spelled *flat terrain*) and was new to the unit. He'd gone through the area familiarization and his unit check ride for A/C, but that was about it. Harry kind of wondered what he was doing on Tac-E with so little time in the area to really learn where things were. Turned out this was a real concern.

Harry went to the mess hall for supper and then on to the flight line. He located the aircraft, and the crew was all there. He asked the FE if the A/C had been around and was told he hadn't. So Harry preflighted the aircraft and started the engines to make sure everything was OK. It was. Harry thanked the crew and hoped not to see them that night. They expressed the same feelings.

He proceeded to the O Club and had a Coke, and he talked with the guys there who were having a good time not having to be on standby.

Along in the evening, well after dark, the phone from operations rang. Whoever answered it called out the A/C's name and Nevling, you're on alert. Go get 'em.

The two of them walked through the officers' area and to operations to see what was up. They learned that they had to take a load of four pallets of 105 mm ammo from Camp Evans to FSB Berchtesgaden. B'gaden was located on a small hill on the north side of the road the 101st had just rebuilt from the coastal plain into the A Shau Valley. The road ran pretty much on the lowest terrain available, so B'gaden was much lower than the surrounding terrain. To the north was the mountain of Eagles Nest at 1,487 meters, or 4,879 feet. It was about five hundred meters, or 1,640 feet above B'gaden. To the south the terrain rose much more slowly into the valley where the road ran, and the terrain didn't rise for nearly two kilometers, or about a mile and a quarter.

Out to the aircraft, go through the start procedure, and off to Camp Evans, about thirty kilometers (nineteen miles) northwest. They called Camp Evans pathfinder who had the load ready and the lights on. Harry was flying, and he went in and hooked up the load. The best way at night to get to B'gaden from there was to stay east of the mountains to near Hue and then into the large valley generally following the road, not that you could see it—or anything else. As Harry turned southwest, the A/C decided to take over the controls. Harry, having been there before, called the pathfinder at B'gaden and told him what was going on. He asked for mortar flares on request, then hand-launched flares on request, and finally three flashlights with red lenses around the landing spot, again on request. *No white light!* The pathfinder confirmed, and Harry called for a flare. Up it came off in the far distance around the shoulder of a mountain. The A/C, for some reason, decided to go out over the A Shau and circle back in to land to the east. Perhaps he thought he'd be able to lose the altitude over the open valley. Sounded like a good idea. Harry called for another flare, and there it was. Almost straight ahead.

As they cleared where they thought the last ridge was, based on the location of the flare, they went out over the A Shau Valley. When the aircraft was turned back to the northeast Harry called to stop the mortar flares and requested a hand-launched flare. Dead ahead. The AC lined up and started dropping off altitude. They had been quite high to avoid any possibility of hitting a mountain. One more hand launch. Good, they were about a half mile out when the flare burned out. Harry called for the flashlights and warned, "*No white light* unless someone wants this ammo on his head!" Been there before too! The red lights are clearly visible in the black dark. The AC does a great job of putting the load right in the middle of the lights.

He then pulled in more power and departed the FSB, turning left. This is good, left is where the road runs due north for almost two kilometers, one and a quarter miles. Plenty of room to get altitude with an empty Chinook. Only problem, he doesn't stop at north and keeps the left turn going. Harry yells into the mic, "Turn back! There's a big fucking mountain over there!" He realizes he is still on transmit, and the AC is on intercom. He can't hear Harry screaming. Harry reaches over, and the fastest thing he can do is turn on the landing light that is still extended from Camp Evans. *Green!* Nothing out there but *green*. Huge fucking trees of *green*. And every one of them reaching out to grab them! The AC quickly jerks the aircraft back to the right and pulls in more power. The *green* disappears. The AC sees Harry turn his radio/intercom selector over to intercom as Harry says, "That's the mountain that Airborne is on. It's a big mother." The AC replies, "It looked plenty big to me. Thanks for the light." Harry told him he was screaming about the mountain—on the radio. The A/C acknowledged he saw Harry switch back to intercom.

With that, and a couple more gray hairs, they proceeded to the refueling point and on to Pachyderm Beach. There was only the one load for that night.

But he was still on Tac-E standby and could not have a drink! Bummer!

# 11th ACR in the A Shau

The 11th ACR joined the 101st with their efforts in the A Shau Valley. They used the reconstructed road the 101st built from Highway 1 near Hue out past Supply Base Birmingham, FSBs Vehgel, and Charlie Brown, and into the mountains. It entered the valley below FSB Berchtesgaden and joined into Route 548. Their armored vehicles roamed down and up the valley. One of these missions was assigned to Harry and an AC we'll call Pete.

Pete was another of those with somewhat questionable judgment. While at Fort Sill (he was not a Playtex; he was there earlier) he failed to replace an oil cap on an engine. Shortly after takeoff, in an empty aircraft, a warning light came on in the cockpit. At least Pete had the good sense to turn around and return to the airfield. When he called the tower the judgment went out the window. He called an emergency. The tower asked him if he wanted to declare an "emergency." This would require the tower to call out the crash trucks and their crews. Pete could have just gone in and landed on the sod area and shut down the aircraft. Instead he told the tower that yes, he was declaring an emergency.

So instead of just going in and landing on the sod near the helicopter area, he chose to land on the runway where the crash trucks and their crews were standing by and shut down the aircraft. He then had to be towed from the runway, down a taxiway, and across a parking apron to the helicopter maintenance area. A lot of unnecessary trouble. Pete got a severe ass-chewing for that.

Harry and Pete had a load of three five-hundred-gallon fuel blivits. A large, heavy load.

As they approached the 11th ACR's bivouac area, they went through the normal procedure and had their identification of the smoke confirmed. The motor pool area was off by itself, northwest of the tents and command APCs (armored personnel carriers). This allowed the supplies to be brought in without "dusting" the mess tent, sleeping area, and command vehicles. On the way in, the pathfinder asked if they would like to join them for a hot meal. Now this was a real treat. Harry had never been invited to lunch with any of the units he supported. However, none of them had the extra space to park a Chinook, either. Pete responded in the affirmative, and the pathfinder identified the mess tent for them. It was what the army called a GP (general purpose) medium. This was the same size tent that Harry had lived in when in base camp on his first tour. Pete dropped off the load, and instead of moving slightly to the side and sitting down, he pulled in pitch and headed for the mess tent! Harry told him to go back to the motor pool area. They would dust the tent, the men, and the food. Pete didn't listen. He proceeded toward the mess tent. Harry yelled at him, "Pete, don't do this! Go back." Pete told him no, that he was going to get close to the mess tent. What an ass. Rather than inconvenience himself by having to walk a couple hundred yards, he was going to inconvenience the entire unit! He hovered over to within a couple hundred feet of the mess tent and set down—in a *huge* dust cloud. Harry was hesitant to even go in the mess tent, but Pete insisted. When they entered, they received a lot of unfriendly looks. One of the guys said, "Thanks a bunch!" In his defense, Harry said, "I told him not to do it."

Harry followed Pete through and got his hot, and now gritty, meal. Pete was unrepentant. Harry was glad that he didn't fly with Pete again.

# ANDY BELMONT'S TALES

Andy could tell a good tale. He regaled the pilots with some of his stories of the more frustrating parts of being a pilot or aircraft commander in Vietnam. Many of us suffered through similar situations. With some minor editing, here are his tales in his words. The first is a night Tac-E with Harry.

# BIRMINGHAM 6

So as to orient all to the military classes of supply—90 percent of what Chinooks do...ah, but that other 10 percent are more war stories:

Class I—Subsistence (food), gratuitous (free) health and comfort items.

Class II—Clothing, individual equipment, tentage, organizational tool sets and kits, hand tools, unclassified maps, administrative and housekeeping supplies and equipment.

Class III—Petroleum, oil, and lubricants (POL) (package and bulk): petroleum, fuels, lubricants, hydraulic and insulating oils, preservatives, liquids and gases, bulk chemical products, coolants, deicer and antifreeze compounds, components, and additives of petroleum and chemical products, and coal.

Class IV—Construction materials, including installed equipment and all fortification and barrier materials.

Class V—Ammunition of all types, bombs, explosives, mines, fuses, detonators, pyrotechnics, missiles, rockets, propellants, and associated items.

Class VI—Personal demand items (such as health and hygiene products, soaps and toothpaste, writing materials, snack foods, beverages, cigarettes, batteries, alcohol, and cameras—nonmilitary sales items).

Class VII—Major end items such as launchers, tanks, mobile machine shops, and vehicles.

Class VIII—Medical material (equipment and consumables) including repair parts peculiar to medical equipment. (Class VIIIa: medical consumable supplies not including blood and blood products; Class VIIIb: blood and blood components (whole blood, platelets, plasma, packed red cells, etc.)

Class IX—Repair parts and components to include kits, assemblies, and subassemblies (repairable or not repairable) required for maintenance support of all equipment.

Class X—Material to support nonmilitary programs such as agriculture and economic development (not included in Classes I through IX).

Miscellaneous—Water, salvage, and captured material.

I Corps, April 1969, 101st Airborne Division. One of the brigades had the previous day made a combat assault and artillery battalion reposition lift onto three new fire support bases, west of Da Nang and at the south end of the A Shau Valley "pipeline." Move, lift, and reorganize about one thousand troops and equipment just for starters.

So in one *not so smooth move* (one Chinook shot down, all crew lost) the division established three FSBs named:

Thor—875 meters (2871 feet) elevation
Pike—1,450 meters (4,758 feet) elevation
Lash—1,809 meters (5,394 feet) elevation

Each FSB was almost directly in a north-south line along ridgelines within sight of one another. However, they were about thirteen kilometers (eight miles) apart in a very, very rugged mountainous region. Navigation was mainly down a river and at an altitude below the peaks, which were usually shrouded in clouds. So on a good day, broken clouds three thousand feet, overcast eight thousand feet, and some clouds lower, and some at or below most mountain peaks. Most of the peaks were above the cloud base.

One would start from the pickup zone, or logistic pad, in this case Supply Point Birmingham, and turn south and follow the river, but not exactly, as that would be a two-hundred-mile trip for each turn and bend in the river, but generally follow the river and keep within the broad V of the river valley.

So the day after they had lost their crew of *five* and aircraft, Belmont and Harry were flying resupply to these newly established FSBs. Since Belmont was a newly minted aircraft commander, he was flying with Harry, most experienced first pilot and "Keep-er Out of Trouble" pilot extraordinaire, classmate, and WO Belmont's serial number was lower than Harry's because B comes before N. Hah!

Very much a Chinook day! Fly to one of the logistic pads that brigades controlled. Thus, support/resupply all the FSBs within the brigade area. Typical day, 110 degrees or more, or even more, loads of ten thousand pounds, or more, divided by eight aircraft for each brigade. Obvious priority is ammo, then food/water, and then construction security stuff.

Figuring the area to be hot, reference the aircraft shot down the previous day and the fact that the troops were just moved in one day earlier. Belmont was surprised and greatly agitated by a conversation he just happened to hear. They were heading back to the log pad at Birmingham and tuned to their frequency when some guy on FSB Thor gets on the net and says, "Was that my PX conex that just went to FSB Pike?" Birmingham 6 replied, "Suppose so, guess the pilot screwed up and went to the wrong LZ. I'll get it brought over to you soon." FSB Thor replied, "Well hurry up. I need some cigarettes."

Well snap, crackle, and pop. That was Belmont blowing a gasket. For starters, the log pad did not tell them it was a PX conex, they disguised it as Class IV, construction materials, and they took it to where they were told, so Belmont got on the radio to Birmingham 6 at the log pad and just went berserk!

Belmont was actually on the controls but was so outraged that he let go and pulled out his six-shooter to ensure he had sufficient rounds to shoot that son of a bitch dead. So Harry's now flying, and Belmont is still foaming at the mouth. He demanded to know where exactly on that log pad this SOB was, as he wanted to talk directly face-to-face. He kept asking where he was, and the response remained vague. As they were getting closer to the log pad, the voice on the other end of the radio changed; now it was Birmingham 99 or some such, and Belmont asked what happened to Birmingham 6! So 99 says, "Do you see that jeep heading down the road toward Camp Eagle? Well that's Birmingham 6." And yes, he did see the Jeep heading east, as they were setting up for landing and most assuredly a *shootout! SOB!* Belmont was left-handed and could probably get off a few good shots through his window!

They shut down for a maintenance check and for Belmont to get his blood pressure back to a readable level. They talked with a sergeant on the pad, and he explained that the 6 was a butter bar second lieutenant and a real prick, but when he heard Belmont coming, he developed an urgent need to be at headquarters at Camp Eagle.

The rest of the day was pretty much the usual, but Belmont did tell the guy on FSB Thor that they would reposition his PX conex but not to expect it until all priority materials were delivered first. They moved it around 1600 hours (4:00 p.m.).

## Yet Another Night Tac-E

(Each day one crew was assigned emergency standby. So you were usually the last one home and any call at 0300 would be yours— this day it was Belmont and Harry.)

In the meantime there was some sort of small unit on the other side, west, of the ridge from the three new FSBs. Maybe a heavy mortar platoon or some such unit but not a full-fledged FSB and no artillery pieces. So being that there were not so many people over there, they got about two or three loads of stuff during the day. But as the day went on, and they were getting ready to close shop, each aircraft commander would call these guys—we'll call them Heavy Platoon—and ask if they needed anything, and the response was always the same: "No, we have all we need." Harry and Belmont were the on-call crew for Tac-E standby, and they were the last to leave. Just like the others, they checked to see if they needed anything. "No thanks!"

Long day, sun setting. Head in to Camp Eagle refuel pad, then pop over to Pachyderm Beach and supper. En route they received a call from battalion; they have a Tac-E. Here's the contact frequency and call sign for more information. OK, Brigade HQ needs a water blivit delivered to Heavy Platoon location. "*Are you sure?*"

"Oh yeah. Emergency request from the location!"

Damn it! OK then, Tac-E requires "gun" cover: "Request guns!" (Belmont's mistake number 1.) He was pissed, and he figured if he was going to be inconvenienced, then so was everyone else. Daylight goes from light to dim to now dark! Sitting at the refuel pad at flight idle for about forty minutes when they finally got a call from a pair of AH1-G Cobras. "What's up?" So Belmont explained that they needed to pick up a blivit of water and deliver to Heavy Platoon. "OK, we don't know where you're talking about, so we will follow you." Belmont knows that the Cobras talk to each other on VHF, whereas the rest of the helicopter units always used UHF radio frequencies. But Chinooks also have a VHF radio, and Belmont tuned them in but maintained communications on the usual UHF frequency.

Chinooks have formation lights on the top of the fuselage. So Belmont turned them to maximum brightness, so they could be seen from above and behind only. He turned all the other lights off as they were flying over Indian country; again reference the aircraft shot down the previous day!

Hook-up load at Birmingham, wondering where the butter bar may be, SOB, and proceed south. Belmont did not do a lot of night flying in Vietnam but enough, and man, it is dark out there! So, broken clouds and some moonlight, but what the hell; he flew this particular path about fifteen times each way this very day. About every sixty seconds, he can see some moonlight reflect off the river, so he knows they are *about* where they need to be. The two Cobras are flying loose formation about two hundred feet aft, one on each side. They were motoring along when it dawned on Belmont that he had not seen a reflection off the river or any other ground reference for some time now. Senses peaked, and sure enough, they were in the clouds, so he did the normal and trained for reaction.

*We'll pause for effect as all rotor head peter pilots digest and figure out what's next.*

Belmont reduced speed, maintained constant altitude and heading, and hoped to get visual reference again.

His next visual clue was a red rotating beacon on each side of them, moving to the front of them, from each Cobra helicopter on each side of them, rapidly moving in front of them, and waaaaay tooooo close! Whereas Belmont was *now* going fifty knots, the Cobras are still going ninety knots; they blew past them at about the time that he realized he made his mistake number two.

They heard all the expletives over their VHF radio and apologized over the UHF radio, but Belmont now had visual with mother earth, and as luck would have it, the clouds cleared, and they had cloudless atmosphere...but again dark, dark terrain but with overhead partial moonlight. At this time, he was pretty sure where he was in relationship to the FSB and the Heavy Platoon and could vaguely see that we were in the valley at a spot wide enough to comfortably maneuver.

They never could get the Cobras to come near them again. Belmont advised them that they were now going to proceed east and deposit the load of water into the Heavy Platoon location. The Cobras said no problem—we will stay here—call us if you need us! So Belmont needs to fly about seven to eight minutes over and then down a mountain ridge that the Cobras are clueless about, and if and when they get shot at...oh yeah, call us. He guessed these guys will be able to tell Belmont's folks what a wonderful guy he was.

Harry and Belmont drove east over the ridge and contacted the Heavy Platoon on the FM radio. The boss man told them that he really did not need any more water, but they could put their load next to the *other blivit*, and since this was such a small LZ, the blivit is taking up most of the room, so they will have to hover some. He further advised them that his people would put out maximum suppression fire at 360 degrees once they were in close to the LZ so that they shouldn't get excited and shoot back!

OK, got you now, Belmont is night adapted and can see where he needs to go; there are lights out, and Belmont can feel Harry on the controls with him, Harry's on the radio and advises the ground boss that we don't need fire suppression, but he either did not hear or it did not fit his plan of action.

They were deep into the interior of northern Vietnam, trying to find a small landing area on a rise but well within ridges and mountains that are up and down and here and there. He had a plan as to where he's going to land when *flash flash flash flash*, brilliant white light in a rhythmic pattern envelops the cockpit! He turns his head ninety degrees left to find some visual clues and sees the tracers outgoing for the maximum suppressive fire, and he's able to orient and come to some sort of a hover...all the while *flash flash.*

Harry has been on the radio and has an eager beaver pathfinder with a strobe light focused on his night-adapted eyes! And after *screaming/pleading* with the guy to turn off the strobe, Harry pulls his pistol and sticks it out the window and announces he is going to *shoot that fucking light out and if you are still there, you die!*

*Flash,* light goes out, thunk, blivit on the ground, release, clear to go, and up and away.

# Epilogue

They survived and rendezvoused with the Cobras. Turned on all their lights and directed them back to Camp Eagle. They refueled and then popped over to Pachyderm Beach, but alas no supper. They usually had the next day off if they were emergency standby the night before. Hard to imagine how tired a twenty-year-old fellow can be after a day like that and *no beer*, as they were still on standby.

# SAM

There was a new guy in the unit, whom we'll call Sam. This fellow was a warrant officer, tall, thin, southern, and antidesegregation, who in his civilian days had been fixed-wing rated and *type rated* in a C-47 (air force designation "Skytrain," used in World War II for cargo and parachute drops).

This guy was forever flapping his gums about being type rated or North Carolina or desegregation, and sometime all three at once. As luck would have it, Sam and Belmont were scheduled to fly together, Belmont as AC, Sam as pilot. Seems Belmont had flown with him a time or two previously and was not impressed with him, but being a FNG (new guy), Belmont cut him a lot of slack. So on this occasion, as Belmont realized that he seemed to be a repeat offender of SOP (standard operating procedure), could not find any fire support bases, remember any radio frequencies, could not fathom artillery operations, and most importantly lacked basic flying skills. He could barely pilot a Chinook! Thus Belmont took it upon himself to instruct him in the art of flying a Chinook. Though he had no formal training as an IP, he had around seven hundred hours in type and about six hundred in-country, Belmont figured Sam needed some instruction, and he needed it *now!*

The division was well into its A Shau Valley campaign, and this day they were supporting the brigade that occupied the valley. FSB Currahee and the east ridge of the Valley. FSB Airborne at 5,820 feet, Eagles Nest at 4,878 feet, Berchtesgaden, Charlie Brown, Rendezvous plus others at the lower end of the ridge.

Pretty much a routine day, sling load hook-up at near sea level, then a short hop to the FSBs along the A Shau Valley ridge or next time into the valley floor. Flying the ridge required awareness of density, altitude, and local wind currents.

Belmont remembered making about three go-arounds at FSB Currahee, located in the valley (low and level terrain and no one shooting at them), and each time "instructing" Sam on how to approach and land. If you can't bring it in here, then how are you goanna deliver up in them thar hills, Mr. North Carolina? As the morning wore on, Sam was starting to respond to his instructions and was demonstrating a modicum of pilot technique with the Chinook.

Lunch time back at the beach.

Back at it around 1300 hours (1:00 p.m.). Likely second mission after lunch, and their load was to FSB Airborne, the highest elevation FSB they had. The winds were out of the southeast, so they approached from over the Song Ta Trach River. Meaning *pinnacle* landing at *maximum.* Approach at a forty-five-degree angle, as mostly aligned with the wind this day, keep above the burble of air currents, and surf it down to the pad on the edge of a "mile-high" cliff. They were looking at mostly a shear drop rock face on the west side of the mountain, but at this time, they were well above the hill and had their act together.

Sam was at the controls, and Belmont was handling the radio, and with minimum verbal input from him as the approach was looking good. Belmont called the FSB, got smoke, added some instruction to Sam, and looked down at the radio console to switch his control from Intercom to FM radio on the FSB frequency. Then he said, "Roger, Green Smoke," and when he looked up, life went to *shit!* Quick!

In the space of three seconds of looking away from their approach path, Sam had a sudden and causeless reaction, *and* at an altitude of over six thousand feet and, oh yeah, out of ground effect by said six thousand feet, he decided to lower thrust to near zero and pull aft cyclic to the maximum.

Yes, Belmont hears what you are saying! Hey, it's a pinnacle to the max, so just turn right ten, twenty, thirty, ninety degrees, and you're high 'n' dry. Good plan, but Sam now has target fixation and is hell-bent on getting onto that little pad on top of the big ass mountain. So at near zero airspeed and near zero pitch on the rotors, he pushes the cyclic forward to the max as if to indicate where he wants his remains buried.

Belmont yelled, "*I've got it!*" and grabbed the controls, knowing he has that slight turn to the right and all is well. Sam will not relinquish the controls, *no way*. Belmont *yelled* again! *And again*!

Belmont unbuckled his seat belt and shoulder harness to be able to move closer to Sam within the cockpit and smash his helmet with his fist, hoping to render him unconscious or otherwise. Just as he had one cheek on his seat and one cheek on the radio console, and now within range of *smacking the shit out of* Sam, he let go of the controls and raised his arms in front of his face. Nice!

Belmont scooted back into his seat, noted that they were about fifty feet from the edge of the mountain with a rate of descent of over three thousand feet per minute or about sixty mph down.

Belmont pulled thrust/pitch up into his armpit. The Chinook moaned and groaned, and he said the Pilot's Prayer: "Oh shit!"

Somehow, Belmont was conscious of the instrument reading just in case he survived. Normal rpm is 232. He was looking at an rpm gauge pointing at his shoes, or six o'clock position, 180 rpm. He looked out his window, and all he could see was earth, rock, and dirt. If he could have let go of the controls and stuck his hand out, he could easily have grabbed a pound of dirt. Belmont looked *up* and the rotors were about twenty-four inches above the ground, and he remembered seeing guys on the mountain looking *down* at him but keeping a distance from the rotor blades, at their ankle height. They were teetering on the edge of the mountain barely supported by aerodynamics.

The Chinook was making really weird noises, but he had stopped their descent. He needed to go up, but there was no more *up* control. If he reduced the pitch on the blades, that would increase rpm, and they can go *up*, but he has to lower the thrust, which means go *down*.

Hmm, what to do. Belmont lowered the thrust/pitch just a bit, and sure enough, the rpm increased a few turns, and they did not go down. He did it again and again and again, and each time the rpm would increase ten or so rpm, and they were holding altitude, but the view out his window was all dirt! In due course the rpm was back up to normal, and they were able to actually maneuver. He now made that thirty-degree turn to the right and flew away. He checked with the crew, and all responded as to being alive. He then asked the ground people if anyone on the hill was injured, and the radio operator was all a-gush at their survival, but no, no one was hurt!

They made it home, and after a change of underwear, Belmont examined the Chinook. It had slight damage on the left foremost pod—battery box door area. The Chinook went to Da Nang for sheet metal repair and returned to action after about two weeks.

Belmont reported to MAJ Butler and requested a ride with a senior pilot so as to make sure he knew what he thought he knew. Turns out that is what he was going to get, requested or not. If one has an "Incident," one's next flight *will be* with a check pilot. So after a short check ride with Herrick, Belmont was signed off as good to go. Sam departed the unit, never to be seen again.

# Aussie USO Ladies in the Shower

Another day where Belmont was Tac-E pilot, in other words last guy home. This particular day was some sort of event/celebration at Pachyderm Beach. Someone must have scored several cases of steaks! May have been the dedication of J. M. Weatherly's new BBQ grill extraordinaire and/or the recently opened new and improved bathhouse and shaving emporium.

He didn't know or care; it was one of those days when nothing went right, and it ran way longer than it should have, and all he wanted to do was stop and rest.

Because of protocol, no one was supposed to eat until all the crews were back at the beach. As he very wearily dragged his ass toward the hooch, a cheer went up from the boys, as now they could start to eat, likely close to an hour after normal dinnertime.

Belmont was so very tired that he had no appetite, and all he wanted to do was shower and go to bed. With a towel wrapped around him and walking in flip-flops, he passed the barbecue grill and walked into the bathhouse.

He heard water running in the shower area but did not think much of it and proceeded to deposit his shaving kit at the sink area, placed his towel on a hook, and walked into the shower area.

Totally zoned out, he did not realize that the shower was being used by a couple of Australian females from one of the USO shows. After maybe fifteen seconds of him getting doused with welcomed wash water, the females realized he was there and started to scream. Belmont was still in a funk, and a couple of guys came in to see what the fuss was all about. They firmly maneuvered him out of the shower and back to his hooch while the females made haste and cleared the area so he could resume his shower. He was now in an agitated funk because he was sure the Pachyderms had one of the few bathroom/shower facilities with a lock on the inside of the door in all of RVN because they often had females in the area. Some days were just longer than others.

# Becoming an Aircraft Commander

O n 5 April 1969, Harry was appointed as Aircraft Commander in a CH-47 Chinook. Wow, all this time and all this work to become and A/C. Harry had been a pilot. He had flown with A/Cs, he had flown with other pilots, and he had flown as Pilot in Command. He had flown in the right seat, and he had flown in the left seat. NOW he was an Aircraft Commander. This meant that the left seat was his. If anyone else wanted to sit there they had to ask his permission—that's ANYONE! (Harry once had his Battalion Commander, a Lieutenant Colonel—LTC—ask his permission to fly left seat.) Wow, this is a great thing!

Moving from the right seat to the left seat is a matter of a slight difference as to how you get into the cockpit, and your butt is now around three and a half feet to the left of where it was. Hmmm. That's not much of a change. However, now whatever goes wrong, and that's *anything that goes wrong, is your fault.*

The sling straps on a load break, and you lose the load—*your fault.* The pilot bumps a load and dings the aircraft—*your fault.* An engine goes bad—*your fault.* Why hell, you come back with a bunch of bullet holes—*your fault.* I did not go out there and shoot a bunch of holes in my aircraft! Doesn't matter, still—*your fault.* Holy shit, can I go back to being a Peter Pilot? Hell no! You're stuck with it!

The up side of it is *you* are in *command.* The aircraft and crew are entirely yours until you land and shut down. Then it goes back to the flight engineer. There are actually some advantages to this. You do not have to land near a mess tent like Pete. You do not have to fly a half mile out to sea. You do not have to refuse a mission that is no more dangerous that what you are already doing. You can go into the "Valley of Death," the A Shau. You also get to train a lot of newer pilots with things that may well save their lives and those of their crew. *That* is what makes all the bullshit worthwhile!

This was a time to reflect on all the things that could kill you. There were a large number of things in this category. Of course the obvious one is the enemy. Whether it's one guy shooting at you from a ridgeline while you are trying to get to the FSBs under the clouds, an NVA soldier popping up from behind a truck, an intentional ambush as had happened on several occasions, or the mortar and artillery fire aimed at the resupply pads at the FSBs. But the enemy was not the only concern. The aircraft could kill you as well. A Chinook is a very complicated compilation of thousands of moving parts. Malfunction or failure of many of those parts would kill you faster than Charlie. If a significant piece one of those six rotor blades separated, you were dead. If the single quill shaft that ran both flight hydraulic systems failed, you were dead. If one of the five transmissions froze, you were dead. A fire was a really bad thing. If it did not kill you directly, it might cause something else that would. A lot of things could go wrong with the aircraft that would kill you. Then there was the "friendly fire." A misnomer if there ever was one. If it's coming your way, it is *not* friendly! You had to know where the artillery was firing from and to and stay out of the way of the fire tracks. Other aircraft could kill you as well. Midair collisions that involved helicopters were normally a fatal event. The weather could kill you. There was an expression of "*cumulo granite*," meaning a mountain shrouded in clouds. Many pilots found out the hard way that one does not run into a mountain and survive. The night could kill you. Most nights it was pitch black out there. One could not see the mountains nor the ridges. Smacking into one of them would not be conducive to longevity. Harry, being a high nighttime pilot was well aware of just how dark it was out in those mountains. Then your pilot could kill you. Sam and the White Knight are examples of near misses. There were many, many things out there that could easily kill you. One had to be aware of all of them and do one's best to avoid them successfully. There were no safe days.

# CREW TO WHITE ELEPHANT

Shortly after Harry became an AC, he drew a mission to Da Nang. Such was to be his pilot. The mission required them to go down in the morning and come back in the afternoon. Aha! A great opportunity to have lunch at the White Elephant, the navy officers' club. Neither of them had been there but had heard what a great place it was. This was a really nice place, especially for Vietnam. China, tablecloths, silverware, waiters. A real restaurant. The food was excellent as well.

Harry and Such planned ahead. They both took their lightweight flight jackets with them. Harry also took an extra Nomex flight shirt.

When they got done with the preflight they called the crew together. They asked if they knew of the White Elephant. All of them had, but none of them had ever been in it. Harry explained what the extra clothes were for. Two of the guys could wear the flight jackets and one the shirt in place of his. With the camouflage name tags, no one would notice there were two Suches and three Nevlings.

When they got to Da Nang and took care of business, they hitched a ride to the White Elephant. It was quite a treat for the crew. There was no place north of Da Nang where one could buy a meal. It was all either mess hall food or canned C rations or dehydrated LRRPs (long-range reconnaissance patrol—dehydrated rations). Having a prepared and served meal was exceptionally rare. They all thoroughly enjoyed having a regular, made-to-order lunch served by waiters on *real china!* When they got back to the aircraft, the crew gave back the jackets and shirt and thanked them for taking them along. Harry and Such told them it was the least they could for all the crew did for them in keeping the aircraft in good working order and flying with them.

# THE WHITE KNIGHT

The Sam that Belmont had the tales about was not the only piss-poor pilot in the unit. One had to wonder how some of these guys made it through flight school and then the transition into the Chinook. Even more curious was how they managed to fool the unit IPs into clearing them to fly as pilot.

# The White Knight and the Flight Crews

Every unit probably had one. You know, a dud. Some worthless piece of crap life dumps on you. Harry's unit had some guys with less than desirable characteristics. They had at least one who was a real loser. We'll call him the White Knight; why will become obvious. This guy was a first lieutenant, fresh out of flight school, fresh in-country. Within a couple of days of getting to Pachyderm, this fool stood up at a pilot's meeting and said that he felt the flight crews weren't working hard enough. He probably hadn't even flown in the unit yet. He probably didn't know they were flying ten, twelve, or more hours a day. That would put the flight crews at what, twelve absolute minimum, if *nothing* went wrong? Probably more like fourteen to eighteen. Without any facts, this fool shoots off his mouth. The pilots shouted him down. He sat down and shut up for the rest of the meeting.

# White Helmet = White Knight

H e was called the White Knight because he had this new air force flight helmet he'd acquired someplace that was shiny white—*bright* shiny white. He was very proud of that *white* helmet. Harry, and probably others, told him to go over to maintenance, get some OD (olive drab or army green) spray paint, and give it at least one coat to take the shine off. He didn't. He was with Harry one day, and they landed for fuel at Supply Point Birmingham. A Playtex ship came in across from them. The pads were thirty, maybe forty yards across from each other. Anyway, the other hook called and asked who they were. Harry told them it was Rat. CW2 Bud Sherrill was in the other hook, and they chatted while getting fuel. Sherrill asked who was in the right seat. Harry told him it was an RLOFNG (real live officer rucking new guy). He asked if the FNG had any idea how bright his helmet was. Harry told Sherrill that he had told him he ought to get it painted, but if he wanted to be the bright target in the cockpit, who was he to argue? He'd rather they shoot at that nice, bright, white target than at him. It was painted that night, and more than one coat!

# Landing Downwind

The White Knight was another RLO who couldn't fly. Harry was the AC when they were resupplying FSB Kolby. The FSB held 175 mm SP (self-propelled) cannons. These were the 'long toms' as they had very long barrels. They were asked to pick up a back haul of empty cargo nets and slings to go to Birmingham. They were in the air, and the pathfinder told them the winds were from the north. So the White Knight went to the north of the FSB to make his approach. Harry's waiting for him to start a loop to his final approach. He doesn't. Harry thinks maybe he's doing an observation pass at about two hundred feet. He does. Harry thinks this is a bit strange, but he seems to be on the right track now. Wrong! He turned north and again flew *past* the pickup point *again*, you know, the one with the smoke grenade that was going on the first pass. He does another 180-degree turn and heads back south, downwind! Harry still doesn't say anything, he's just trying to figure out what the hell the White Knight is doing. This time he begins a shallow descent—*downwind*—and comes to a one-hundred-foot hover over the pickup point. *Out of ground effect!* The aircraft immediately began to fall through the hover. Harry grabbed the controls and pushed the nose over and to the right, added power, and recovered before they met with something more solid than air or themselves. Harry told him, "Contrary to popular belief, these things do not descend well vertically. Especially when you're *downwind **and** out of ground effect*! Weren't you paying any attention to the pathfinder's instructions or the smoke?" He said something that didn't make much sense so Harry told him that he needed to pay attention to what was going on, plan ahead, and stay ahead of the aircraft and the situation. Harry was very glad that they hadn't been carrying a load. The extra weight would have caused serious trouble.

# NEAR MIDAIR COLLISION

A few days later Harry was again assigned as his AC. (Maybe he pissed Cooper off about something to get this punishment, or maybe it was Captain Paul.) They picked up a load of three, five-hundred-gallon fuel blivits for the 11th ACR unit in the northern A Shau Valley. Harry told him to head out roughly along the road into the valley, then turn north over the middle of the A Shau. When they got there and turned northwest, a Huey came off Eagle's Nest headed southwest across the valley. He's in a very slow descent—and on a direct intercept course. Harry tells the White Knight, "Huey at two o'clock." He looks but doesn't say anything. They close. "Huey at one thirty, coming to our altitude." Still nothing. "Huey at one o'clock, our altitude." Still nothing. Harry can see that he's looking at the Huey, and they are about to have a midair. He grabs the controls and tells him, "I have the aircraft." Nothing. "*I have the aircraft!*" Still nothing—and Harry can't move the controls—he has literally a death grip on them. By now the Huey is about 12:10 and closing fast. Harry screams at him, "*I have the aircraft! Let go of the controls!*" He's still staring at the Huey with his death grip on the controls. Thankfully, the chief had changed out a radio/intercom control head on the center console and left a large screwdriver there. Harry picked it up by the blade and backhanded the handle into his face. He let go, and Harry bottomed the pitch and rolled left. The Huey went by with his blades overlapping theirs. Harry saw the Huey A/C with a look of horror on his face flash by. What the hell they were looking at Harry didn't know, but it's hard to not see a hook with three five-hundred-gallon blivits slung underneath. After they changed their drawers, Harry would bet they paid more attention to the airspace. He figured by then that was enough of the White Knight and kept him off the controls the rest of the day. Harry related to Cooper what had happened. He did not fly with the White Knight again. Harry thought they put him back with the IPs. Harry owed Jack Herrick and Tracy Montee an apology for having to deal with this idiot. Of course, one of them cleared him as pilot in the first place.

## The White Knight and the Flare

No one liked this guy. Most couldn't stand him. Harry thought he'd managed to piss off every pilot in the unit. One evening the White Knight headed for the latrine. The latrine was a small, screened-in building with a bench over four half-fifty-five gallon drums. Every evening at the same time he went in and sat down for a half an hour or so. Somebody used a trip flare to booby-trap the latrine on him. He opened the door, and the bright white light filled the building. The White Knight came out like a rocket and disappeared. *No one* saw him for three days!

When Harry returned on a parts scrounging run in the fall, he asked Such what happened to the White Knight. Such told him, "Oh, they came and took him away." When Harry asked who had come, Such replied, "The guys in the white jackets with the restraints."

# WILLIE

They had another pretty much worthless guy in the unit. Willy had been with the original Playtex at Fort Sill. He came in sometime after Harry and quickly showed he was pretty much worthless. When an emergency levy order came down for two pilots to go directly to Vietnam, the senior officers picked the two who were the least valuable to the unit. Willie was the first choice to go.

As luck would have it, he was assigned to Varsity before it became B Company, 159th Aviation Battalion, 101st Airborne Division. After a few months, and after they moved north and joined the 101st, Varsity tired of him and had him transferred to battalion. Well, wonder of wonders, they got tired of him and sent him to Pachyderm. Those pilots who knew him from Playtex didn't want him, either. Now Willie was the only pilot to serve in all three companies as well as battalion on the 159th Assault Support Helicopter Battalion.

Willie was summed up extremely well in a comment on an officer's evaluation report written at Fort Sill. It stated, "This officer, when highly motivated, is barely adequate." That was Willie.

So now, with Pachyderm having him, Willie had been in all three Chinook companies as well as battalion headquarters. There just was no place left for him to go. Pachyderm was stuck with him.

Harry had been AC for a while. He had also flown with junior pilots fairly often. He hadn't been assigned Willie as a pilot. There was good reason Willie wasn't an AC yet.

One morning, after the operations runner had gotten Harry up, he stopped at operations to see who his pilot was for the day and where they were going. His pilot was Willie, and they were going to the A Shau Valley. The A Shau was OK; Willie was another matter. Oh, well. Harry had never flown with Willie, so had no idea of what kind of pilot he was. With his general lack of concern, attention to detail, lackadaisical manner, and so forth, Harry was not particularly looking forward to the day.

He got the rest of the information for the aircraft and the mission and went to the mess hall for some breakfast. He noticed that Willie wasn't there. Oh well, some of the guys didn't have breakfast. Harry finished eating and went to the aircraft. Hmm, no Willie. Now Harry is wondering where the hell he is. He should be at the aircraft for the preflight. Harry rushed through the preflight and was ready to go fifteen minutes before the scheduled takeoff time. Still no Willie.

Knowing Willie, Harry did not go to the mess hall but went to Willie's hooch, and sure enough, there he was, still asleep. Harry woke him up, he mumbled something about going away and leaving him alone. He went back to sleep. Harry woke him again and in no uncertain terms told him to get his ass out of bed and to the aircraft. Willie again mumbled something and made no move to get out of bed.

Now Harry's really pissed. This lazy SOB has been woken *three* times. Once by the operations runner and twice by Harry. He still made no move to get his ass out of bed. Harry went over to the shower area, filled one of the washbasins with several quarts of cold water, and returned to Willie's hooch. Upon entry, he dumped the entire contents on Willie's head. That got him up! He came out of the bed sputtering and cussing. He asked, "What the hell did you do that for? Now my bed's all wet!"

Harry hollered back, "You've got to be kidding. I woke you up nicely once! I woke you a second time! I shouldn't have had to do that! If there's a next time, the water comes with the first visit! Now you've got five minutes to have your ass strapped into that seat! I'm taking off on time in ten minutes. If you're not there, I go without you." He left.

Harry wouldn't have left without him. The Chinook requires two pilots. While Harry had flown Hueys by himself, and he knew he could fly a Chinook solo, there was no way he'd go into Indian country with one pilot. Too many things could happen that would take two pilots to handle.

Harry returned to the aircraft, and a couple of minutes later, he saw Willie rounding the corner of the hooches, still getting dressed, and in a quick shuffle for the aircraft. Harry got in the AC's seat and strapped in before Willie got on board. While Willie was getting in his seat and strapped in, Harry completed the preflight checklist and had the APU running. Harry did not say anything and started the aircraft by himself. He just had Willie sitting there like a lump.

Harry taxied out to the takeoff pad and lifted off. As he flew to Supply Point Birmingham to pick up a load, he called for artillery clearance and then to the resupply point to let them know he was coming in. Harry picked up the load and departed for the designated FSB. For the entire morning, he did not let Willie touch anything. No time on the controls, no radio calls, nothing. Around 1130 hours (11:30 a.m.), Willie pressed the intercom button and asked, "I get it that you're mad at me. You ever going to let me fly?"

Harry responded, "You want to fly with me you get your ass out of bed and to the aircraft *on time*. You take care of your part of the preflight procedure, and you act like a *pilot*! Then I'll let you fly."

For the remainder of the day, Harry flew and took care of all the other duties in the cockpit. Willie sat in the pilot's seat and did nothing. Which he was pretty good at. When they returned to the beach, Harry dismissed him with, "Willie, if we fly together again, do not pull that stunt. You show up on time and ready." He took care of all the after-flight duties as well.

He thought it appropriate to notify Cooper in operations of what happened. He told him what had happened that day and informed him that he was not refusing to fly with Willie. However, if he shirked his duties as pilot again, Harry was done with him. Cooper thought that was appropriate.

Several day later, Harry went into operations after being roused by the runner and saw he had Willie as pilot again. He went to the mess hall for some breakfast and noticed that Willie wasn't there. Hmm. Is this going to be a repeat? He went to the aircraft, and there was Willie. He told Harry the he had done the complete preflight. Harry confirmed this with the FE. They climbed into the cockpit and had a normal AC and pilot day. Willie had learned his lesson with Harry.

# AGENT ORANGE

Most people have heard of Agent Orange. This is a defoliant used by the US military as part of Operation Ranch Hand in Vietnam. It was a mixture of equal parts of herbicides 2.4.5-T and 2.4-D. The really bad thing was that it contained the most toxic of the dioxins, TCDD. This is what has caused all the problems in Vietnam and with the US forces that served there.

Harry was flying support for the 101st this morning. He was taking ammo out to the FSBs along the road being constructed into the A Shau Valley. He had picked up a load of 105 mm ammo at Camp Eagle and was headed west. There was a solid overcast at about 300 feet.

He flew south into the large coastal plain that extended back to the mountains. This gave him some ground clearance and allowed him to be further away from any enemy fire that may be directed at him. With the solid overcast he would have to try to work his way to the FSB under the clouds. There were no holes in the overcast.

He followed the road around the shoulder of the first mountain at the end of the valley west of FSB Vehgle and southwest of FSB Son. As he was going around the mountain there suddenly appeared two C-123 Provider aircraft rigged as spray planes. They were spraying along the road to defoliate the jungle on either side.

When Harry spotted these airplanes they were at his altitude and about a quarter of a mile distant. Way too close! Harry immediately bottomed the pitch and dove down and to his right. The C-123s both pulled back on their controls and went up and to their left into the clouds.

Harry's immediate assessment that they would go for the clouds, away from the ground, was correct.

The spray planes were busy avoiding a mid-air collision and did not turn off their sprayers. They were still putting out Agent Orange as they disappeared into the clouds. Harry's aircraft received a good dousing of the chemicals.

Harry recovered from his dive and continued around in a 360 degree turn before proceeding along the road out to the FSB. Except for the mess on the windshield and the smell in the aircraft Harry did not think much of the chemicals at the time. He was far more concerned with the near mid-air collision. They are not conducive to longevity.

It wasn't until much later that he would learn that Agent Orange would kill him.

# Record Number of Sorties

Harry was awoken this day to fly. He followed his normal routine of checking in at operations before going to the mess hall. He found that he was to relocate an ARVN battery from the north point across a saddle in the ridgeline to the southern point. OK, this should be interesting. When the ARVNs went to the field, they took pretty much everything with them. Everything. They would take not only their military equipment but pigs, ducks, chickens rice, and of course, the cooking pots. They would have bags of charcoal and who knows what else. Just a tremendous amount of stuff.

After getting the details on the mission, he proceeded to the mess hall for some breakfast. Then on to the flight line to get his aircraft for the day and, with his pilot, preflight it. Everything was good. Harry briefed the crew on what they were going to be doing and that it should be fairly simple and relatively safe. The ARVNs were seldom near where the action was.

They started up the aircraft and headed for the mountains. The ARVN 105 mm artillery battery was only about the third ridgeline in. Far from the A Shau Valley where all the action was at the time. They called ahead and got ahold of the artillery unit, called for a smoke on the first load, and went in to pick it up. Harry had the controls and told his pilot that he'd fly the first couple of loads to see how things were. Harry picked up the first load, a 105 mm howitzer cannon. He had already seen the other peak that was only slightly higher than the one where the battery was already located. As it was not far, perhaps 150 yards, he simply pulled in a bit more power, eased the nose over a bit and actually did a fast hover to the other peak. By the time he got to twenty knots, it was time to bring the nose up for the landing of the cannon. The ARVNs had sent a few men over to the other peak, and they had popped a smoke. Harry set the load down in the gun pit they had ready for it. He repeated the maneuver to get back to the pickup point. A cargo net of 105 mm ammo. Same thing back to the new FSB. He dropped this off next to the gun they had just positioned. Time elapsed—less than ten minutes from the first pick up.

In aviation, a sortie is defined as one takeoff and one landing. With a Chinook this if further defined as either the aircraft itself or the external load. Harry had just completed four sorties in less than ten minutes.

Harry told his pilot to watch closely what he was doing because this was an unusual situation where you just got the aircraft to fly, and you had to stop. He was also ignoring the very light breeze that would have little, if any impact on the aircraft. He would pick up a load and bend a bit to the west, land it, take off, bend a bit to the east, and pick up another. Sort of a football-shaped flight. By the fourth load, Harry had placed two of the six cannons and turned the controls over to his pilot. He thought this would be an easy and short day. Wrong. The fifth load was a cargo net with some stuff. Not a lot; just a collection of stuff. Harry wondered if it even weighed one thousand pounds. Oh well.

They took load after load after load the short distance until they needed fuel. They had "back hauled" empty nets and cargo straps several times so the ARVNs could make up new loads. They had moved three of the six cannons and had the other three to go. They informed the battery that they were going to refuel. They had been out there over two and a half hours. Even at only one load per five minutes that is over forty-eight sorties. There may have been more than that.

They made the short trip to Birmingham and refueled. The normal procedure for refueling is that the CE and gunner would both go out the ramp at the rear of the aircraft, and each would refuel one side's three tanks. The center tank was the main, and the fore and aft tanks were much smaller. The main tanks would provide two hours of flying time and the other four an additional hour and a half. The refueling took longer than four or six sorties.

After refueling, they went back to the ridge and moved more stuff. A lot of stuff. Not a lot in each load, but a lot of loads. They also moved the remaining three cannons and their ammo. Another load of fuel and time to head for Birmingham. They informed the battery that they would be back to finish up. By this time they had well over ninety-six sorties for the day. Surely a record. A normal heavy day would be fifteen.

They refueled and went back to finish off the move. On the way, Harry called operations and told them they were almost done and he'd call on his way back to Pachyderm Beach. They asked what was taking so long, so Harry informed them that they had moved all six cannons plus the ammo, then the normal retinue of ARVN "ash and trash."

Following the second refueling, they went back and finished moving the ARVNs to their new home. They went back to Birmingham to top off the tanks as was customary so the next flight would have full tanks.

Harry wasn't sure just how many sorties they had made that day but certainly over one hundred. Had to be one hell of a record. Unsure that it actually accomplished anything but setting a record, but at least it was good for something.

# TIGER MOUNTAIN INCIDENT

In a nutshell, Belmont was doing the usual sling load resupply to FSBs when he got a call from Pachyderm Operations to contact battalion. Battalion told him C Company was involved in a 105 howitzer battery move and because of mechanical problems could not get enough aircraft for the lift, so he was to fill in one of the slots for C Company. Here is a frequency and contact, "Press On." (The battalion motto.)

He showed up at a location near the coast and found out it was an ARVN move and to take guns to XYZ123 location.

He looked on the map and…"Oh shit!" Tiger Mountain across *the* valley from Airborne. Part of the adventure this day was that the flight engineer was a hard stripe E-5 who was getting his four hours of flight time for pay. Bit of an arrogant ass and not the best load spotter.

So not having any more info than point A to B and guns at A need to be at B. He picked up the first 105 mm howitzer, and off he went. He went west, crossed the mountains, and crossed *the* valley to Tiger Mountain. He was not sure what they were calling this operation and the new FSB designation, but the old marine FSB was the last to be evacuated and then bombed as the marines withdrew to Vandergrift back in March. (Another war story there.)

As he approached the FSB with his load, he noticed a lot of activity on the mountaintop—unusual, as most battery moves were organized and secure operations because it's not good form to supply the enemy with big firepower. As he got closer to the touchdown, he could see troops scurrying around and some not in normal uniforms. He put the load over the smoke, and the FE is telling him to "Hold! Hold! Hold!" What the fuck is going on?

"Can't put it down because tracers are flying all around," the FE calls out.

Andy replies, "Chief, coming down *now!*"

Load number one is on the ground and "Ta-ta," he's off and out of there. He flew back to the coast and picked up another gun. This time he was a little better prepared for what is in store, so he briefed the crew and especially the FE. "Let's put it down on the smoke and get out." The number two gun was a slam, bam, thank you ma'am delivery and check out his tail pipes. He went back and picked up number three gun and called battalion, "Where is Playtex, and do you know what is going on top of that mountain?" There are NVA at or inside the perimeter, and we are taking hits with each load." Battalion responds, "Roger we'll pass this info on to Playtex when they report airborne." Thanks a pant load.

He moved four of the six guns for the battery. Van Opstal, from Playtex, arrived with gun number five, lost an engine over the FSB, and crashed onto it. This closed the FSB because a big ass CH-47 was hogging the remaining room and the battery move was then canceled, and he was sent back to doing what he had been doing.

Now, about the crash. This incident involved CW2 Rick Van Opstal, Playtex, and LTC Billy Odneal, from Liftmaster, battalion getting his four hours of flight time for the month. They were hauling a 105mm howitzer to Tiger Mountain when Charlie hit the ninety-degree gearbox as they were on approach. Of course they lost thrust, and the LTC panicked and shut down both engines, and they settled on the gun. They were able to set the hook down on top of the howitzer in a bomb crater on top of FSB Tiger Mountain at the very edge of the cliff. Actually spearing the Chinook with a howitzer is a better way to describe it. Fortunately, the bakes were locked on the howitzer, which probably kept them on the mountain. When they shut it down and un-assed the hook, the front blades hit the edge of the bomb crater. MAJ Larry Karjula and CW3 Bud Sherrill, Playtex, took a crew out to attempt to recover the helicopter.

The first thing they did was dig a dead-man and chain the Chinook to it to keep it from sliding off the mountain. The maintenance guys had to strap themselves to the helicopter while they were working on it. They changed the cliff side gearbox, dug out space for the front blades and replaced them. When it was repaired enough to fly, Karjula flew it out.

He took off his door on the theory that if anything happened he could jump out and still be on the mountain. When he cranked it, the Chinook shifted slightly. When he went to flight, it shifted some more, and when they unhooked the deadman chain, it shifted again. He appeared to start out his door each time until they unhooked the deadman when he no doubt said to hell with it and pulled pitch. The Chinook lifted, and the howitzer gun tube came out of the fuselage. He hovered over to a spot where he could set it down. Sherrill put all his guys in for an award, which they deserved and received. The hook was evacuated to the rear and sent back to the States for repair.

# BACK TO ANDY

Belmont's pilot was a new guy and with not much flight time in country. Belmont flew the first load as was customary because of it being a "new" LZ. After things got hot, he would let the pilot fly back to the coast, as they were empty, and he had the shakes. Belmont did not say much to him and handled all the radios and all the flying with the load. He felt a little sorry for the pilot but just did not have time to schmooze. He was running on adrenaline, trying to keep the folks at the PZ (pickup zone) informed, and calling battalion about where Playtex was.

After the end of the day, the SGT FE informed Belmont that he had struck one of the guns and punched a hole in the aircraft. He took a look, and exactly down the center line of the aircraft, starting at about one foot from the very nose, was a straight-line scratch that got more pronounced and a deeper groove as it traveled aft to a one-inch hole about two feet from the cargo hook bay. "Looks like a bullet hole to me, Sarge," said Belmont.

"Oh no, sir, you contacted the barrel of one of the guns and punched a hole in the belly," says he.

About ten days later, that FE knocked on Belmont's hooch door and informed him that during a one-hundred-hour inspection they had to pull some of the floor panels. They found a .51-caliber slug embedded in the cross former ahead of the cargo bay, and since said former is a main structural element of the whole aircraft, they needed to get it repaired at Da Nang, and it would be out of service for about two weeks.

# Tomahawk to Bach Ma—and Back

Bach Ma is a Buddhist shrine and retreat in the mountains about twenty-nine kilometers, or eighteen miles south, of Phu Bai. It sits at an elevation of 1448 meters, or 4,750 feet. Just east of Bach Ma is a ridgeline that goes up to 1528 meters, or 5,013 feet. The mountains extend farther to the east to about two kilometers from the sea, and then the terrain drops rapidly to the South China Sea. FSB Tomahawk is about eleven kilometers, or seven miles to the east of Bach Ma, and is about twenty feet in elevation. Now religious shrines were supposed to be "off limits." The NVA knew this and used them as caches for their weapons and materials.

Someone in the 101st decided they should stage an artillery raid at Back Ma and run a sweep through the rugged terrain to the west. Pachyderm was tasked to relocate the six 105 mm howitzers from FSB Tomahawk to Bach Ma. So, early one morning Harry took off from Pachyderm Beach and headed south to FSB Tomahawk. After hooking up his first 105, he took off to the north, as that was where the breeze was from. He kept going north at around fifty knots and maximum rate of climb with that airspeed and load. At around three thousand feet, he turned to his left and headed back toward Bach Ma. It had taken him quite a ways north to get up to even half the altitude he'd need to clear the ridge.

As he approached Bach Ma, he flew on past to turn back into the wind. It was flowing over the ridge behind Bach Ma, and Harry did not want any surprise downdrafts on final approach. He sat up for a shallow approach. The mountains dropped to the west, and he had plenty of ground clearance. This allowed him to get in most of the power needed for landing or to go around if something went wrong. Nothing did. He put the gun down on the smoke grenade the pathfinder had used to mark the spot and took off to pick up another gun. Once he went past the last ridge, he bottomed the pitch to get down to Tomahawk. He flew, or rather autorotated, to the east, past Tomahawk and out to sea. He turned back to the west, still in autorotation. Finally, he was able to pull in some pitch and approach Tomahawk for another gun.

This was an interesting and different day. Harry was used to flying in the mountains. However, this was very rugged. Very steep ups and downs and very close to the sea. Harry had not had to "bottom-out" the pitch to get from point A to point B before.

The artillery was up at Bach Ma for a short period before they wanted it moved back to FSB Tomahawk. Pachyderm was again called upon, and Harry was to head south again. He had a long way to get the altitude needed so it was a much faster trip there at one hundred plus knots. Again the breeze was from the north, so past Bach Ma and approach from the southwest. Again careful for the winds coming over the ridge. Spot the gun, hook up, and take off, paralleling the ridge until well clear of it. Then the turn to the east in a direct line with Tomahawk. Once Harry cleared the last ridge, he again bottomed out the pitch, and he was actually autorotating toward Tomahawk. Even with the 105 hanging from the aircraft, Harry could see he would not lose enough altitude to land the gun. He turned a bit south and did a couple of S turns to lose even more altitude, so he could approach the FSB. He started pulling the power back in at about a quarter mile and got the gun set down where they wanted it.

The climb back up to get the next one was at near maximum power, and he still had to go north, turn, and come back to get the altitude needed to clear the ridge. Another interesting day with maximum descents and climbs.

# R&R Platoon to FSB

While most of their missions were taking cannon ammo to the various FSBs, they flew a lot of other missions as well. Some of the missions were food, water, mortar rounds, and small arms ammo. They took the FSBs about everything they needed. In addition to ammo (for their cannons, mortars, machine guns, rifles, hand grenades, and anything else), they also took mail, hot food, replacements, bunker and defensive materials, SP packs, you name it. They also did medical evacuations to field hospitals, hospital ships, and to the big hospital at Da Nang. They even flew prisoners from the field to the rear areas. They dropped fifty-five-gallon drums of "Phu Gas," a homemade napalm. They brought back captured weapons and other supplies. They inserted FSBs, moved them, and brought them back to the base camps. Anything the army or marines needed, they were available to take care of. And the Chinooks rarely, very rarely flew in formations or pairs. They did not have a wingman. They were nearly all single-ship missions. If things went south, they were on their own until help could get to them.

One of the troop movements turned out a bit strange. One of the guys was told to go pick up a load of troops and take them to FSB Airborne. This was just below Eagle's Nest, a communications site on the tallest mountain on the east side of the A Shau Valley. So he swept into Camp Evans and landed by the identified smoke. He saw about a platoon of troops but didn't pay much attention. Just another routine mission from a rear area to a forward area. The troops loaded, the FE said, "Ramp is up, cleared for takeoff." Off they went.

223

Climb up to altitude and head for FSB Airborne. Call the pathfinder, confirm the smoke, and land. Ramp down, and troops exit. Troops return. Hey, what the hey? A staff sergeant went to the FE and told him they were headed for Eagle Beach, a piece of coastline for one day R&R (rest and relaxation). What the hell were they doing on an FSB? The AC turned and looked in the back. None of the men had their combat gear, most didn't have rifles, and many had beach towels. Oops! Somewhere somebody's wires got crossed big-time.

The AC told the FE to make sure everyone was back onboard and took off. He called Pachyderm Operations and told them what was going on. Then he called the people he had talked to at Camp Evans prior to picking up the troops and asked what was going on. It took a few minutes, but they got it figured out and told him to take them to Eagle Beach.

So that's where they went, this time. When the troops got off the aircraft at the beach, they were much happier and stayed off the ship.

# SHOWER TEAMS

One of the more interesting missions was the transporting of "shower teams." The team consisted of four or five men, a portable, gas-operated pump, a five-gallon can of gasoline, some hose, a stand that was a pipe about five feet tall with four extensions on top in an X, each with a shower head and a five-hundred-gallon blivit of water. They would go in and land, and then the "team" would load the pump, gas can, shower pipe, and connecting hose. Then they would lift off and hover over to hook up the blivit. They would go through the same procedure as taking any other load to a FSB, including notification of what they were carrying. Usually the FSB had been notified in advance of their arrival so the men could be ready.

Upon arrival, they would drop the blivit on the smoke marker, hover to the side and set down. The team would gather their equipment and go off the ramp at the rear of the aircraft.

The team would set up the shower in a spot with good drainage and start up the pump. The water from the black blivit would not be hot, but it was warm. All the men on the FSB would rotate through and get a shower. Even the perimeter guards would be relieved for their shower. It was a really nice thing for the men. Most of the crews really enjoyed taking the shower teams out so the men on the FSBs could get a shower.

# BLIND DRUNK

Harry had always thought "blind drunk" was just an expression. He found out different one night. He wasn't scheduled to fly the following day, so after supper he went to the O Club and had a few drinks. He was drinking sloe gin and Coke. Tasted like cherry Coke.

Around 2000 (8:00 p.m.) Harry checked with operations to see if there were any changes. There weren't any, so he had a few more drinks. At 2200, another check with no changes and a few more drinks. Harry was more than a bit drunk at this point. He saw his roommate, Such, at the bar and sat down beside him. He asked if Such would make sure he got back to the hooch, and Such said he would. Harry had a few more drinks. At midnight he had someone else check as he didn't think he could make it to the field phone and back. Still not on the flight schedule, so he had another drink.

About this time Harry realized he couldn't see anything. It was just black. Now this should have panicked a pilot. Going blind would end it all. Harry was too far gone to care. He reached over and poked Such on the arm and again asked he make sure that he got back to the hooch because he was blind. Such assured him he would. Harry had another drink.

When Such got ready to leave, he took Harry by the arm and led him out of the O Club. Harry got about halfway and lost awareness of anything beyond that point. Around 0600 (6:00 a.m.) the door to the hooch opened and the operations runner said, "Mr. Nevling, you have to fly today." Harry was lying on the floor. Such had gotten him back to the hooch, but Harry missed the last step and crashed onto the floor. Such couldn't get him to move, so he covered him and let him sleep it off.

Harry opened his eyes and found that he could see again. Good thing. Then it hit him. He had to fly. Not a good thing. He asked the operations runner, "I checked as late as midnight and wasn't on the board to fly today. Who changed it and when?" The runner said he didn't know. Harry asked where he was scheduled to go. "The A Shau," the runner replied. Harry said, "That goddamned Paul did it again!"

It wasn't bad enough that Harry had to fly with a hangover; it was totally unnecessary. Paul seemed to have a routine of checking the flight schedule board, and if he were scheduled for a nasty area, he'd sneak back in during the night and change it. He'd either take his name off the bad area flight and trade it with a safe area or just replace his name with someone else's. Harry thought it was just him that this happened to but found out he also did it to at least Belmont as well. What an ass! Harry really didn't care if there were chickenshits who wouldn't fly into harm's way. He did mind when they were devious and underhanded about it.

Harry was sure that in any aviation unit there would be pilots who would prefer not to go into harm's way—but not very many. It was a dangerous profession, and they knew that going in. Most of the pilots were young and more than a bit crazy. Harry, at twenty-two, was older than most of his comrades. He wondered how many of the less-than-brave pilots were low enough to sneak into flight operations in the middle of the night to change the flight schedule.

Harry calmed down, got some coffee, and went off for the day.

# Weird and Davis, Plus Nevel, Combs, and Shellum

On 18 April, as a new A/C, Harry was hauling ammo from Birmingham out to the FSBs along the east side of the A Shau Valley, Airborne, Eagle, Berchtesgaden, Whip, and Thor, north to south along the east side on the high ground overlooking the valley. One of those wonderful days of flying, clear weather, light breeze, and no one shooting at you. It looked like it might be a light day of flying. Not a lot of loads going out to the valley. Harry had started after 7:00 a.m. and had made several sorties carrying mostly 105 mm ammo with other supplies to the northern FSBs. He had not gone to Whip or Thor that morning. Seemed it was Weird Harold's area that day. The loads were not assigned to a specific aircrft. Anyone flying that day could have wound up with the load Weird took to FSB Thor.

Around 1000 hours (10:00 a.m.), Harry was on his way with another load and about three-quarters of his way to Airborne when a distress call came over the "Guard" channel. Guard was a radio frequency preset into the radios. All one had to do was select "Trans/Rec+Guard," and you were monitoring 243.0 megahertz. They *always* had the radio on this setting. This allowed them to hear others call for help. Weird called out "I'm hit!" Knowing Weird, they knew that he personally was hit, not just the aircraft. There was nothing Harry could do until he dropped off his load, which he did expeditiously, and headed south. He had heard on Guard that Weird had been ambushed going into FSB Thor, much like he and Such had been ambushed a month previously at FSB Whip. This time they had brought along an RPG (rocket-propelled grenade, bazooka, if you wish). The NVA had not only shot up the aircraft and Weird with AK-47s but also put an RPG round in the left main fuel cell. The JP-4 came out so fast it did not catch fire but put out the number one engine. With Weird incapacitated, his pilot, Davis, took over the aircraft. Davis was the company administrative officer. He spent his time in the company orderly room taking care of all the paperwork. As such, he flew his four hours per month for flight pay requirements. However, this did not allow one to become or remain proficient with the aircraft. It appeared that with one engine out, Davis tried to pull too much power from the number two engine, either without "beeping" in the extra needed or the number two not being able to put out the power requested. In either case, the rotor rpm dropped off, and when it got below the minimum of 214, he was in trouble. Somewhere around 160 rpm, the blades lose their rigidity and begin to fold up. They do this until they break or tangle up and the aircraft drops like a rock. In this case, it hit in the side of a ravine full of Punji stakes (sharpened bamboo stakes planted as a booby trap) and rolled to the bottom. There were no survivors.

All this happened as Harry was dropping off his load at FSB Airborne and going south to see if he could help. By the time he was nearing Whip, it was all over, and he was told to go back to his regular missions.

Later that day they got teams into the ravine to recover the bodies and the aircraft.

That day Pachyderm lost KIA (killed in action): CW2 Harold Lee Eckert Jr., AC (Panel 27 west, line 108), CW2 Thomas Arthur Davis, P (Panel 27 west, line 107), SGT Robert Joseph Nevel FE (Panel 26 west, line 2), SGT John Beechley Combs, CE (Panel 27 west, line 106), and SP4 John Charles Shellum (Panel 26 west, line 4). This was a terrible loss to Pachyderm and to Harry. He had not had the opportunity to fly with Weird or with Tom Davis. He knew them both from the pilots' meetings and the O Club as well as other encounters in the company area. He had flown with Nevel, Combs, and Shellum.

# Flying through the Saddle

Yet another of those days with marginal weather. Harry, as AC, was flying with 1LT Randy Ramsden. They'd drawn missions from Camp Sally to the northern A Shau. As they were going up to Sally to pick up a load, Harry was keeping an eye on the mountains out his left window. There was a rather solid overcast over the coastal plain, but it was high enough that gaps indicated saddles in the ridgeline. It looked like they could get past the first ridge. If this were possible, they could fly the valleys to other saddles and work their way out to the A Shau. The break that Harry saw was fairly narrow, perhaps two hundred yards wide, and with their load on slings below the aircraft, there would not be much vertical space, either.

They flew in to Camp Sally resupply area and picked up their first load. It was another load of 105 mm cannon ammunition. These were rather nice loads. While heavy, they were very stable. One could fly as fast as the density altitude would allow. This was always over one hundred knots. That was nice, as a target moving that fast was difficult to hit. Especially if you were close to the ground, as the tree cover would not give someone on the ground much of a view of the aircraft going by. Problem was that someone siting near the cloud base on the side of a ridge did not need much of an opening to have time for a good look, and a good shot, at you.

Harry was flying, as he wanted to find a route that they could use and reuse. He headed back south, then turned west up a valley toward the saddle. As he got closer, he could see it was going to be snug. To allow for the load below the aircraft the width of the opening was now about 150 yards. This would be a great spot for an NVA soldier to take potshots as they were flying through. Harry shot the gap near the right (north) side as fast as he could go. He did not see any muzzle flashes nor hear any *pops* from rounds going through the aircraft. Once through the saddle, the ceiling was actually higher so there was no problem getting out to the valley, and they dropped off their load. Coming back, Harry was still flying, and this time he shot the gap close to the right (now south) side again.

Ramsden pressed a floor switch and said over the intercom, "Why is it when you go through that gap you always put me next to the trees?"

Harry replied, "If someone is going to take a potshot at us I want to be as far away from him as possible. That puts you close. When you're flying you can go through that saddle anyplace you want—as long as you keep the load out of the trees."

# GETTING LOST ON THE WAY BACK FROM CUNNINGHAM

The weather had finally started to clear a bit. There were no longer the sucker holes to have to find and fly down through to find the FSBs. Now they were flying through broken clouds. It still sucked, as the visibility was still limited, but it was one hell of an improvement over the crap they had been flying in.

It seemed to clear off quickly, just a matter of a few days. One afternoon Harry was flying with a newbie, 1LT Randy Ramsden. Ramsden was one of the good RLOs. He didn't try to use his rank and paid close attention to what the WOs were trying to teach him. Harry enjoyed flying with him in the right seat.

They had been flying from Vandergrift to the marine FSBs just north of the A Shau Valley. That morning they had to take the route up the coast to Quang Tri, then turn inland and fly the valley to Vandergrift. As the day progressed, the weather cleared.

Around 1600 hours they had picked up their last load of the day. The marines at Vandergrift told them that after they dropped it off they were finished for the day. Good news! They'd be back to the beach in time to get a meal in the mess hall. No C rations warmed by the aft transmission tonight!

They dropped off the load at FSB Cunningham, and Harry climbed out to the west, turned quickly left, and kept climbing to the southeast. Ramsden asked, "Where are you going?"

Harry said, "What? You want to go back past Vandy, then around to Quang Tri? Look, *no clouds!*"

Ramsden had to ask, "You think you can find it?" Neither of them had flown this route in either direction. In the mornings they had to go to one of the resupply points at Birmingham, Camp Evans, Camp Sally, Quang Tri, or Vandergrift. Once they picked up a load, it was a question of what clouds they had to dodge around or below to find the FSB where their load was supposed to go. This was new and very different. Even with the haze, they could see twenty miles or more. Problem was neither had had that view, so nothing looked familiar.

Harry told Ramsden, "No sweat. I got this." Ramsden wasn't convinced. There were no radio navigation aids, so Harry was navigating by the seat of his pants.

Ramsden then asked Harry, "What if you're wrong?"

Harry's response was, "Oh ye of little faith! I won't miss it, but if I do we'll just keep heading southeast till we see the South China Sea. Then we turn north or south till we see something we recognize. We have plenty of fuel so no sweat. Besides, I'm not going to miss it."

Harry kept the same heading he'd picked up after leaving FSB Cunningham and climbed to be above the ridgelines they would have to cross. It was a wonderful afternoon for flying. Finally some good visibility and no turbulence. No one shooting at them. And they should be home for supper. Ah, life was good.

As they approached another ridgeline, Harry thought he could see the coast way off in the distance. He called this to Ramsden's attention. As they got over the ridgeline and could see down into the next valley, there was Birmingham. Just slightly off the left nose. It was in a perfect position for Harry to descend and turn left into one of the refueling pads, just like he'd do if he had approached the refueling area from anyplace.

Harry touched down, settled in, and the FE dropped the ramp to go out and refuel the aircraft. Harry turned to Ramsden and said, "How about that?"

Ramsden said, "You were just lucky."

"Maybe," Harry said, "But here we are, right where I aimed for from Cunningham." Ramsden did not have a reply for that.

# LOW LEVEL ON HIGHWAY 1

One afternoon when Harry had 1LT Randy Ramsden as pilot they finished early. As they flew south from Quang Tri Ramsden asked Harry if he could go low level. Harry replied, "You remember the two rules of low level?" Ramsden affirmed with, "Yes, low and fast." Harry told him 175 Knots is max today. Go for it." Ramsden rolled the nose over, picked up speed and dropped down to about 30 feet over highway one. When he got to 175 knots harry told him, "Lower." He went down to about 20 feet over the highway. Harry gave him a thumbs down sign and he lowered the aircraft to about 10 feet. Harry said, "That's good. Any lower and we'll be landing."

As they came around a curve north of Camp Sally there was a small motorcycle, perhaps a Honda 50, with two men riding it. As they were doing about 200 miles an hour they were closing on the motorcycle very fast. When they were about 200 feet behind it the passenger on the back of the motorcycle turned his head and saw the Chinook bearing down on them. He immediately reached around the driver, grabbed the handlebars and headed for the right side ditch. Harry and Ramsden were not low enough to have struck the men on the motorcycle but they were low enough to scare the crap out of the passenger.

As they neared Camp Evans Harry told Ramsden, "Enough fun for one day. Take her up." All Ramsden had to do was ease back on the stick and they were at 500 feet in a matter of seconds.

They went to Birmingham to refuel and then to Pachyderm Beach. Ramsden was quite happy with his low level flight down Highway 1. They had to take their entertainment where they could find it.

## Landing on the *Repose*

Harry had flown several medevac missions. The big one being getting the marines out of Laos to Charlie med at Combat Base Vandergrift. Regardless of the pickup location or the destination they had all had the same general characteristics. Get the wounded on board as fast as you can and get them to a hospital as soon as you can. The pilots were all aware of the golden hour, that hour after an injury when it was critical to get the wounded to a hospital. If they got there in that time frame the fatality rate dropped dramatically. So, grab 'em and go! Get there now! Get them out of the boonies and to the hospital.

So just to prove that nothing's the same, Harry got a call to pick up some wounded. Fine, where are they, and where are they going? The pickup point was a spot on the map in the A Shau Valley." The drop-off was the *Repose*.

The *Repose* was a US Navy hospital ship. One of two that alternated being on station in the South China Sea off the coast of Vietnam. They had a helicopter landing pad for medevac flights and an NDB (nondirectional beacon) to locate them. Harry was given the frequency call sign for the ship and the frequency and identifier for their beacon.

Harry got to the pickup point in short order, and three men were loaded on with a medic. Ramp up, and off they went, headed for "feet wet." The pilot dialed in the frequency, and they confirmed the Morse code identifier. The *Repose* was quite a ways out in international waters. Harry flew out and past the ship to get into the wind for landing. As he passed the ship he looked down at the postage-stamp-size landing pad. Harry began to wonder if it would even hold a Chinook. He had already notified the ship that he was inbound but now asked if a Chinook could land on their pad. He was told the yes, there was room. As he made the turn back into the wind and began the final descent, the pad just got smaller and smaller and even smaller. He saw that there was some sort of mast to the aft of the landing pad and a boom crane forward. Oh, oh, this is getting smaller by the second!

Harry started to hover forward over the ship's rail. He was looking at the landing pad that was smaller than the parking area inside the revetments back at the beach. The mast on his left looked about three feet outside the rotor path, and the boom on the right was about the same distance. He had the gunner and CE keep an eye on the obstructions on their respective sides and moved slowly forward over the pad. As he was going over the pad, he realized that it was not much wider or longer than the landing gear. Oh, wonderful!

Now he had the gunner and CE also watching for when the aft gear got on the pad. Slowly forward, slowly. Finally, the FE called out that the aft gear were over the pad. The aft gear were about twenty feet below Harry and over forty-five feet behind him. He slowly let the aircraft down. Bump! The ship's roll had hit the right aft gear and knocked the aircraft up off the pad. Stabilize the aircraft and try again. Harry, sitting in the cockpit, was over the edge of the ship. Below him was nothing but water. The ship was behind him. To get visual reference he had to look out the left window and down to the deck and railing. He had to look up and to the left to keep an eye on the mast and up to the right through the overhead canopy to watch the cargo boom. Try again. This time as soon as he felt a touch from the pad he dropped the pitch to firmly plant the Chinook on the pad. Success!

The FE called and asked, "Sir, can you move forward? The ramp is over the rail."

Harry replied, "No, if I move forward, the main gear will go off the pad."

The chief came back with, "We'll have to pass the litters off the side of the ramp and back to the deck."

Harry watched as they passed the litters off the right side of the ramp and back onto the deck. All three were successfully passed to the navy medics.

The FE pulled the ramp up, and Harry jerked in some pitch to clear the pad and deck as quickly as possible.

They cleared the *Repose* and headed for "feet dry" and on to the next mission. This one was, at the very least, quite interesting. Harry would not care to have to do it again.

## Air Medal Awarded

On 24 April 1969 orders were issued awarding Chief Warrant Officer 2 Harry R. Nevling the Air Medal. This was awarded for activities from 9 January to 14 February 1969. The pilots referred to this as the basic Air Medal, as nearly every pilot received numerous oak leaf clusters as additional awards with the Air Medal. Harry was later told he had twenty-two oak leaf clusters due him, but he did not receive the orders.

## Operations Runner to Crew Engineer

Harry was sound asleep in his hooch. He'd had a fair amount to drink in the O Club the night before and kept checking the flight board to see if he had to fly. He didn't. When he finally went to bed around midnight he made a final check of the board, and his name was not on it. OK, a day off.

About 0630 hours (6:30 a.m.) the door to his hooch opened, and Harry raised his head to get a flashlight in his eyes. He grabbed a boot, hurled it at the face in the door, and said, "Get that damned flashlight out of my eyes!" The door closed before the boot hit. The door opened again, slowly. It was the operations runner who went around in the morning to get the pilots up who were to fly that day. This was a new one. "Yes, sir. Sir, it's time to get up," the runner said.

"What?" Harry demanded. "I checked the board at midnight, and I wasn't on it."

"Sir, you are now."

Harry thought CPT Paul had struck again. He put his feet on the floor, and the runner left to get the other pilots up.

Harry got up, dressed, and headed for the mess hall by way of operations to see where he was going, what he was to do, who his pilot was, and what ship they had that day. In operations was a large board that could be written on with grease pencils and wiped clean. It showed the two pilots, AC or pilot in command first, the aircraft, where they would be working, and an estimate of how many hours of flight time it would take. As Harry looked at the board, he did not see his name. The runner was seated at a desk beside the board. Harry glowered at him and said, "I'm not on the board. Why the hell did you get me up?"

The runner meekly replied, "Sorry, sir. I made a mistake."

Harry responded, "That's one!" and left.

About two weeks later, pretty much the same thing happened but with the flashlight toward the floor. No fly. Plenty of drinks. Woken early. No fly. This time Harry put both hands on the runner's desk, leaned over, and said, "That's *two*!"

Within another couple of weeks the runner came in. (There were two of them and the other one had gotten Harry up correctly on several occasions during this time.) This time at 0600 hours (6:00 a.m.). "You're flying today, Mr. Nevling."

"Shit!" Harry said. It wasn't that he didn't love to fly, he just didn't like it as a surprise after he'd been up late and been drinking. So again, up, get dressed, and off to the mess hall. Stop in operations to get the information, and he's *not on the board—again*! This time he just glared at the runner who was cowering behind his desk, apologizing profusely. Harry said, "That's *three*!" He picked up an M-16 rifle hanging on a hook, checked the magazine, put it back in the rifle, and turned to the runner, who by this time was backed tightly into the corner.

CPT Cooper was standing there and said, "Harry, I don't think he knows you're kidding."

Without taking his eyes off the runner, Harry said, "What makes you think I'm kidding?" About this time, the runner probably shit his pants. Harry kept glowering at the runner for a few more seconds, then put the rifle back and left. He was not awoken by accident again!

A few weeks later Harry was awoken to fly. This time he had known about it since the evening before. He'd had only a couple of drinks and a good night's sleep. All went well until he got on the aircraft. There was the operations runner mounting an M-60 machine gun in the gunner's window on the left of the aircraft. He asked the FE, "What the hell is he doing on my aircraft?"

The FE replied, "He's my new gunner."

Harry inquired, "Do you know what a fuck-up this guy is? He can't even get the right pilots up to go fly!"

The FE informed him that he was a good gunner and very helpful with the aircraft. Harry told the FE and the new gunner that if the gunner fucked up in the aircraft like he did on the ground he'd be tossed out. He said, "Our lives may well depend on you and your guns. If they don't work, we have nothing to shoot back with. Are you sure you have the operating rods in correctly?" (An M-60 has a rod about two feet long that uses the pressure from the fired round to cycle the breech for another round to go into the chamber. Both ends look similar, but if it is in backward, you have only one shot. Then you would have to manually cock it to get another single round off. The weapon has to be disassembled—the rod put in correctly—and then reassembled.)

Harry said, "When we take off we're going over the water, and when I say it's clear, I want to hear both those guns fire on automatic." When Harry took off, instead of heading west they went east over the South China Sea. There were no sampans in sight, so he said, "Clear." He listened and could easily identify that both guns were firing. "Good," he said, and they turned back west to do their missions for the day.

Within a fairly short time, Harry got on the same aircraft one morning to see the operations runner/gunner at the right door/window. He asked the FE, "What's he doing over there?"

The FE said, "He just made CE."

Harry walked over to him, patted him on the back, and said, "Congratulations! It looks as though you have found what you are good at."

He had a big smile on his face as he replied, "Yes, sir, I have!"

A good lesson in people. Here was a guy who couldn't take a list of names off a board and wake up the right people but could handle the mechanics of not only a machine gun but a Chinook, an incredibly complex machine.

# Evac of Marine FSB

Pachyderm was again flying support for the marines. They had expanded their FSBs out into a new area on what was probably a follow-up operation to Operation Dewey Canyon. Perhaps it was another phase of Dewy Canyon. Regardless, Pachyderm was back in the northwest corner of South Vietnam supporting the 3rd Marine Division. When they decided to withdraw from some of the farthest-out areas, Pachyderm was there to assist with the withdrawal.

This was another FSB on top of a mountain close to the Laotian border. The west side of it dropped off sharply into a valley, probably with a river in the bottom. For Harry this was an add-on mission. He was called on his way back to the beach and told to go help with the evacuation. Harry had not been to this particular FSB before but had the coordinates, frequency, and call sign for the pathfinder.

Wonderful. That meant that Harry would be the last ship in—and the last one out. Two problems with that: it was already dusk, and by the time he got there and got loaded—it would be an internal load of the last security forces—it would be dark. Harry had had enough of night flying in the mountains. The other problem was that it would be the last security forces. If the NVA were anywhere in the area they would see what was going on. It would be easy for them to attack as the last of the forces were leaving. This sucked already, and Harry wasn't even there yet.

As he approached the FSB, he observed a cannon being slung back to Vandergrift. There was another aircraft just lifting off with a sling load of just stuff. There was another Pachyderm waiting to go in. Harry made a wide turn to allow time for the other Pachyderm to go in and pick up another load of stuff. These loads were the remnants of the FSB. Stuff like leftover ammo and rations, tents, and just junk that someone thought was important.

When the FSB was clear and Harry went in, it was the far side of dusk. As he landed, he could still make out the terrain features, but it was getting darker quickly.

The CE dropped the ramp, and the marines started getting on board. Harry was looking out over the valley they would have to take off toward. Harry was thinking that the far side of that valley was Laos. If not, it was damned close. The loading seemed to be taking a long time. Harry looked up in the cockpit rearview mirror, and all he could see were marine helmets. Lots and lots of helmets. Harry asked the CE, "How many Jarheads you got back there, Chief?"

"Sir, I stopped counting at ninety," he replied.

Harry told him to find someone in charge and get at least half the marines off the aircraft. The FE acknowledged this. A couple of minutes later the FE came back on the line and said, "Sir, there's a gunny (gunnery sergeant, senior NCO ) back here who says he's already lit the fuse. You'd better get out of here. Oh shit."

When the marines evacuated an FSB, they would plant explosives to destroy any equipment and fortifications remaining. They did a good job of it. Harry figured that much of the top of the mountain was about to disappear.

He pulled up on the thrust lever. Nothing happened. He pulled in more pitch and could feel it starting to get light on the gear. He pulled in power to the red line and was still on the ground. *Oh shit!*

Harry told the pilot to watch the clock. He wanted five-second intervals called out when he said "Mark." He was going to go to emergency power *again* to get all those marines off that mountain. Harry pulled the power up to the red line of 875 foot pounds of torque, called "Mark," and pulled in the extra torque for his emergency power. The aircraft slowly lifted off the ground. There was not enough power to take off, so Harry hovered to the edge and "fell" off the mountain. He was able to maintain forward momentum as they went down the side of the mountain, and the aircraft got past translational lift and started flying. Harry eased back on the stick, stopped the descent, and started to climb. By the time they reached the fifty-five second mark, the aircraft was flying fine. They were maintaining airspeed and a good rate of climb. Harry had turned to the right to stay in the valley as they climbed high enough to clear the ridgeline. Once over the ridge, he lowered the thrust level to below the normal red line and headed for Vandergrift to drop off the marines. He knew there was a large mountain northwest of Khe Shan, so he went east to make sure he would get enough altitude to miss it. When they arrived in the Vandergrift area, the pilot called for clearance, and it was approved. They both turned on their landing/searchlights. These were nestled in the belly of the aircraft and could be run out and swiveled for illumination of the ground. They spotted the landing area, and Harry told the pilot he was going to make a "running landing," as he didn't think he had the power to make a normal approach to the ground and sure as hell didn't have enough to come to a hover.

Harry approached the landing area in a shallow descent, and as he was about to touch down, he pulled the nose up and pulled the power back into the red line. The aircraft slowed even further as the aft gear touched down. The aircraft rolled to a stop, and Harry pulled the stick farther back as he lowered the thrust to ease the main gear onto the ground.

The FE lowered the ramp, and the marines exited the aircraft. They probably knew there was a problem from the antics the aircraft went through to get them from the FSB to Vandergrift.

Harry still had to fly over the mountains to refuel and return to Pachyderm Beach. He pulled thrust and took off. Clearing the mountains was not difficult with the aircraft empty. Harry maintained fifty knots and used the rest of the power to climb to six thousand feet to be well above any of the mountains and headed east to the coast. Then down the coast to the Camp Eagle refuel pad and a hop over to Pachyderm Beach and home. Harry was really sick of this night-flying shit!

## MARINES OUT OF THE VALLEY

Another afternoon mission add-on. There was a marine ground unit on patrol who needed to be picked up and taken in to Vandergrift. "Roger that. Where are they, and what is their frequency and call sign?" Harry got the information. They checked their tactical maps and located the grid coordinates. Hmm. Indian country. The grid coordinates were in a remote, rugged area that was not mountainous or jungle. It was mostly grass and shrubs with small trees. A series of valleys and ravines ran through the area.

They took off and headed for the location, getting artillery clearance on the way. They called the marines on the frequency given them and got a quick response. They asked for smoke and identified red smoke. The marines confirmed, so Harry set up an approach into the bottom of a small, grass-filled valley. It's getting on in the afternoon, and with the mountains to the west, it's going to be dusk in minutes. From there to dark is pretty quick. Then it just gets *black!*

Harry was feeling pretty good about this. He should be able to load the marines, be out in just a few minutes, and probably get to Vandergrift before dark. As the marines were starting to load, a lieutenant came up to the cockpit. Oh, oh, Harry thought, this can't be good. The LT told Harry that they would not be able to get another marine helicopter in to pick up the rest of his men before dark. Whatever did not fit on the Chinook would have to stay. He would not split his force, so they were all going or all staying. Harry respected this. The LT was more interested in his men than getting his ass back to Vandergrift.

Harry asked him how many men he had. Fifty-two was the response. Hell, Harry had picked up a lot more than that. He looked out the windshield and saw that the valley was straight for about a quarter mile and then turned to his left. It looked as though it narrowed at the turn as well. Harry turned to the lieutenant and told him to get his men on board. He said thanks and left. He looked up in the mirror and did not see any more marines getting on. The LT had just stepped off the ramp and appeared to be calling his men. Five minutes, and no more marines. Dusk was getting duskier. Harry asked the FE if he could see the marine LT. He stepped off the ramp and found him. Harry asked the FE to ask the LT where the rest of his men were. He came back shortly with, "He said they were on the ridges on either side pulling security. They're on their way." Oh shit! Yet another night flight! Harry told him to have the lieutenant put a rush on it. It was getting dark fast. Another anxious ten minutes, and the FE called, "Ramp up. Ready for takeoff."

Harry was thinking he didn't know what was on the other side of either ridge. He didn't know what was in the curve of the valley, and he didn't know what was on the other side of the ridge at the curve where he intended to depart past. That's a lot of no knowledge. Harry went through what by now was his standard pilot briefing about an emergency power takeoff. There is still enough light to see the terrain. So, power up to red line, "Mark," emergency power up and nose over, keep it low and below the ridges on either side, accelerate, accelerate, accelerate. Harry got the maximum speed possible when he got to the ridge ahead of them. The pilot was calling off the five-second intervals, and they approached the ridge. Harry pulled back on the stick, and they shot nearly straight up. By the time the climb indicator caught up with them, the pilot was calling, "Sixty," and Harry dropped the power back below the red line as he rolled the nose over and again accelerated.

They delivered the marines to Vandergrift without incident and left for Pachyderm Beach. The tops of the mountains were still in enough light to navigate safely past them to the coast, down to refuel, and to go to the beach. Another day done.

## Smoke in the Avionics Closet

Yet another morning in wonderful downtown Phu Bai! Just kidding. Actually, Harry had never been into Phu Bai. Oh, well.

The routine. The operations runner comes to your hooch and wakes you an hour and a half before takeoff. The pilots have that time to get up, get dressed, get some coffee and/or breakfast, check in at operations if they are the AC, and preflight the aircraft. Same ole stuff this day.

Harry got up when the runner opened his door. He put on his Nomex fire-retardant flight suit, brushed his teeth, and went to operations. Harry saw that they were again going to take supplies out to the FSBs around the A Shau Valley. Next stop the mess hall for some breakfast, then on to the flight line. Talk to the crew, check the logbook for any noted problems, and preflight the aircraft with the pilot and crew. The gunner mounted the two M-60 7.62 mm (.308 caliber) machine guns, one in the left window behind the AC and avionics compartment, the other in the front door behind the pilot and the heater/winch closet. Preflight check complete. Climb into the cockpit, and strap in. A four-inch-wide lap belt with a two-inch shoulder belt over each shoulder attached to the lap belt buckle. Check to make sure the locking mechanism for the shoulder belts works. Go through the starting procedure, and get the aircraft running. Check the parking area for other aircraft moving, and taxi to the take-off portion of the pad. A Chinook is steered by the left rear wheel. The control is a small knob on the left rear of the center console. Either pilot can reach it, but it is normally operated from the left seat. Check left, right, and overhead; get the all clear from the crew; and pull in power with the thrust lever. As the aircraft lifts off, ease back on the stick until clear of the ground, then roll the nose over and climb out. Stop the climb at about two hundred feet, and head toward the resupply point you are going to use that day. Today it was Supply Point Birmingham. Call the loadmaster at the resupply point, and get your load information. Pick up your load, and head for the FSB it's supposed to go to. So far so good. Just another beautiful day…oh, oh! What's that smell? Smells like something burning.

Harry asked, "Chief, is something burning back there?"

"No, sir," came the response. "Why? Do you smell something?"

Harry told him he thought he smelled smoke, like from an electrical fire. The FE stuck his head into the cockpit but couldn't smell anything. A Chinook is like a station wagon with the back window down. Everything from the back comes to the front and out the side windows. If there's anything burning back there it will be smelled in the cockpit. Harry told the FE it was OK. Maybe it was a whiff of something else. But Harry could still smell it. You do not want a fire in a Chinook. The entire aircraft is a combination of different exotic alloys, and it burns very nicely and very, very HOT! Harry saw the remains of one they lost from an engine fire. You could have swept up the leftovers and put them in a bushel basket.

The smell got worse, and Harry called the FE back to the cockpit. This time he could smell it. He thought it may be something in the avionics closet behind Harry and went to check. Shortly he called Harry on the intercom and told him it was the gyro for the artificial horizon. It was extremely hot and nearly burned his hand through his glove. Harry told him to unplug the power. When the FE did this, they could hear the gyro screech to a stop. The smell quickly dissipated, and Harry was relieved. With clear weather they really didn't need the artificial horizon, so they carried on and performed the day's missions. Perhaps another close call. Had the defective gyro started a fire in the avionics closet, it would have been a really bad thing!

# Race with a Cobra

One morning doing his routine of taking loads of ammunition, water, food, and other materials to the FSBs and other ground units, Harry was picking up yet another load of four pallets of 105 mm howitzer ammunition from Supply Point Birmingham. Just after he lifted off the load and reached about three hundred feet of altitude, an AH-1 Huey Cobra gunship sailed past his left window. The Cobra was a replacement for the UH 1C and M gunships. Rather than being shaped like the Huey, it was a slim and trim fighting machine designed to be a gunship, not a modified something else. It was only thirty-six inches wide at its widest point, and that was to accommodate the transmission mounts for the Huey transmission it used. It had a turret on the front, usually containing a three-barrel, 20 mm Gatling gun capable of putting out several thousand rounds a minute. Under its stubby "wing" hard points, it carried rocket tubes for 2.75-inch folding fin rockets, usually with ten-pound warheads of high explosive. A formidable weapons platform. The two pilots were seated front and back. The forward pilot was also the gunner and controlled the rotation and elevation of the gun turret. The aft pilot was the designated pilot and usually fired the rockets. The guys who flew the Cobra thought they were pretty hot shit flying a "hotrod." Harry thought differently.

As the Cobra passed Harry on the left at a pretty good clip, the gunner looked over with a grin and waved bye-bye. OK, Harry thought, let's see what you got! He added power up to the red line and rolled the nose over to build up his airspeed. It took a while, but as the two helicopters were flying over the eastern mountains to the A Shau Valley, Harry sailed past the Cobra and waved bye-bye to them. The gunner's jaw dropped, as he couldn't believe that a Chinook carrying four pallets of ammo was actually passing them! Ha! Still think you're hot shit? Thought not.

That evening in the O Club, Harry was regaling his tale of passing a Cobra when one of the guys who had been in the unit down south at Bear Cat before they joined the 101st and was the 200th Assault Support Aviation Company told him they had an "official" race between an A model Chinook and a Cobra. The two units got together and set up the rules and course for the race. Of course there was a bet or two to go along with the race. Now, a Cobra is limited by VNE (velocity never exceeded) because of the airframe or some such thing. The VNE on a Chinook is a made-up number to hold down some of the stress factors but really can be exceeded. The maintenance officers and crews tweaked the engines to put out even more power and got ready for the race. Came the big day, and the two aircraft lined up at the start. They were to race to another base camp (Bien Hoa perhaps, sixteen kilometers to the northeast.) in the area, circle the perimeter, and return. (If it were Bien Hoa, it would be over thirty-two kilometers for the track, or about twenty miles.)

On the day of the big race all was prepared and set for takeoff. Now an empty Chinook can really haul ass from the ground. You pull in all the power and pick it up. Not necessary to use aft cyclic to get it up on the aft gear in this situation. You just pull it up, roll the nose, and *go!* That's just what happened. The Cobra saw nothing but the tail and ramp of the Chinook as it "left him in the dust." As the tale goes, the Chinook was back to the start/end point and shut down before the Cobra touched down. So much for the hotrod.

# Radar AA

Harry had been flying support for the Marines-again. This day he had been carrying loads out of Quang Tri to the FSBs north of the A Shau Valley and southwest of Khe Sahn. It had been a busy but quiet day. No one had shot at him, to the best of his knowledge. To tracer rounds, no mortars. The clouds had pretty much cleared so there was good visibility.

Harry had returned to Quang Tri for another load in the mid afternoon when he was told he was done for the day. All missions out of Quang Tri had been completed.

Harry had enough fuel to get to Supply Point Birmingham easily. There he could fill his tanks and return to Pachyderm Beach for the day. With the cleared weather, he decided rather than take the longer route roughly following Highway 1 he would make a straight route to Birmingham. Probably not the best idea.

The straight route would take him west of Camp Evans and Camp Sally, over the foothills and along the front of the first chain of mountains. This was Indian country.

While us forces pretty well controlled the corridor along Highway 1 and the coast the terrain to the west quickly became jungle covered hills then the mountains. There were no US bases in these foothills. Indian country.

With no sling load Harry had climbed to about three thousand feet and 150 knots. The mountain ridges to his right, west, were near his altitude but quite a bit further west. He figured that if anyone started popping at him with an AK-47 he had enough altitude to minimize and damage from a depleted round.

As he neared Camp Evans to its northwest he head a beep on his FM radio. He was still tuned into Vandy DASK for artillery clearance and hadn't changed over to the 101st clearance center. They had no FSBs that would be firing in his direction. Just a couple of seconds later there was another beep. Oh, Oh!

The pilots had been told that the NVA had reportedly moved radar controlled anti-aircraft artillery (AA) into the area. The tell-tale was that they could hear the pulses from the radar as beeps on their FM radios. It would take at least three beeps for the radar to lock the gun on target. If you heard these beeps the best thing to do was change direction and/or altitude to evade the radar lock.

Just as Harry heard the third beep he was turning east and climbing. The regular beep, beep, beep continued and Harry continued to fly an erratic route to avoid any radar lock. This AA would be either 20 mm or 40 mm cannon rounds. Harry did not wish to tangle with either. He continued his evasive flight and the regular beep, beep, beep continued as well.

This went on for about ten minutes, a long ten minutes, until Harry got near Camp Evans when the beeping suddenly stopped. Harry had warned the crew of what was going on. No one saw any sign of AA fire coming their way. Harry wasn't sure if this was the real thing or perhaps just a test. He was glad that it did not involve any rounds coming his way.

# Troops in the open

This day Harry had been taking resupplies from Quang Tri to FSB Cunningham and other marine FSBs in that area. His last load of the day was a back haul of empty cargo nets to Quang Tri resupply. As the weather was clear, Harry could take a direct route from FSB Cunningham to Quang Tri.

Empty cargo nets are not a desired load. They don't have enough weight to streamline and will take off on their own if you get above about 50 knots. So Harry departed FSB Cunningham with his slow load and rapidly got to 50 knots. He kept in extra power to climb over the mountains between there and the coast.

He levelled off about 5,000 feet where he'd have plenty of clearance for the mountains. A beautiful day. The only thing hampering visibility was the ever present haze. They could see at least twenty miles. Nice.

As they crossed the last ridge Harry started bleeding off altitude over the rugged foothills. He looked down and saw a large clearing in the jungle to his left front. It was at least 2,000 feet below him. There was a trail going across the clearings long axis from southwest to northeast. And there was movement!

As Harry looked closer at the trail he could make out a column of soldiers stretched across the entire clearing. There were about sixty soldiers dressed in khaki uniforms. Holy shit! These had to be NVA soldiers headed in the direction of Quang Tri.

Harry quickly called Vandy DASK to find if there was any friendly activity in the area. There was none. Harry explained what he was looking at and requested guns come to the area. The controller told him he'd get them there as soon as possible.

Harry climbed up a bit and began an orbit south of the clearing. He did not want to attract any attention to his being up there. As the far troops reentered the jungle more would appear coming into the clearing.

Troops in the open are an artillery man's wet dream. They have no place to go, no place to hide. Harry was not going anywhere near these guys with only two M-60 popguns for assault. He hoped that help would arrive before the troops got into the jungle on the far side of the clearing.

Harry continued to orbit while he waited, and waited, and waited. He watched as the last man entered the clearing and still no guns.

When the last man was past the midpoint he got a call from a pair of ariel rocket artillery aircraft. These were Hueys with forty eight 2.75 inch folding fin rockets plus two door gunners. Harry explained what was going on to them. By the time they got over the clearing the last man had gone into the jungle on the far side. Harry told them that the last man had just disappeared into the trees and if they could follow the trail into the trees they could locate the troops.

Harry was getting low on fuel and left the area with his best wishes for good hunting.

## Best Area North of Da Nang

By the time the pilots, under the guidance of Weatherly, had finished the pit barbecue on their new outdoor patio, they had a really nice and very comfortable place to come back to at the end of the day. There were lot of concrete walkways and patios throughout the company area. Pachyderm had built a new shower building located behind the officers' hooches and to the right. They replaced the old one with a cement floor and a regular building on top. The drains just went out into a drainage ditch, but it was a great improvement over the previous shower. The showers were gravity fed from tanks on top of the building. Hot water was provided by running the water through a barrel with an emersion heater. This meant that someone had to go up there and regularly check the water supply to ensure it was sufficient. They also had to check the fuel for the immersion heaters; if the fuel that dripped onto the plate in the heater ran out, there was no hot water.

After Pachyderm had been flying support for the marines for a couple of months there was an award ceremony. Lt. GEN Richard G. Stillwell, XXIIII Corps commander, made the presentations. Maj. GEN Raymond G. Davis, commander, 3rd Marine Division, was also in attendance. Most of the medals awarded that day were for actions in support of the marines.

Following the ceremony, General Davis approached Major Burns and thanked him for the fine job that Pachyderm had done in support of his marines. He also asked if there were anything he could do for the major or Pachyderm. Burns replied that there was. The marines on the other side of the Phu Bai Airfield had running water. He asked the general if it were possible to run a line over to their area. The general granted his request. Pachyderm had running water! In Vietnam that was a really big deal. It wasn't potable but was great for washing. The first things that were hooked into the water supply were the showers and the mess hall. Eventually it was run into the field grade officers' hooches. The wash basins were replaced with sinks and faucets. Cold water only that simply drained into the sand underneath the buildings, but a significant increase in comfort. As Harry and Such were in one of these hooches, they rather enjoyed running water.

Many USO troupes stayed with Pachyderm, as it was probably the nicest area north of Da Nang. One of the troupes, a group of Australians, spent several stays at Pachyderm Beach a number of times. This was where themural on the wall of the screened patio came from. This artwork really enhanced the patio.

Another advantage of all the USO troupes coming through was that many of them would do a special show just for the Pachyderms. They had built a stage for the performers. The audience either sat on the sand or brought their own seats. The officers and enlisted men of Pachyderm thoroughly enjoyed these special performances. Another perk of Pachyderm Beach!

# Lookin' for an RLO (Real Live Officer)

One morning there was a delay at the resupply pad at Vandergrift. Harry set his aircraft down near the Pachyderm Operations shack to wait. Two other Pachyderms joined him. This was one of the extremely rare occurrences where Harry shut down his aircraft during the day. Normally it was running constantly from the time he left Pachyderm Beach or wherever until he returned to his base for the night. The six pilots were standing off to the side, smoking and talking. While they were standing there, shooting the shit, a pair of marine CH-46s approached and landed beside the pilots. A marine major exited one of the aircraft and approached Harry and the other pilots. Harry and the others came to attention, and Harry said, "Good morning, sir." The major looked at the group. We were all warrant officers. After scanning the group a couple of times, he asked who the flight leader was. Harry looked at the others standing there and realized that he was the senior warrant there. He turned to the major and said, "Sir, we don't work like that. We're all single ship flights."

He looked over the group again and asked, "Who's in charge?"

Harry responded, "I'm the senior officer of these three aircraft." The major's jaw dropped. He said, "You mean you're in charge of these three Chinooks?"

"No sir," he replied, "I told you we don't work that way. But I am the senior officer."

The major didn't know quite what to say. There he was, a major with a flight of two CH-6s (with the approximate capabilities of a Huey) talking to a CW2 he thought was in charge of three CH-47s. It seemed to be a bit much for him. He started trying to say something, but he was stumbling about, so Harry asked, pointing, "Sir, if you're looking for a real live officer, Captain Cooper, our operations officer, is in that shack over there." He hurried toward the shack. When the major entered the building, the warrants all had a good laugh.

# RECOVERING LURCH

Harry was in the O Club late one afternoon on a day off from flying. Captain Cooper came in and asked if he'd been drinking. Harry knew what that meant. He told Coop, "No sir, just drinking a Coke."

"How would you like to go on a mission this afternoon?"

"Sure. What is it?"

"Well, you know about the raid into Elephant Valley today?" Harry did. There were several aircraft assigned to pick up a company of infantry and take them into Elephant Valley to conduct a surprise raid on suspected NVA positions. Each of the aircraft was to take thirty or so infantry and drop them into a spot in the valley in a daisy chain. Several aircraft would follow one another, go in, drop off the infantry, and take off quickly to let the next one in. Cooper told him that one of the aircraft, with Larry Lurch Hines as AC and 1LT Ramsden as pilot, had an engine shot out, and crashed. It appeared that everyone was OK, but the crash resulted in all the blades being ripped off. They had taken in a recovery team to prepare the aircraft. A Chinook couldn't lift another Chinook unless some of the major components were removed. Captain Dickey, maintenance officer, was in charge of the recovery crew.

They planned to remove both engines and both rotor transmissions with the rotor heads, then take out the airframe. They had an aircraft assigned to do this, but it was getting late, and they wouldn't be able to get the airframe to Red Beach at Da Nang and back to pick up the recovery team and the infantry security force before dark. Cooper told Harry that CW2 Al Tatman was going as pilot and if he wished he could go with him. Harry told him that he'd be glad to help out and headed for the flight line.

He found Tatman at the aircraft with the crew, and it had already been preflighted. Harry and Tatman got into the cockpit and cranked up the aircraft.

Elephant Valley runs southeast from the A Shau Valley toward the north side of Da Nang. It seemed a logical route for the bad guys to take to get to that side of Da Nang. The northwest end of it is about forty-four kilometers (twenty-seven miles) almost due south from Phu Bai. As Harry and Tatman headed there, Harry told him that he wanted to scout the crash site before landing. Harry had never been in Elephant Valley, although he was familiar with where it was and its reputation as a nasty area. Harry flew toward the head of the narrow valley, so he could fly down it and take a look. He contacted the soldiers on the ground and told them he was inbound. They told him the other aircraft had left with the airframe. He asked for a smoke grenade to easily locate the site. Harry spotted the smoke, confirmed the color, and flew toward it at around one hundred fifty knots about five hundred feet above the valley floor. Wow! Very narrow valley. A true V with steep sides rising into mountains. Harry spotted the wreck on what had been a road along the south side of the valley. It was overgrown with grass and brush. Lurch had done an excellent job getting the aircraft in there and turning about ninety degrees to the right to line up with the road. To the left of the aircraft the side of the valley rose steeply, and that was what ripped the blades off.

Harry asked the ground if they had any enemy activity and learned they hadn't had any contact. The infantry was out on perimeter security and hadn't seen or heard anything. That was good news. Harry told them he was going to make a couple of passes to see if he drew any fire and try to spot a landing area. He turned the aircraft, dropped to about fifty feet, and went down the valley at around 150 knots. If anyone was going to shoot at them, Harry didn't want to give them an easy target. The pass was uneventful so Harry pulled up, turned around, and flew up the valley at around fifty knots. Still nothing, so he turned around again and approached the site. One could only see the overgrown road once you knew it was there. It was obscured by overgrowth of grass and brush. He hovered around the site, trying to find a place to land without tearing the blades off. Harry was amazed that Lurch was able to find a spot to put his aircraft down after losing an engine to enemy fire and only suffering two minor casualties. He finally found a suitable spot about two hundred feet up the valley in front of the crashed aircraft. Being very careful and having the entire crew watching the terrain, he successfully set the aircraft down.

It was already dusk, and Harry knew the light would disappear rapidly in the mountains.

Captain Dickey and his recovery crew started loading their tools, parts, and pieces they had removed. Then they loaded more. And then they loaded more. By now it's getting dark. Harry did not want to be flying out of that spot in the dark. Too narrow and too likely that the bad guys had moved in for an ambush. Now would be the time to strike, as there were the fewest US soldiers left. Harry looked back and saw they were loading quilted material insulation panels on the aircraft. It was getting dark rapidly, and Harry considered this a waste of time. He told the FE to have Captain Dickey get everyone on board; they were leaving. It took another ten minutes or so, and by then it was dark. Damn!

Harry could just make out the sides of the valley. Harry asked Tatman to monitor the clock and notify him every five seconds after he told him "Mark." The Chinook had a red line on the amount of power you could pull from the engines. The normal red line was at 875 foot pounds of torque. This limit could be exceeded to the second red line of 995 pounds for ten minutes. That difference of 120 pounds is a 13.7 percent increase in useable power. With it being near dark, having a lot of activity at the crash site all day, and not knowing what was out there, Harry considered it an emergency situation. Now that 13.7 percent makes a noticeable and significant difference in the performance of the aircraft. Harry started pulling in the power with the thrust lever and lifted off. He continued pulling power, and as the torque gauge passed the first red line, Harry called, "Mark!" He kept a steady increase in the thrust until it was at the second red line. As he was doing this, the aircraft came off the ground. As soon as he was clear of the shrubs, he turned the aircraft about eighty degrees to the right using pedals, rotated the nose over to keep near the ground, and rapidly picked up speed. He wanted to stay close to the ground until he had enough speed to turn it into a lot of altitude rapidly. If someone was going to start shooting at them, he wanted the most difficult target possible. When Tatman called, "Thirty!" Harry was heading up the valley and picking up speed rapidly. At "One!" they were moving right along just above the treetops. Now they could make out ahead where the valley took a sharp turn to the left and had a ridgeline directly ahead. "One thirty!" The airspeed was increasing rapidly, and as they approached the ridgeline, Harry pulled back on the stick, and the aircraft rapidly rose as Harry bled off the airspeed for altitude. He kept climbing as Tatman called out, "Two!" When they got about five hundred feet above the terrain, Harry decreased the power to the lower red line but kept climbing as he accelerated again to get up to 120 knots, a nice cruising airspeed, and headed for Camp Eagle to drop off the infantry. They did not take any hits, and no one saw any muzzle flashes. Whew!

They dropped off the infantry where they wanted to go at Camp Eagle, refueled, and returned to Pachyderm Beach. Another interesting day.

Harry later learned that he and Tatman were to receive Air Medals with Valor Device for their actions that day. Harry wondered where that came from and asked Tatman. He told Harry that he had submitted them for the award. Harry was a bit surprised. He never put himself in for a medal. Had he done so, he was sure he would have received an award for evacuating the marine FSB and taking the marine infantry out of that valley late in the evening. There were other actions Harry was involved in that may have gotten him awards. However, he just didn't feel it was right to put himself in for a medal.

# Number 1 N1

The next time Ramsden flew after Lurch and he crashed in Elephant Valley was the following week, and it was with Harry. He was a bit nervous. (*Surprise!*) They had the good fortune to draw a ship that had a weird problem. Harry had never seen it before or after.

After takeoff from Pachyderm Beach, they were headed northwest. As they were crossing Highway 1, Harry asked Ramsden if he heard anything. He didn't and asked what Harry heard. Harry then asked the FE if he heard anything. Again no. Harry told them he wasn't sure what it was, but something happened that shouldn't have. Another thirty seconds or so, and he heard it again. No one else had. About every thirty seconds he'd hear something strange but couldn't put his finger on it. After the fifth or sixth time, the FE said that he'd heard it as well. A couple more times and Ramsden picked it up also. Harry was scanning the instruments and gauges and finally caught it. The number one engine N1 tachymeter was fluctuating. This measures the speed of the engine's turbine. The thing that generates the power that allows the aircraft to fly. The fluctuation was not much, but with each cycle, it got worse. When Harry first saw it, it went up 1.5 percent, then down 3.0, then back up to stable. Each cycle it would gain or lose another quarter percent or so. Harry had the FE come up to the cockpit, so he could show him what was going on. When Harry showed the FE the number one engine's N1 gauge, he looked over at Ramsden. He was getting a bit pale. He asked what they were going to do. Harry said he wanted to watch this but started a slow right turn to avoid Camp Eagle and headed back to Pachyderm

Beach. When it got to fluctuating plus and minus 5 percent, Ramsden was white, and Harry pulled the circuit breaker. The engine steadied up, they landed at the beach, and got another ship to fly. Harry never did find out what caused it, but it never happened to him again, and he never heard of it happening to anyone else. Ah, yet another interesting day in 'Nam!

## Phony Problem Cooper Had Harry Check

One morning when Harry went into operations to check on his aircraft and mission assignment, Captain Cooper called him aside. He asked Harry for a favor. He had an aircraft that had been brought back the previous morning with a mechanical problem. It had been checked over by maintenance, and nothing was found. Cooper wanted to know if Harry was willing to take the aircraft and see if he could find anything wrong with it. Harry agreed. Neither one of them wanted Harry to know what the problem was. If it were there he'd find it.

Harry went out to the aircraft and preflighted it with his pilot and the FE. Everything looked fine, so they did the cockpit check and started it up. No sign of anything wrong, so Harry took the controls, and they left the beach and headed for Supply Point Birmingham to pick up a load. On the way, Harry kept a very close eye, and ear, on everything. He made a variety of maneuvers to see if he could stimulate anything with the aircraft. No sign of anything wrong. He called operations and informed Cooper. He told him he'd check in again after the first mission.

They picked up a load of supplies and headed for an FSB along the A Shau Valley. After dropping the load off and going back to Birmingham there was still no sign of a problem, even with his efforts to find one. He called in to Cooper again and gave him the info. Cooper told him that's what he thought. Harry said, "You have one of those to deal with?" Cooper told him yes but did not name anyone. Harry didn't want to know. He could certainly guess. It had to have been an AC to bring a ship back. It could only have been one of three: Paul or Pete or perhaps…

# BILL CRISTOBOL'S PISTOL

Harry was flying with Bill Cristobol that day. Bill had come into the unit after Harry and the other Playtex pilots. Cristobol was on his second tour as a pilot having flown Hueys his first trip. He was a really nice guy, friendly, gentle, and helpful. And, Harry thought, a bit crazy. He wanted to get discharged from the army in Vietnam and stay there as a missionary. Harry wished him luck with that plan.

On this day Harry got into the left seat first, then Cristobol got into the right seat. He carried his sidearm in a civilian belt and holster he must have bought in Vietnam. After he sat down he lifted it up and rotated the belt and holster so the pistol was now in his crotch. His sidearm was a .45-caliber semiautomatic pistol with a seven-round magazine. Harry had to ask, "Bill, why do you put your pistol there?"

He answered, "It's to protect the family jewels. If a round comes up through the chin bubble and into my crotch, it will hit the pistol and not me."

"Well, Harry came back, "what do you suppose will happen if that round hits the ammo in your pistol?"

He thought about that for a few seconds, lifted up and shifted the pistol back to his right side.

## CALLED BACK—TOO MANY HOURS

The army had rules on how many hours a pilot could fly in any thirty-day period. In operations there was a board with all the pilots' names listed. To the right were columns for the thirty days. The last column was for the total hours. Each day this board was updated. Any hours flown the day before were added, and any hours flown thirty-one days prior were erased. Then the totals were adjusted accordingly. The pilots were not to fly more than one hundred hours in any thirty-day period without talking to a flight surgeon (doctor). At 110 hours they had to be actually seen by a flight surgeon. In no case were they to fly more than 120 hours in that time period.

On 22 June Harry was flying as AC with his hooch mate and friend Such. They had already taken several loads of resupply out to the FSBs along the A Shau Valley when around 1400 (2:00 p.m.) they received a radio call from operations. It was CPT Cooper telling them to return to base. Harry said they still had several loads to deliver and requested the reason for the orders. Cooper replied, "You have too many hours. Return to base now." Harry did not think it wise to argue the point.

Upon his return, COL Ted "Chrome Dome" Crozier, the 101st Airborne Aviation Group commander was in operations. He wanted to make sure that Harry returned. When he left, Harry looked at the board and saw that he had 109.4 hours with that day's time added in. Had he stayed out to finish the missions he would have been over the 110 hour limit. Wouldn't have mattered much as he had not talked with a flight surgeon. (There was one based at battalion.)

Later Harry took a look at his hours for June. He had five days with over eight hours and two with over ten hours. During the month he had carried over one hundred hours for twenty-five days and 110 or more hours for fourteen of those days.

This had been building over time. In January, he flew only twenty-eight hours. Some of this may have been because they had just arrived, the weather was shitty, he went to Varsity for in-country orientation, back to Playtex for a brief time, then on to Pachyderm on 1 February.

February saw a total of 67.5 flight hours, then up to 90.6 in March. April he had 83.0 hours, and in May it went to 106. The high hours in May combined with the hours in June to get him a lot of days over the army limits.

When Harry got back to Pachyderm Beach on the twenty-second, he was grounded for the rest of the month to get his total down. It took until the twenty-sixth to get him below one hundred hours, and he was at 79.6 by the end of the month. Harry would have preferred to fly any or all of those days. He loved flying the Chinook. However, he had learned how tired one could get, so it was probably a good thing. But then it wasn't his decision to make.

## ALL THE SMOKES IN THE VALLEY

One lovely afternoon Harry was taking resupplies from Supply Point Birmingham to the FSBs located along the east side of the A Shau Valley again. It was another of those great days for flying, light breeze, no clouds, unlimited visibility, and no one shooting at him!

As he approached Birmingham, he called for his next load. The pathfinder told him he had three five-hundred gallon blivits (a cylinder shaped, rubber-like bladder) of gasoline to take the A Shau Valley. Ah, another load for the 11th ACR. He never understood why they were called blivits. The normal definition of a blivit is ten pounds of shit in a five-pound bag. These things were pretty neat. They had tow rings on each end so that they could be towed, at low speeds, behind a vehicle. They had a fill/drain valve on one end, and as they were emptied, they collapsed in on themselves, which made it easy to carry them empty, especially in a cargo net.

Five hundred gallons of gasoline weighs 3,150 pounds. The three blivits were 9,450 pounds plus the weight of the blivits themselves. This did not make a particularly heavy load. Because of the weight, the load would not swing below the aircraft, so he could go as fast as the density altitude allowed.

Brief lesson in aerodynamics that was very important in Vietnam. Density altitude is standard pressure altitude as it is affected by an increase in temperature, a decrease in atmospheric pressure, and to a small degree, the humidity. All these factors will increase the density altitude, which is what the aircraft thinks it is flying at. As an example,

271

at five thousand feet and eighty degrees the helicopter behaves as if it at seven thousand feet, a 40 percent increase in elevation. In Vietnam on most days, all these factors adversely affected the aircraft's performance, no matter what you were flying. In the Chinook the above example at forty thousand pounds gross weight (forty-five thousand maximum gross weight) would limit your airspeed to 115 knots (132 mph). This was significantly below the normal maximum of 175 knots (200 mph). You could actually fly faster than these limits. However, it was hard on the air-craft, and Harry did *not* believe in abusing what was keeping him in the sky! He flew at or near the maximum speed to get to where he was going quickly and return. Thus he could accomplish the maximum number of missions in the time available.

Harry cleared the eastern edge of the valley and called the path-finder on the assigned radio frequency. He responded, and Harry asked for smoke, as he was nearing the map coordinates where he was told to go. The pathfinder replied, "Smoke out." As usual, Harry would identify the color of the smoke.

He called back and said, "I have banana (yellow). Um, and goofy grape (purple), hmm, and another grape, and two more grapes, a red, and another grape." Harry had seven smoke grenades going at the same time scattered over an area of about a square mile.

The pathfinder called back and said, "I'm standing next to *my* ba-nana smoke waving my arms."

Harry quickly identified the correct location and took the fuel blivits in and dropped them off. As he left, he called back to the Pathfinder and told him, "It looks like Charlie stole a bunch of grape smokes. Keep using different colors than that."

"Roger that!" came the reply.

This drove home the need for the protocol that the pilot confirm the color of the smoke. Landing at the wrong one could get you hurt—bad.

# .50 Caliber

I t was another very nice day for flying. The weather was clear, and the visibility was only impeded by the haze that is a permanent fixture in Vietnam. Regardless, the visibility was about forty miles or more. There was a light breeze out of the northwest but not enough to cause any difficulties. Harry and his pilot had been taking resupply to the FSBs along the A Shau Valley. As was normal, procedure they called for artillery warnings to find out what FSBs were firing in what direction and where the shells were landing. It would not be a good thing to fly through their path of flight.

Some days the artillery was firing from a number of locations to a variety of targets. This could require the aircraft to fly rather circuitous routes to get to the FSBs. This day the artillery was firing from a couple of FSBs on the edge into the valley. No problem with having to fly around any of the flight paths. He just had to plan ahead as to how they would approach the FSB with the load.

By early afternoon the mission loads were dwindling, and Harry picked up a load of bunker materials, timber, and concertina wire, to take down to FSB Lash. With the weather being so clear, rather than flying west and then south, he thought that maybe they could just fly a straight line from Supply Point Birmingham to FSB Lash. Harry radioed the artillery warning center to see what they may have to fly around. *Nothing was firing!* Every FSB in the 101st Area of Operations was quiet. This was a first for Harry. He had never flown during daylight hours without any artillery warnings. Perhaps things were beginning to quiet down. One could always hope.

Because of the amount of timber in the cargo net, it would provide a lot of wind resistance. One of those loads that had to be flown slowly. So, trade airspeed for altitude and fly higher. Harry climbed to about two thousand feet above ground level as he headed southwest to FSB Lash. The mountains that he would have to cross were lower than in the central and northern part of the valley.

About a third of the way along their route, Harry saw tracer rounds floating up to the right front of the aircraft. As they were red, he figured they were .50-caliber American rounds. The NVA used .51 caliber with green tracer rounds. However, if they could get American weapons, ammo, or equipment, they would gladly use them. The rounds were not really close to the aircraft, but Harry started zigzagging the aircraft to make it more difficult to track and hit. He told the CE on the right machine gun to send a couple of bursts down at the guy shooting at them. It would probably do no good at that range, but maybe the slugs dropping around would dissuade the machine gunner from shooting at them. It didn't. Harry then asked if the CE could see exactly where the fire was coming from. Harry could not see it, as it was behind the chin bubble. The FE said that he could see exactly where it was coming from. So Harry asked him to come into the cockpit and locate it on his tactical map. The CE pointed to the neck in a large bend of the Song Hieu Trach river below them. He told Harry the gun was right in the middle of the smallest part of the neck. Harry thanked him. He checked the position and saw the land was quite flat there. He then got the grid coordinates for the location. While doing this, he again called artillery warning to see if any of the FSBs were firing. He was told no, there were no fire missions at that time. Harry knew there were no friendlies in the area, so he told the warning center, "We have a guy below us shooting a fifty-caliber at us. If you can, we'd appreciate it if you could dissuade the son of a bitch from shooting at us on our way back from Lash."

"Roger," he responded. "I'll see what can do."

They got their load the rest of the way to FSB Lash without any further incidents and put it on the smoke. As they departed, Harry called for artillery warnings again. Holy shit! Every FSB in the area was firing into the same location. The one Harry had given the warning center just a few minutes ago. Harry figured they were all bored and looking for something to do. There were at least four batteries—that's twenty-four guns—firing on the machine gun location. Man, that should sure as hell dissuade the son of a bitch! He was probably wondering which gods he had pissed off—if he were still alive. As they flew past the location to the southeast, Harry looked down. It appeared as if the river had changed course and was now flowing though the neck instead of around the large loop. Even if each battery had fired only three rounds, that would be seventy-two rounds of 105 and 155 mm dropped into a pretty small area. There would be a lot of craters for the river to now flow into.

# Founder's Day Picnic

One beautiful day Pachyderm had a picnic. Harry wasn't sure if it were founder's day. The date the unit was first organized, or something else. He really didn't care. It was a day off with beer and sodas and steaks and fun and...it started early in the afternoon and went till dark.

There was a jeep trailer full of beer, sodas, and ice. Everyone was having a great time. A great day of letdown, relaxation, and having a good time. Harry had cut part of the legs off a pair of jungle fatigue pants to for a makeshift pair of shorts. This and a T-shirt were his uniform for the day. Many of the guys had swimsuits or shorts. Others made do with what they could make or just wore fatigue pants. The army does not provide for any part of the body to be uncovered except the top of the ears and forearms. Everything else is covered by headgear, a shirt of some type, and socks with shoes or boots. They do not like sunburn. Matter of fact, there is an army regulation prohibiting sunburn. None of the guys were thinking of that on this particular day.

During the afternoon there was a softball game that Harry sat and watched, cheering and jeering for both teams. A lot of the guys really didn't care who won; they were just having a good time hollering at whoever was at bat.

In the late afternoon there was a big barbecue with grilled steaks and side dishes from the mess hall. It was really a great day.

The next morning Harry woke up, swung his legs out of bed, and put them on the floor. He screamed and put them back up on the bed.

When his legs dropped, more blood flowed into them and stretched his sun burned skin. It hurt! A lot!

He was scheduled to fly, so he knew he had to get up. It took him fifteen minutes to get his legs on the floor and stand up. Once he got that far, the pain was manageable, so he put on his Nomex (a highly fire-resistant material) flight uniform and went out to fly. It was a very uncomfortable day.

When he got back to the beach, he managed to get some cream from one of the guys and put it on his legs. He couldn't go to the medic because of the army rules. It was several days before he could stand without pain. No more shorts!

# LIEUTENANT FUZZ

L T Fuzz is that guy you meet only in the army and typify *"How in the hell did this guy ever get in charge of anything other than latrine cleanup?"* LT Fuzz who, by the power of "Fuck Up and Move Up," got assigned to battalion. For his flight pay, he was authorized to fly the Colonel's LOH. One day he was flying it with a CPT from battalion with no more sense than he had. During their flight, they had to refuel. LT Fuzz promptly landed at the Chinook refueling pad, which had higher-horsepower pumps and higher-flow rates than Huey pads because Chinooks have more than double the fuel capacity requirements. He put the fuel nozzle into the oil tank filler. It was too big to fit in the hole, so he held it against the side of the aircraft and shot the fuel into the oil tank! It was reported that the noise of the engine now with *no* oil was something to be witnessed, and the flame out of the exhaust was similar to an F-4 on afterburner! And here Harry had thought Floyd was dense! The only way these two survived was by never going into harm's way.

# R&R

Harry had planned to take his R&R (rest and relaxation) leave in early August. This time off and away from the combat zone was a welcome relief by most of the men. Pretty much anyplace you were in Vietnam was a combat zone. It wasn't like World War II where the average infantryman in the Pacific Theatre saw forty days of combat in a three-year tour. In Vietnam he saw an average of 240 days of combat. Even when you were in a rear area, you were still subject to rockets, mortars, and/or sappers. A welcome relief to not have to concern yourself with your safety twenty-four hours a day.

Harry had arranged to meet his wife in Honolulu. There were a lot of other R&R destinations throughout the wide region from Australia to Bangkok, Singapore, and Japan with others in between. A lot of the married men chose Hawaii, as their wives could get there fairly easily. The penalty was that Hawaii R&R was five days while all the rest were seven.`

Harry got a ride to Da Nang in a Pachyderm Chinook and from there a Boeing 707 to Honolulu. He had scheduled his wife's flight so she would arrive before him and depart shortly after he did. He felt his time away from Vietnam was more critical than hers away from Minnesota. Imagine his surprise and disappointment when he arrived at their hotel room and no one was there. His first thought was, "Oh shit! Something happened to her airplane." He called the airport and found that the flight she was supposed to be on arrived on time a few hours before. Now what? He would just have to wait and see what was going on. He had brought a bottle of Seagram's *Crown Royal.* It was a very smooth premium whiskey. In Vietnam booze was very inexpensive. *Crown Royal* and *Chivas Regal* Scotch were six dollars a bottle.

Anyway, Harry had a drink while waiting. He called back to Minnesota to see if he could find out what was going on. He learned that his wife took a later flight than was planned. Didn't know why. Neither did Harry. He had another drink. And another. This went on for several hours until he heard a key in the door.

Finally his wife had arrived! He asked her what the hell had happened. She told him that she found that she could save twenty dollars by taking the later flight. Twenty dollars—are you kidding me? That was a fair amount of money at the time. But the time available was worth far more.

They made love a couple of times, then went and got something to eat, as by then it was into the evening. They went back to the hotel and spent the rest of the night in each other's arms. That was nice!

The following morning they slept in a bit. Made love again, and finally got out of the room around noon. They walked along the beach side of the hotels on the bay. There was an outdoor restaurant that had draft Michelob. *Draft Michelob! Wow!*

They wandered around a bit more, had some lunch, and went back to the hotel. It was evening before they left the room again. They had supper and returned to the room.

The following day they wanted to do some exploring. It felt good to be able to just go where you wanted to. Not have to worry about who or what you would encounter along the way. Harry rented a Camaro, and they went out to the USS *Arizona* memorial at Pearl Harbor. This was very impressive. You have to take a boat shuttle to the memorial. The memorial is built to straddle the sunken ship. You can look down into the water and see where they removed the gun turrets. They also removed some of the superstructure of the ship to keep everything underwater and allow the building of the memorial. There was still oil leaking from the fuel bunkers aboard the ship. Every few seconds another drop would float up and make a rainbow of color on the surface of the water.

The names of the 1,177 men who were killed aboard the USS *Arizona* on 7 December 1941 are engraved on the far (south) wall of the memorial. This is nearly half of the twenty-four hundred lives lost on that "Day of Infamy." This was a very moving experience for Harry.

When they returned to the dock, Harry wanted to go into the navy officers' club for a drink. A very nice one-story structure not far from the memorial. Very relaxing and a good place to contemplate the memorial.

After that they went back to the hotel for the remainder of the day and evening.

The next morning they took off counterclockwise around the island. A beautiful drive. Past Diamond Head and up the east coast. They had stopped at the military cemetery in the Punchbowl and paid their respects to fallen comrades, mostly from World War II. There are the unidentified remains of twenty-seven members of the USS *Arizona* crew buried there as well as thousands of soldiers, sailors, and marines who lost their lives in World War II.

Along the coast they stopped at several of the beaches on the way—Waimanalo, Kaneohe, and Laie—to watch the people in the ocean and the ocean itself. As they got near the northwest point, the road deteriorated and became a track. Then there was a sign, "Roadway Not Maintained—Travel at Own Risk." This was a path across the lava beds, not a road at all. In some places, you could make out where other vehicles had traveled; in others, not so much. At the northwest point of the island there was a lighthouse. Harry wondered how many tourists to the Islands had seen this. Probably not many.

As they continued across the lava bed, now on the west side of the island the road gradually improved until they were back on asphalt. They did not find any beaches on the west side of the island. They went down though Haleiwa, past Kaena Point, and on through Makaha, Waiana, and Nanapulc. Then they proceeded around the north side of Pearl Harbor and back into Honolulu. Upon returning to the hotel, they spent another late afternoon and evening in their room.

Late in the morning of the next day they decided to go up the center of the island. The climb north of Honolulu was spectacular. Looking back upon the city and the bay was breathtaking. Once getting into the central plateau it was all pineapple in fields of red volcanic deposits. The pineapples were growing out of the ground with the fruit right at ground level. Harry hadn't thought about it before, but the pineapple is a succulent, a type of cactus if you will. It's amazing how sweet and juicy a cactus can be. There was a road off to their right that went to Pali Lookout. This is the escarpment on the east side of the plateau and at this point it is a near vertical drop of around a thousand feet. This gives one a spectacular view of the eastern lowlands and the Pacific Ocean. The road down had been rebuilt, but Harry pulled off on the old road that went down the face of the cliff. There was only a pull out area, as the roadway was missing for a hundred feet. Then one could see where it used to run down the mountains. Wow! That must have been a thrill driving that road!

They got back into the car and continued down to the coastal plain on the east side of the island. They wandered around a bit as they worked their way back to Honolulu and their hotel.

The following day's adventure was to go up to the central plateau and west. Another road led from the plateau to the western coast. There was nowhere near as much lowland on the west as on the east, but it seemed like an interesting drive. As they went over the crest and started down the west side, the windward side, the flora changed dramatically. It was all cactus and desert plants. Harry stopped to take pictures of the plants. Who would ever think one would see desert plants on Hawaii? After all, it is a tropical isle. Rain forest and jungle plants are what he expected.

Harry had noticed a sign at the top stating that this was a Naval Reserve. At the bottom there was a gate with a guard. The guard approached Harry and stated that it had been reported that he had been taking pictures. Harry confirmed this. The guard asked if he had seen the sign at the top stating the pictures were not allowed. Harry said to the guard, "Oh, you have nukes stored here." The guard replied, "Sir, I can neither confirm nor deny that there are nuclear weapons at this installation." Harry told him that confirmed that there were. He apologized that he had not seen the sign, as he was fascinated by the flora on the ground. He told the guard that he had not photographed any of the installations. In fact, all his pictures had been facing the other direction, and they were of the plants. The guard gave him a warning about paying attention to the notices, did not confiscate his film, and let them pass.

They proceeded down the west coast at a leisurely pace and returned to Honolulu and their hotel.

The next day was the last day. Harry had to return to Vietnam and his wife to Minnesota. Harry had tried to schedule it to have the maximum amount of time with his wife, so her flight was shortly after his. They packed their bags and went to the airport to await their flights.

Harry's welcome back gift at Pachyderm Beach were orders of transfer.

# Goin' South

At the end of July Harry received orders to join the 242nd Assault Support Helicopter Company at Chu Chi, Base Camp of the 25th Infantry Division. All nondivisional aviation aircraft assets that were not organic to (a part of) a specific division were under the control of the 1st AVN BDE (1st Aviation Brigade). This involved a tremendous number of aircraft of numerous types, both rotary winged (helicopters) and fixed wing (airplanes). Most of these assets, especially helicopters, were formed into battalions. Some of this made no sense to Harry. The 242nd for example was part of the 145th Aviation Battalion. This battalion also included gunships, slick, medevac, and observation companies. Fortunately, Harry did not have anything to do with battalion. All his contact was with the Muleskinners or the units he was supporting.

On 22 August 1969 Harry left his beloved Pachyderm and headed south to his new unit. The move from Playtex was difficult. He was used to the unit and the other pilots and crews. With that move, however, a lot of both went with him. Eleven other pilots were transferred with him to Pachyderm. This time there were several pilots leaving the 159th ASHB, including Andy Belmont, Tom Andrews, and Larry Lurch Hines. This allowed the import of pilots with varying rotation dates so there would not be a lot of them leaving at the same time. With Harry were CW2 John Michael Weatherly, an original Playtex, and CPT Craig Knutzen. They were assigned to the 12th AVN GP (aviation group) part of the 1ˢᵗ AVN BDE. Harry and Weatherly were further assigned to the 242nd ASHC

(Assault Support Helicopter Company). Now there would only be one other of the original Playtex with him.

They were all flown down to Da Nang in a Chinook where they caught an in-country shuttle hop on an air force C-123 "Provider" to Tan Sun Nhut airport outside of Saigon. This was a major replacement depot and transfer point in Vietnam. After processing in, a bunch of them went into Saigon for a last evening together.

The following day they went back to the repo-depot (replacement depot) to see about transportation to their final destinations. Harry and Weatherly were picked up by a Muleskinner Chinook and taken to Cu Chi

Most of the pilots were aware that the marines had submitted a bunch of them for different awards from all the support provided to them and the actions involved. Harry was one of these and had already been presented with a DFC (Distinguished Flying Cross) for his participation in rescuing the marines from Laos. However, without the citation and orders acknowledging this, the presentation would not matter. He had also been told that that the marines had submitted the recommendations and commendations on marine forms to the army. He was informed that they had to be on army forms. Upon arrival at Cu Chi, he took it upon himself to go back to Pachyderm and see that they were on the correct forms and get them to the 101st Headquarters at Bien Hoa. He told his platoon leader what he was up to and left.

Harry hitched a ride into Bien Hoa about thirty kilometers (twenty miles) east of Saigon and from there caught a flight on an air force C-7A "Caribou" to Cam Ranh Bay. This was a major deep-water port for Vietnam, and a lot of the military equipment and supplies flowed through it. It is located approximately 290 kilometers (180 miles) northeast of Saigon. By the time Harry arrived there, it was late afternoon, and he was told there were no more flights going north that day. He had no orders for this trip and was stuck. No quarters available without travel orders. Fortunately there was another chief warrant officer standing nearby, and he asked Harry if he could offer him quarters with his unit for the night. This warrant was an army boat captain. He was piloting boats around Cam Ranh Bay off-loading ships. Harry thanked him and accepted the offer. They caught a three-wheeled Lambretta motor scooter taxi, and it took them to the gate of the warrant's compound.

Cam Ranh Bay was a relatively safe place in Vietnam. Nothing ever happened there in the line of enemy activity. For some reason they left it alone.

In the morning Harry went back to the airfield and caught a ride all the way up to Da Nang in another C-123. From there he hitched a helicopter to Phu Bai and got them to land at Pachyderm Beach. Harry was back "home."

Maybe not quite "home." A new pilot to the unit had been assigned with Such in Harry's former hooch. However, he was able to find an empty bunk with one of the pilots he knew.

Harry went to the orderly room and found the awards and decorations clerk. He told Harry that he had the marine recommendation forms and was trying to transfer them to army forms. Harry informed him that he was in fact AWOL (absent without leave) from his new unit but really wanted to hand carry the recommendations to Bien Hoa. The clerk dropped everything else and processed the marine forms. This still took three or four days. On the third evening he was there, he received a phone call from his new commanding officer. He asked Harry if and when he was going to return. Harry apologized profusely and explained the situation. He seemed to take it very well and told Harry to get back as soon as he could. Harry told him he would and gave an estimate of the time it would take at Pachyderm and Bien Hoa.

When the clerk was finished, Harry took the forms and went to the airport at Da Nang again. From there he was fortunate to catch a direct flight to Bien Hoa. He took the forms into the Divisional Awards and Decorations Section and handed them over to a clerk. In discussing them he found out from the clerk that they did not have to be on army forms. They were acceptable on the marine forms. Wonderful! Four days wasted.

Harry wanted the orders and certificates for the awards to be able to take a copy with him, so he could make sure the guys got them. This took another couple of days. Harry was able, even with no order *nice* club. Very nice, well decorated with a real bar and real bartenders, one soldier, and a Vietnamese worker. Harry ordered a drink and sat at the bar looking around. One wall was all slot machines. The furniture was in great shape and matched. All the pieces were matching. They must have come directly from the States for this O Club. As he was sitting there, a sergeant first class came over to talk to him. Seeing a sergeant in the officers' club was a bit of a surprise, but Harry really didn't give a shit. If he wanted a cold beer or a drink, this was the place to be.

Beer it was. He took the can of beer from the bartender and sat down next to Harry. A bit of small talk, then the sergeant asked if Harry were a pilot. Harry told him that, yes, he was a helicopter pilot. He then asked Harry if he knew anything about Hueys. Harry told him that he'd flown them in the States but was flying Chinooks now. Then the real question: "Could you put one together? One that is in the condition it was in when it was brought over?"

Harry asked, "You have a new Huey?"

The sergeant explained that he was a mess sergeant and ran a nearby mess hall. Some unit had come through and gotten themselves set up, then left. For some reason they left behind a brand-new Huey all packed up for shipping. So the sergeant managed to wrangle the thing into a large supply tent he had for mess supplies. *Hmm*, putting together a new Huey. Blades, tail boom, antitorque rotor, driveshaft, plus a lot of things Harry couldn't even think of. Harry thought about it for a minute, then told the mess sergeant no way. There was just too much technical information and skills that he did not have. What the sergeant needed was a helicopter maintenance officer. The sergeant was disappointed. "I really wanted to get that thing put together and have someone take me for a ride in it before I go home."

Harry knew a bunch of people who could put that Huey together. But how would he get them to Bien Hoa? There was the problem. Oh well. He suggested to the sergeant that he contact a Huey unit and trade the Huey he had for a ride in it. He said he would consider that.

Then Harry thought about the situation and thought, "Man! Is this a weird war or what?"

Harry spent a couple of nights at Bien Hoa before the awards were prepared. He had gone over to the PX and bought a small black Samsonite briefcase to carry the paperwork. When he finally got the paperwork and award certificates in their folders the pile was more than the briefcase could comfortably hold. He had to sit on it to get it to latch.

So off to the airfield. He sat the case on a bench while he waited for his transportation to Cu Chi. The heat from the sun warped the cover on the briefcase. Harry still used it for many years.

When he got back to Cu Chi, he hitched a ride to Muleskinner and reported in to the commander. He showed the major the contents of the briefcase to validate his story. The major forgave the AWOL transgression, and Harry went to his hooch, ready to fly whenever Muleskinner needed him.

# WELCOME TO THE MULESKINNERS

When Harry arrived at the Muleskinners, he found a well-established company area. Again the officers' quarters, hooches, were close to the helipad but not as close as at Pachyderm Beach. They were also two parallel buildings but much farther apart. The courtyard between was wide enough for a volleyball court with plenty of room left over on both sides as well as the ends. The showers and latrine were between the helipad and the hooches, while the O Club was beyond them. The club was a large single building with an outside enclosed entry area. The bar was in the left rear. The near wall left of the door had booths, and there were ample tables and chairs. The men were able to show movies in the building once a week without being crowded. To the right of the door were five-by-seven-inch photos of all the pilots in the company. They were in the order of rotation back to the States. The photo closest to the door was the next pilot to rotate home. When Harry and John Michael Weatherly showed up from Pachyderm, all but three of the pilots were moved two spaces farther from the door. This pissed some of them off. Understandable. Several were angry with Harry and Weatherly. Not understandable, they had not requested to be there.

The company orderly room (headquarters) and operations were across form the flight line before the officers' hooches, and the mess hall was beyond those hooches and to the right.

The hooches had two pilots assigned to each. There were no tech reps at the Muleskinners. (This was probably because the Muleskinner aircraft were A models and did not need to be studied.) The interiors were the same size as the normal hooches at Pachyderm, enough room but by no means spacious. Harry was assigned as a hooch mate to CW2 Al Smith. Smith was significantly older than Harry. This didn't bother him, but it seemed to take Smith a while to warm up to his new hooch mate.

The room had an entry area with the two beds along either side wall at the rear. At the head of the bed at the left, Smith's, there was a small closet. Later on Harry bought a small refrigerator at the PX, and they put it in this closet. Cold beverages in the hooch. Nice! On the right there was a half wall with shelves on the bed side. Over each of the beds there was an oscillating fan mounted on the wall. These were necessary; it was hot at Cu Chi. The fan would oscillate from the head to the feet and back. Took a bit of getting used to but was much better than the heat. Cu Chi was much warmer than Phu Bai, which was actually cool—for Vietnam.

Another thing that Harry had a lot of trouble getting used to was that the perimeter guards would randomly fire their weapons into the barbed wire perimeter at night. The perimeter was just beyond the land/parking area of Muleskinner. There was a .50-caliber machine gun in a nearby bunker, and every time they started firing it, Harry would wake up. At Pachyderm Beach, Harry never heard a round fired.

One really neat thing at Muleskinner was that one Sunday morning a month Smokey Gerhardt, a Hispanic pilot, would make fresh Mexican food for the pilots. He would set up in the entry area to the O Club and make fresh fried tacos or burritos or tamales or enchiladas or whatever. Yum! He would have the items he needed sent over from the States and get the staples, such as cooking oil, lettuce, tomatoes, onions, and other things from the mess hall. It was all freshly made and very good. A real treat!

Harry settled in and got ready to start flying for the Muleskinners.

# FLYING IN THE FLATLANDS IN A MODELS

When Harry started flying for the Muleskinners, he saw that they were flying the older A Model Chinooks. He had not noticed the difference in the flight characteristics between the A Model and C Model at Fort Sill. It was probably because he wasn't familiar enough with the aircraft to notice the difference. He found it early on at Muleskinner.

Whenever a pilot went to a new unit, he first flew with an IP (instructor pilot). It was the IP's job to see that the pilot was familiar with the AO and safe to fly the aircraft. Neither of these things was a challenge for Harry. He learned the AO quickly and demonstrated that he was safe to fly the aircraft.

The next step was to fly as pilot for more familiarization before becoming an AC. The only problem Harry had was that everything was FLAT. No mountains, not even a hill. On one of his early missions, he was flying as pilot for his hooch mate Al Smith. They were taking a load of general supplies to a FSB northeast of Cu Chi. Nothing unusual, nothing special. Until Harry got on final approach. The A Model started to "float." His descent just stopped, and he was still moving forward toward the smoke grenade marker. The best thing to do would probably have been to go around and start over. Harry, though, thought he could save the approach. Well, almost.

He pulled the nose up a bit and dropped pitch from the rotors. It worked; he dropped. When he did, he hit a paddy dike with the net and dumped the entire load outside the perimeter of the FSB. There was nothing he could do but apologize to the pathfinder and the AC. On the way back, Harry asked Smith if it was common for the A Model to "float" like that. He said yes. It was just something you got used to and flew through it. Harry took it to heart, paid more attention to the final approach, and did not do that again.

Harry really missed the mountains. First, there was no place to hide. No mountains to go behind, no valleys to fly through. Just the wide open spaces. They could see you coming for miles. Second, there were no spots to hit with the load. On a mountain you had a spot on the mountain or ridge to hit with the load. If you missed, all you had was air. In the flats the spot was miles and miles of flat terrain. If you had a problem you couldn't fall off the mountain while you tried to fix it.

Now, the pilots who were used to the flats probably loved it. They didn't have to worry about the air currents, the turbulence, or the cloud cover you may have to fly over, under, around, or through. In the aspect of the sky trying to kill you, it was a lot safer in the flats.

Another thing that was very different was what was called "blade time." That was the amount of time the rotor blades were turning at operating rpm. Up north they'd start the aircraft in the morning, and after going through the starting process, the engines were pushed up to "Flight." They stayed there until they were done with the day's missions and back at their home base. If an aircraft was gone for eight hours, that's what was usually logged as flight time. In the south, it was not uncommon to shut down the aircraft someplace and sit and wait for something to get ready or put together or whatever. It was common to sit someplace at "Flight Idle" if it were a short wait. If you were gone from your home base for eight hours, you may only log six hours, or five and a half hours, or whatever.

# Tay Ninh

Early on Harry was flying one day and went to operations to get the information on the day's activities. They had a late departure of 1000 hours (10:00 a.m.). He saw that they were going up to Tay Ninh first to pick up a load for Nui Ba Dinh. As a newbie, he was the pilot and had to preflight the top of the aircraft. Not his favorite thing. This was his first trip to either Tay Ninh or Nui Ba Dinh. None of the other guys wanted to go to Nui Ba Dinh. It was a *mountain*! As it was the only one in the AO, it was something of a mystery to them.

Upon their arrival, the pathfinder informed them the load was not ready yet. It would be at least a half hour. So they landed and shut down the aircraft. As the blades were winding down, one of the supply point NCOs (sergeant) came up to the door and asked if anyone wanted anything from the canteen. Harry said, "You have a canteen here?" A canteen is like a short-order restaurant. Tay Ninh was a smaller base, and it really surprised Harry that there would be anything like that there. There were NO canteens in the north. The NCO said yes. Harry then asked if he could get a grilled ham and cheese with a *Coke* or *Pepsi*. The response was yes, and he went on to take orders for the rest of the crew. In about twenty minutes he was back with the food for the crew. Harry was still in shock. He said to the AC, "Man, this place is way too civilized." He replied, "Nope, maybe more than you're used to but still not enough."

As they finished their food, Harry thought it was a whole lot better than C rations heated by the aft transmission. The NCO came back and said they were ready. They started the aircraft, picked up the load, and headed for the Mountain of the Black Virgin. It wasn't very far from Tay Ninh, but the communications site was on the other side of the mountain. Harry flew around the south of the mountain and spotted the site. As the AC called for a smoke grenade marker, Harry made a 270-degree right-hand turn while he surveyed the site. As one would expect there were a lot of antennas. They were all to the north of the helipad where the smoke marker was. Because of the size and cone shape of the mountain, Harry didn't think there would be any significant wind currents or turbulence. He continued his approach to the west and set the load down right on the smoke. Beautiful. After releasing the load Harry backed up a bit to clear the mountain, made a left pedal turn, and dropped off the mountain. He had enough power to climb out, but dropping out prevented any rotor wash going to the site, and it was more fun! The AC was duly impressed.

# PURPLE JESUS

Purple Jesus had only two ingredients. *Wyler's* grape drink mix and *Everclear*, 180 proof grain alcohol. This made it purple, and Jesus, it really didn't taste all that good, but it sure did the job! Harry's Mom regularly sent him "goodie" packages of treats from home. The box normally contained homemade cookies in six- packs in twist-tie baggies and packed in popcorn. On one occasion she did not have time to pop the popcorn so she used orange packaging "peanuts" she had brought home from her job at IBM. Harry thought they were "Cheetos" and had a handful. Bad mistake. It wasn't that they tasted bad, they had no taste. They also did not chew. They simply turned into a wad in his mouth. There were also usually several packets of *Wyler's*. The *Everclear* came from his oldest sister's husband, a North Dakota native. One could buy *Everclear* in North Dakota, but not in Minnesota, so his brother-in-law would get a bottle when he visited his folks and send it to Harry. A bottle of *Everclear* would go a long ways.

On one Saturday he had off, Harry went out into the "courtyard" between the officers' hooches. Several of the pilots were playing a game of volleyball, and Harry asked if he could join in. They said yes, and he joined them.

After a half hour or so someone called a break. Several of the guys asked if anyone had something cold to drink. Several guys had water or Kool-Aid that they brought out from their hooches. Harry brought out a square quart bottle of "Purple Jesus." He warned the guys what it was, so they took it pretty easy on the bottle.

While they were shooting the breeze, the company XO (executive officer), a captain, came by. Without asking, he picked up the bottle of Purple Jesus and took a big swig of it. He asked whose it was. After Harry told him it was his, he asked if there was any alcohol in it. Harry simply said, "Sir, It's Purple Jesus. It's made with Wyler's Grape Drink mix. So it's purple, and Jesus, with this water it doesn't taste all that good." Without asking, again, he helped himself to another big swig.

As it was Saturday it was movie night at the O Club. It was only an hour or so after the encounter in the courtyard when Harry walked by the booth where the XO was sitting with a glass of sloe gin and Coke. The XO asked him what it was. Harry couldn't resist, he said it was cherry Coke. The XO didn't drink and had no idea what Purple Jesus or sloe gin was. The XO said, "Give me a taste." Again, not a request. This was just an order. On top of not liking this guy much in the first place, the demand did not sit well with Harry. So Harry asked if he'd like one. He asked if there was any alcohol in the drink. Harry evaded the question by asking back, "Sir, have you ever seen me drink anything other than pop or beer?" He responded, "Guess not. Get me one." Another order, not a request, so Harry did.

During the intermission to change reels on the projector, Harry went by and asked the XO if he'd like another. He said yes. Every time Harry could he would pass by the XO's booth and ply him with another drink.

After the movie and later into the evening, Harry made another pass. The XO wasn't there, so Harry asked where he'd gone. One of the guys sitting there told him that he was out behind the O Club puking his guts out in the drainage ditch. Harry figured that it served him right for being such a jerk!

Harry wasn't sure if he ever figured out what had happened to him.

# My Lai Massacre

The news of the My Lai Massacre got out in November of 1969. The actual event was on 16 March 1968, some twenty months earlier. Allegedly there were from 347 to 504 "unarmed civilians" killed. One has to wonder, the way the Viet Cong worked, how many of those were really "civilians"?

More curiously was that on the same day the four-inch headline in the *Stars and Stripes* newspaper of "Massacre at My Lai" appeared with most of the remainder of the front page dedicated to the related story. A four-column-inch article appeared on page four or six. It went something like this: "Elements of the 503rd Infantry of the 101st Airborne Division discovered over three thousand bodies in a ravine off Highway 1 approximately seventeen kilometers south of Hue. It appeared that the civilians had been taken from Hue during the 1968 Tet Offensive, tied together with wire and rope and marched the seventeen kilometers. Then they were led into a ravine in the mountains and shot. It appeared that only about half of the people died from wounds. The others died from exposure, dehydration, and/or starvation." There was more information in the article, but that about sums it up.

So, how is it that 347 to 504 alleged civilians rate a four-inch headline, and three thousand true civilians rate only four column inches? Why is it that the My Lai Massacre was front-page news for months and the "Hue Massacre" never hit the media at all? Curious, is it not?

Oh, by the way, sometime that summer the *Chicago Sun-Times* ran a headline about how horrible it was that US forces were using CS gas on the VC and NVA (this is a super tear gas-type of chemical named after the two men, Corson and Stoughton, who invented it in 1928). Now CS gas is nasty stuff. It will make your eyes tear so you cannot see, it will gag you and make you cough. It may make you puke. It will temporarily incapacitate you if you get a full dose. The key thing is "temporarily." It is not deadly. It is a debilitating agent, not a death agent. Why is it that the *Chicago Sun-Times* had nothing to say about the NVA using nerve gas at marine FSB Fuller? The news the people got back in the States was what the media wanted them to hear. Anything bad about the United States and its troops was front-page stuff. Anything bad about the VC and NVA was not mentioned. The US population was spoon-fed propaganda presented from the North Vietnam government and the Soviet Union. The above are only two examples of this. Glaring examples.

# Scrounge Mission

One afternoon Harry was sitting in the air conditioning of the O Club when the operations and maintenance officers came in. They asked if Harry was qualified in the B model Chinook. He said that he was. The only difference being that when shutting down the aircraft, one had to put a bungee cord over the thrust lever in a B model. They said they were aware of this, but one still had to be signed off officially by a B model IP. Harry told them he had flown B models for his in-country orientation with Varsity and had therefore been qualified in the B model. He asked them what was up. They told him they had a scrounge mission to go up north to see if they could get extra spare parts for the aircraft and anything else they might be able to trade for or pick up. They told Harry that he was the only B model qualified pilot in the company so he was going. He had been "voluntold" for the mission. Harry wondered where they were going to get a B model, as Muleskinner had all A models. By this time Harry was again an AC so the success or failure on anything on the mission would be his fault.

They were planning on going to Da Nang where there was a repair depot for helicopters. Harry told them he had been there and suggested that they continue on to Pachyderm Beach and see what they could do with C Company and perhaps the entire 159th Aviation Battalion. They talked this over and thought it was a good idea. Wonderful, Harry thought. He'd be able to see Such and the other guys still at Pachyderm.

The day before departure, the maintenance officer informed Harry that they were now going to use a Muleskinner aircraft, but Harry would still be the AC for the mission. Great!

The next morning they met at the aircraft. The maintenance officer and a maintenance enlisted man were there along with a civilian tech rep whom Harry had never seen before. Harry and his pilot preflighted the aircraft, and they took off on their planned route. They flew east to the coast and refueled at Phan Rang, an air force base. They then proceeded up the coast, planning to refuel at Chu Lai. About twenty kilometers south of Chu Lai they ran into rain. Heavy rain that reduced visibility drastically. Harry was flying at just above a hover when he spotted the river that passed Chu Lai on its way to the coast. He hovered up the river and contacted the pathfinder at their resupply point. The pathfinder told him he could see the aircraft, but Harry could not see him. He gave instructions, and the perimeter wire came into view. They refueled and went back down the river to the coast and proceeded north—slowly. The rain cleared significantly by the time they got to Da Nang. Harry went up the east side of the peninsula that formed Da Nang Bay and then around it and across the mouth of the bay to Red Beach. It was early afternoon when they departed for Pachyderm Beach.

Upon arrival Harry was told where to park the aircraft and did so. They shut it down and proceeded to maintenance. Harry saw Such and said hi. He did not want to interrupt the conversation regarding parts and swaps. He told Such he'd see him later in the O Club.

One of the maintenance men took the crew to where they'd be quartered, and a Warrant Officer pilot took Harry and his pilot to the officers' area and showed them to their hooches. Harry's old hooch was occupied by Such and a new pilot, so Harry was put in a room a few doors down the row.

After getting some supper in the mess hall, Harry and his pilot went to the club. Harry introduced him to the guys he knew and had a nice conversation with them. Such arrived later, and Harry had a long chat with him. This was when he found out that the "White Knight had been taken away." It was good to be back! Pachyderm Beach felt like home.

During the night, the guys from Pachyderm put 101st Screaming Eagle decals on the aft pylon of the Muleskinner aircraft. The crew thought it was really neat, but the maintenance officer not so much.

They got the aircraft ready and took off south for refueling again at Chu Lai, then on to Phan Rang. They were instructed where to park for the refueling, beside a revetment for air force fighter bombers. Harry parked close to the revetment so as to be out of the way as much as possible. As the blades were turning down, the civilian tech rep came up to the cockpit and asked Harry if he was too close to the revetment and would get a blade strike. Harry told him no, the blades were three feet from the revetment. Evidently not believing Harry, the tech rep went out the back of the aircraft and walked over to the revetment. As the blades slowed, they approached the level of the top of the revetment. The tech rep watched. Harry could still tell they would be about three feet from the metal wall. As the blades dipped below the level of the revetment, the tech rep came back on the aircraft. Harry said, "Three feet, right?" The tech rep replied, "Give or take an inch." Harry knew where the tip of those blades were.

By the time they had refueled, it was dark. Harry took off and headed west for the final leg to Muleskinner. It is again black out there. Harry remembered that there was a large mountain west of the base, and they were not very high. He simultaneously pulled in more pitch and eased the nose up to increase rate of climb while running out his landing/search light. When he turned the light on, there was a lot of green in front of them. He turned to the right to pass the mountain. That was just in time. Running into that mountain would not have been a good thing. Yet another of those things that is not conducive to longevity.

Harry realized that there was no way he'd be able to find Muleskinner nor even Cu Chi Base Camp in that dark, so he called Tan Son Nhut radar and got a vector to Cu Chi.

Ahead of them a series of bright flashes appeared. As they were moving closer to him a rapid rate Harry knew it was not any kind of ground fire. As they passed to his right front he thought it must be some kind of photo reconnaissance taking pictures at night.

Radar told them they were approaching Cu Chi Base Camp. They both turned on their landing lights and searched for the perimeter wire. They quickly found it and then located the Muleskinner pad, where they landed the aircraft, taxied to a revetment parking place, and shut it down. It had been an interesting and eventful trip.

# FSB Roy

Harry continued to fly resupply missions throughout the AO. No one shot at him. That was a good thing. As all good things come to an end, there was FSB Roy. Roy was way east of Chu Chi. In fact, Harry was convinced it was outside of their normal AO. He was right. It was actually an FSB with a 1st Air Cavalry Division artillery battery. Now FSB Roy was waaaay out in the boonies. There was no other base anywhere in the area. The one exception was a SF (Special Forces) B Camp a couple of kilometers north. This camp was on the border with Cambodia. In fact, it was so close to the border the aircraft landing on the airstrip there had to land to the north and take off to the south. If they departed to the north there was no way they could avoid going into Cambodia.

Harry's mission was to pick up 105 mm ammo at the Special Forces base and take it to FSB Roy. As they had to go past FSB Roy to get to the SF Camp, Harry tried to get in contact with the pathfinder. He changed the radio to the proper frequency and called, and called, and called. No reply. He finally had to change to the SF frequency. They told him to land at the southeast corner to the side of the runway. Harry did so. There was an air force C-130 'Hercules' at the north end of the runway. It sounded as though they were having difficulty with one of the engines, as it just sat there running up the engines and taking them back down. They had obviously just unloaded a bunch of pallets of 105 mm ammunition that was just north of where Harry was parked. There were several men stacking the crates on cargo nets. No forklifts out here. The crates were individually placed on the nets.

No one was telling Harry anything, so he put the engines to "Flight Idle" and got out of the aircraft. He saw what appeared to be an officer with a 1st Air Cav unit patch on his sleeve. As Harry approached, he saw that he was a brigadier general (one star). Oh shit, Harry thought. This guy has to be the assistant division commander. What the hell is he doing out here? Oh well, even though one does not disturb generals, he's the only person Harry saw who could help. As he approached, the general turned to face him. Harry had the presence to not salute him out here in the field. He said, "Good morning, sir."

The general replied, "Good Morning, Mister. What can I do for you?"

Harry told him, "Sir, I see that your men are getting the loads ready. Now if you can just get me a frequency and call sign that someone at FSB Jerry will actually answer, I'll be able to get their ammo to them." The general went over to his radioman and came back in a couple of minutes with a slip of paper with a call sign and a radio frequency different than those that Harry had. Harry thanked him for the information and returned to his aircraft.

After getting the engines and rotors up to speed, Harry picked up the aircraft and started hovering over to the first load of ammo. Just before he got there he saw the telltale puff of a mortar round exploding just a bit farther up the side of the runway. What the hell! Then he thought, "They're not shooting at me; they're shooting at the C-130. They're just really lousy shots." About then, the C-130 revved up its engines and headed down the runway. They must have figured out what had just happened too and did not want to give the bad guys a chance to get a round in the right place. As they got to the end of the runway they lifted off and departed the area. Whatever problem they were having appeared to have suddenly lost its importance!

This is the only time that Harry, to his knowledge, was shot at down south. That was just fine with him. Having learned that a cockpit full of weapons did one no good, Harry had taken the .45-caliber semiautomatic pistol he was issued, without a holster, cleaned and oiled it, wrapped it in a handkerchief, and put it on a shelf above the head of his bed. There it stayed until he turned it back in to the company armorer just before he left Muleskinner.

Harry picked up the load and headed for FSB Roy. It wasn't far enough to get much past a hover. He called the pathfinder and got a smoke – only. No radio communication. As all the guns in the battery were pointed northwest, Harry went around to the east and put the load down on the far side of the battery where the smoke was. He hopped back up and picked up another load. Same thing, battery firing to the northwest (it had to be going into Cambodia) and just a smoke grenade. Harry figured fine. He just picked up the loads as fast as he could and took them to the FSB. No communications. By the time they got the loads moved, it was time to go back for fuel. With the two-hour maximum fuel endurance and the hour and a half or so of flying time and the distance from the fuel point to FSB Roy, it did not leave a lot of time for the moving of ammunition.

By the time they got back to the SF Camp, another C-130 must have come and gone, as there was another planeload of ammo. Harry did not even try to call the pathfinder. He just moved all the ammo and went back to Cu Chi. He was done for the day.

# GOAT MILKING CONTESTS

Another big difference was what the pilots referred to as "goat fucking contests." This was a takeoff on a derogatory phrase used by army drill instructors that went something like "I've been around the world, been in war, even saw a goat milking contest in the state of Missouri, but I ain't ever seen no shit like this!" There were a lot of the goat fucks up north. Matter of fact, one night a bunch of the guys in the O Club, after a few drinks, got together and dreamed up a mission for division air. They called Division G-3 (operations) Air and requested a U-6 Beaver (fixed-wing airplane) mission from Camp Evans (which had an airstrip) to FSB Spear (A closed FSB on a ridgeline that was all up and down. When the FSB was open every gun was at a different elevation.) The load they requested was more than the gross weight (the total *maximum* weight of the aircraft, fuel, and load) of the aircraft. About two hours later G-3 Air called back and told them they could not accept the mission, as FSB Spear was closed. No mention that there was no way to land an airplane there! No mention that the load was far more than the airplane was capable of carrying! That explained a lot about what the guys were going through with stupid instructions and information.

Down south it was a bit different. An example was one day when Harry was assigned to relocate an artillery battery about five kilometers. He had other missions in the morning so it was early afternoon when he got to the FSB. This mission was not a very long haul. He flew out to the pickup FSB, picked up a bunch of men and a 105 mm howitzer, and took them to the new FSB. On approach he saw that there were men already there, probably infantry. He set down the gun, then moved to the side and landed the troops. Fine. Back to the old base and picked up another gun. To the new base and placed the gun where they wanted it. So far so good. Back for load number three. OK, this one is a cargo net with 105 mm ammo and other materials. Return for load number four. It's not ready? How long have you guys known about this move? How can you not be ready? Oh well, Harry told them he'd go refuel and wait a bit. He'd be back in an hour. So off they went to the refueling point. After topping off the tanks, they moved to the side and shut down the aircraft. Harry waited a full hour there before starting up the aircraft and going back to the base that was to be moved. Fine, a load of "ash and trash," a cargo net full of a wide variety of stuff. They hauled it off and came back for another load. More ash and trash. Load number three on this round was another gun. OK, to the new FSB and on the smoke. Back for the next load. What? Again with no load? OK, how about two hours this time. You call the other base and tell them we're coming for the nets and straps. We'll bring them all back here so you can get the rest of your gear ready to move. They went down and back-hauled the nets and straps, dropped them off and went back to the refueling point. By then it was getting on into the afternoon. Operations called as Harry should have been done. They asked if he needed any assistance with the move. He told them no. "This is just one big goat fuck. They really don't have their shit together. We've spent more time shut down waiting than we have moving them. This battery commander is going to wind up having his forces split for the night at this rate." There was no way they were going to do this at night, not down south.

They didn't need it but topped off the tanks anyway. And shut down again. When they returned to the FSB there were another three loads that they moved before running out. By then it was dusk. Harry told them someone would be back the next day, and it would really help if they got their shit together and had their loads ready to be moved.

Upon returning to Muleskinner, the CO and operations officer were waiting for him at the edge of the helipad. The CO asked what had happened. Harry told them the blow-by-blow of the mess it was trying to move a battery that was not ready to be moved. They thanked him for the information. Then, the CO, who had flown Chinooks in I Corps on a prior tour, said, "Harry, I know you're used to flying in I Corps. Things are a bit more civilized down here. Don't use foul language on the radio down here."

"Yes, sir!"

# THE TRIFECTA

Another fun mission was when there were three FSBs in fairly close proximity along a river southwest of Cu Chi. Every afternoon these three bases would get a cargo net of supplies. None of the individual loads was very heavy, so they would put three different doughnuts (a multilayered circle of canvas webbing that the cargo straps were attached to that would fit over the cargo hook). They'd hook up the third load first, then the second, and finally the first. The pilots would pick up the three loads and go to the first FSB. There they'd set the three loads down, and the FE would use his shepherd's hook (a metal shaft with a flat hook on the end they could pick up doughnuts with if necessary) to hold the second and third doughnuts in place while the first load was released from the cargo hook. Off to the second FSB and the same routine, keeping the third doughnut on the hook. The third was a quick in, set down the load, release, and depart. Pretty slick. Someone was using his head when he came up with that one. As much as things got screwed up for the pilots it was surprising that they were able to do this. Must have been a pilot who came up with this maneuver.

Now the stupid part. The northern of these three FSBs was on a gentle turn in a river from southeast to south. Predominant winds in the area were from the north or northwest. The resupply pad was outside the main perimeter on the north side of the FSB. OK, everything is well—until.

Until they decide to build a "shitter" on the edge of the resupply pad. This was a simplified version with only a bench box with four holes and four half drums. Whenever they went in there, they would kick up a significant dust and dirt cloud, so Harry warned the pathfinder that anyone sitting on the shitter when they came in would get a serious dusting.

All is still at least OK. One afternoon when Harry went in, there was a man on the shitter, and he did get seriously dusted.

Then it got seriously bad. They built a three-sided shelter over the shitter. They now had something that would catch the wind from the blades' downdraft. A Chinook can generate a tremendous amount of downdraft. To make it as bad as they possibly could the open side faced the resupply pad! This would really catch the downdraft wind well! Now that was beyond stupid!

Harry called the pathfinder and warned him. He told him that it was very dangerous to have the wind from the downdraft catching the open side of the shitter shelter facing the resupply pad. He told him that some afternoon someone was going to come in with maybe a bit heavier load and/or a slight breeze across the pad toward the shitter, and it was going to wind up in the outer perimeter concertina wire.

Sure as shit, a few days later Harry had that run again. The loads were a bit heavier, *and* there was a quartering breeze coming across the pad directly into the shitter shelter. When Harry flared the helicopter to stop his forward motion and his descent, there went the shitter—and the soldier in it! Harry saw the shitter and soldier hit the wire and invert. By the time they got the first load released, and Harry was lifting up and backing off the pad, he saw the soldier crawl out from under the shitter and out of the wire. He was a mess! The drums had emptied when the shitter capsized and covered the guy.

Harry called the pathfinder and told him he was sorry the shitter and guy had gone into the wire. He also reminded him that he had repeatedly warned him about its position.

Harry did not say anything to his company operations although he probably should have. He heard nothing more about the incident, but a few days later he drew the mission again, and the shitter was moved away from the pad. He also had an OH-6 Cayuse (commonly called a "Loach" from the Light Observation Helicopter acronym) follow him around the entire day. Someone must have wanted to see if he was hotdogging the aircraft. Never heard anything from that, either.

## Stuck in the Mud

It seemed to Harry that he got all the far away missions. He'd be sent to FSB Roy, then FSB Jerry, both way off to the northeast. He'd be sent to Nui Ba Din, way to the north. This day he was sent on a mission in support of the 9th Infantry Division way off to the southwest. This was way out of their AO. The 9th Infantry was operating in the flat rice paddy terrain along the Mekong River.

Harry had an internal load of replacement troops and equipment. This place was in the middle of rice paddies. Nothing but paddies as far as you could see. Sort of the middle of nowhere.

Harry had gotten his artillery clearance and contacted the pathfinder. A smoke grenade was set off where they wanted him to land. In another rice paddy. Harry made a normal approach and set down on the smoke. The FE lowered the ramp and the troops and equipment left the aircraft. The FE said, "Ramp's up. Ready for takeoff."

Harry pulled in enough pitch to lift off but not extra so he wouldn't blow the troops away.

Nothing happened.

He could feel the aircraft lighten but it was still on the ground.

He added a bit more power and still nothing.

"Hey, Chief Harry called, what's going on? We're still on the ground with plenty of power to be gone." "Well sir, you're stuck in the mud."

The ground looked firm but it was extremely soft and the aircraft gear had sunken in until the fuselage was on the ground. Man! Can you imagine having to dig a Chinook out of the mud? Not a pleasant thought.

Another new experience for Harry. He had not had to deal with mud before. Yet another lesson learned. Keep power in when landing in soft areas.

So Harry pulled in even more power and wiggled the cyclic to wiggle the aircraft loose form the mud. He could feel it move but it still took a bit for it to break free. Lift off. All is well.

Maybe not. They had only gone a couple of kilometers when the MASTER CAUTION lights lit up. These orange lights are located on the center of each pilot's instrument panel so they get one's attention immediately. Then you have to look to the center column to see which caution set off the master.

Harry looked at the caution panel as saw *xmsn chip det*. This meant that one of the five transmissions had metal floating in the oil and had shorted across a magnetic plug. Not a good thing. This could mean one of the transmissions was disintegrating. Should that happen and one of the transmissions lock up one or both rotor heads would immediately stop. Another thing that was not conducive to longevity.

Harry started a turn back to the FSB for security while the checked the transmissions and immediately realized that was not a good idea. He needed to be on the ground-now!

He lowered the pitch and headed for the nearest spot. Not hard to find as everything was flat. He sat the aircraft down but kept some additional power in so it was light on the gear. He didn't want to sink into the mud again. The FE pulled the chip detector plug form the aft transmission, the easiest to get to and found the problem. He brought the plug up to the cockpit and showed it to Harry. There were fine metal shavings, fuzz, on the plug. Enough to short across the doctor but nothing to worry about. The FE wiped the plug and reinserted it into the transmission. Harry gave it a minute to make sure there wasn't more metal floating around in the oil. The *xmsn chip det* had gone out and remained that way. Harry breathed a sigh of relief and they departed back to their own AO.

# FLYING FOR THE AUSSIES

Another faraway place Harry was sent to was the 1st Australian Task Force at Nui Dat in Phuc Tuy Province. This was located southeast of Saigon and northeast of Vung Tau. A long way from Cu Chi and his normal AO. That was alright though. Flying for the Aussies was a real treat. They were very organized and highly efficient. Harry would go down to their base at Nui Dat and take ammo and resupplies to a FSB north of the base camp. The loads were always ready and the trips were fairly quick. The FSB was located in a large clearing with jungle to its north. They had a single strand of concertina wire as a premier as if daring the bad guys to try something.

One day Harry witnessed an Australian Canberra bomber making low level bombing runs just north of the FSB. It was very interesting to watch the wide-winged bomber release a pair of bombs and see them arc to the ground and explode.

A real good thing was that the Aussies insisted that the pilots dine in their officers' mess. This was really a nice mess. It was laid out with white tablecloths, china, silverware, and white jacketed mess stewards. This place was at least as nice as the White Elephant in Da Nang. The major difference was you did not have a menu to select from. Didn't matter. The food was always great.

One day Harry was leaning against the rail of the veranda around the officers' mess when an Australian officer came around the corner. As he approached Harry, wiping his brow with a handkerchief, he commented "Bloody awful hot!" Harry replied, "Not too bad today. In fact it's a bit cool. It must be only eighty degrees or so." The officer, who Harry at first thought was an Aussie warrant but was actually a major gave him a strange look. Harry quickly added, "That does sound a bit strange, but it is a bit cool. You'll notice I'm wearing a lightweight flight jacket." The Aussie, who must have just arrived in-country, responded, "You mean it gets worse?' "Oh yes", said Harry, "It's been running over 100." "Oh my God", was the response.

# Nui Ba Dinh

Nui Ba Dinh, the Mountain of the Black Virgin, is located about sixteen kilometers (ten miles) north-northeast of Tay Ninh City, in Tay Ninh Province. It is also about ninety kilometers (fifty-six miles) northwest of Cu Chi. It is a religious and historical site. It also has a good-size communications site involving fifteen or so different military units. Oh, it is the *only* mountain in the entire AO. The surrounding area has an altitude of about 340 feet. Nui Ba Dinh is 3,235 feet high. It is a huge round cone-shaped granite mountain covered in jungle and often clouds. On the southeast side there was a shoulder that had the major communication site on it.

The pilots who flew in the southern rice lands didn't know what to do with a mountain. In fact, if they transitioned onto the Chinook at Fort Rucker, Alabama, the only location other than Fort Sill, Oklahoma, the only pinnacle they saw was a bulldozed pile of dirt! No mountains in southern Alabama. So it was understandable if they seemed to be in awe of Nui Ba Dinh.

As there was no artillery up there the only ammo was small arms and mortar ammo, and of course, food, water, and sundries. It seemed that most of the resupply was done by Hueys as there were not a lot of Chinook missions up there. However when there was one it was tasked to the Muleskinners and then to Harry. It seemed to him that every mission to Nui Ba Dinh was flown by him. He didn't know if they ever selected Weatherly to go up there and didn't think to ask.

Actually, Harry preferred the mountains to the flats. If something went wrong and you lost power on a true pinnacle you could always dive off the side of the mountain. If you were in the flats, you just crashed, as almost happened to Harry. We'll get to that.

So, Harry had been in the unit long enough to get familiarized with the AO and have his AC check ride. Now he's back to being responsible for the crew, the aircraft, and the mission. Most of it was fairly simple and routine work. Hauling ammo and resupply to the various FSBs in the area. To Harry, after flying in northern I Corps, this area seemed rather quiet. He'd been there several weeks and had not been shot at yet, except for the one mortar round at the Special Forces camp. No night Tac-Es. Just nice flying weather and conditions. He'd been into Nui Ba Dinh a couple of times and found it not much different from many of the FSBs he'd gone into regularly flying with the 101st Airborne. In fact, the signal site on Nui Ba Dinh was a lot like FSB Airborne, only it was not on the top of the mountain but on a shoulder below the peak. The terrain sloped away from most of the site but to the northwest was the rest of the mountain. You could not approach it from the west or northwest.

Harry checked his missions for the day and saw he would be flying out of Tay Ninh. That was fine with him. The resupply people up there seemed to always have their shit together and were a pleasure to work with. The same couldn't be said for some of the marines at Vandergrift.

Harry and his pilot checked out the assigned A Model aircraft, fired her up, and headed northwest. As they checked in with Tay Ninh they received information about what most of the loads would be. One was a fifty-kilowatt generator to be taken to the signal site on Nui Ba Dinh. Harry knew that the generator would not be as heavy as a cannon or four pallets of ammo, but it still was heavy. Harry requested they give it to him early on when the temperature was a little cooler and the density altitude better. They told him they'd have it ready when he got back from his first load. Harry thanked them, picked up the load, and left.

When they returned, the generator was rigged just like they promised. Harry picked it up and headed north-northeast for the mountain. He didn't have to look hard. The mountain is clearly visible from Tay Ninh or just about any place else in the AO. He climbed out just south of the mountain, as that was the shortest route to the site. As he was approaching the mountain, he called the site, told them what he had for them, got the winds on the ground, and went past the mountain. He turned left to come around at the site and saw the smoke marker for where they wanted the generator.

Harry approached from above and pulled up at a high hover. The generator was rigged with fifty-foot slings to clear the antennas in the spot they wanted to position it. He was hovering out of ground effect with the generator about another fifty feet above the ground. He got right over the spot, and just as he started a slow descent, things went to shit. The number two engine N1 started to unwind, the torque from that engine dropped off, and he immediately heard the telltale pop-pop-pop-pop-pop of bleed band popping.

When the pressure in the combustion chamber gets too high, there is a band around it that will open and close, bleeding off some of the pressure. Sometimes the band screws up and just keeps popping open and closed rapidly. This does a lot of bad things. It causes the engine to lose power through less-efficient combustion, and it allows the fireball in the combustion chamber to expand and touch the metal sides of the combustion chamber. It is *very* hot, and it will start an engine fire. Excessive bleed band popping is not a good thing. Sometimes the engine will correct itself with a small change in power requirements. Sometimes it just keeps going, and you have to shut down the engine and try starting it again. That's another special situation that requires very close monitoring of the EGT (exhaust gas temperature) to make sure the band has closed.

The aircraft began to settle in, and Harry knew he didn't have long until things were going to get really bad. He wanted to try to save the generator, so he called the FE and said, "Chief, when that generator is about five feet off the ground, pull the release."

"Yes, sir, was the reply."

The rotor rpm was continuing to decline, although it was still in the green arc. He was beeping up the other engine to take up some of the lost power, and at the same time, he was using the pedals to turn the nose to the right and off the mountain. The FE pulled the release. Harry could see the "*cargo hook open*" caution light. The FE called, "Load clear!" Harry dropped the nose and fell down the side of the mountain. His primary concern was to get the rotor rpm back up, then deal with the bleed band popping. As he fell off the mountain, the pressure came off the rotor blades, and he dropped the thrust to try to shock the engine back into working order. It didn't work. He shut it down before there was any serious damage. All this took a matter of a few seconds. Who was it that said, "Combat is a matter of hours, sometimes days, of extreme boredom interspersed with moments of terror." Well, sometimes you don't even need the combat.

Harry got the aircraft stabilized and was heading for Tay Ninh. He called back to Muleskinner and told them what happened. He requested that another aircraft be sent up and maintenance could fly this one back. This should have taken less time than it would for Harry to fly to Cu Chi, pick up the aircraft and fly back up to Tay Ninh. Wrong! It took them three hours to get there. When they finally got there, one of the maintenance officers, a numb-nuts first lieutenant, made a comment about having to fly up there. Harry told him, "It's not my job to fly broke-dick aircraft. I take my chances flying the boonies. Besides, if you'd gotten off your dead ass, it would have taken a lot less time than me making the round trip—sir!" Harry had never liked this guy. He was one of those pilots who got his four hours of flying a month for flight pay qualification, and that on milk runs. In addition to that, he would use one of those printed tape machines and put messages to the real pilots on the cockpit dashboard. Things like "*Engage mind before engaging rotor.*" In some helicopters the pilot must engage the rotor. The Chinook does it automatically. Idiot!

# BLEED BAND—AGAIN!

A few days later, Harry drew the same aircraft, and a brand-new pilot. This pilot had just arrived in the unit and was probably on his first day with an AC after being released by one of the unit's IPs. Harry led him through the preflight to make sure he had it down pat. They completed the cockpit check and started the aircraft. Off they went. One of the missions was to relocate a "paddy pad" from Cu Chi Base Camp to a FSB to the southwest. This was a very heavy load. Harry called the Cu Chi location and told them he had to burn off some of the fuel before trying to pick up the pad. He gave them an approximate time they'd be ready to relocate the pad. They uneventfully completed several missions, then went to pick up the paddy pad. He had the fuel down to where he could get the pad, take it to its new location, and get back to refuel.

Harry took the load, as he didn't yet trust the newbie with this maximum load. They went to the unit's location at the 25th Infantry Division's Base Camp at Cu Chi. The pad was ready, and Harry hovered over it, speared the doughnut, and pulled the straps tight. He slowly added pitch to see how much power it would take to lift it. He had enough and pulled in the rest to start lifting the pad off the ground. He had a fair amount of clear area and was able to get enough altitude to clear all obstacles and slowly climbed out. They slowly climbed to about five hundred feet as they headed toward the FSB where the pad was to be placed. The pilot called the pathfinder and got a smoke grenade to mark the spot. He confirmed the color of the smoke, and Harry started his descent into the FSB. He made a slow and shallow approach and stopped over the smoke at about ten feet. Down with the load, on the ground, slack in the straps, and release. Done. All was well.

Harry turned a bit to the left and pulled pitch to leave the FSB. Ahead was a narrow tree line, but without a load the obstacle posed no problem—yet. As Harry was at around twenty-five knots and just approaching the tree line, the bleed band started popping again. Severely. This time the number two engine just dropped all power and the "Number 2 Engine Fire" light illuminated. Shit!

Harry dropped the thrust lever, pulled the nose up to get the rotor rpm back up, and headed for the ground just past the trees. At the same time he called to the pilot, "Number two to Ground and Stop. Pull number two fire handle, fire number two fire bottle into number two engine." The pilot, thank God, did exactly that. As they were headed for the ground, the rotor rpm started coming back so Harry beeped up the number one engine and started pulling power back in. It seemed to be holding, so he rolled the nose over to level. It still held, so all was at least OK. Harry steadied the airspeed and was able to start a climb.

All this took a matter of seconds, just a few seconds. Time is extremely critical in a situation such as that. Any hesitation will get you hurt, or worse.

Harry called the crew on the intercom and told them to take a look at the number two engine and see if they could tell the fire was out. Neither the CE at the right door nor the FE looking out one of the porthole windows could see any fire or smoke. Whew! Good thing.

Harry nursed the aircraft back to Cu Chi and the Muleskinner pad. He called ahead and told them maintenance hadn't fixed the aircraft, and number two had failed completely. He took it in, landed, and was able to get it back into the revetments he had taken it from several hours before.

It's bad enough the enemy is trying to kill you. They *do not* need help from the weather, the aircraft, the pilot in the other seat, or another aircraft or artillery in the sky. Harry had now had all of these attempt it!

Operations said they'd have another aircraft take care of the few missions Harry had left. He was released for the day. Great! He took the pilot to the O Club, and they had a drink, maybe more. Harry bought.

Harry was very happy with the newbie and told him so. He did just as he was told with no hesitation, no questions. Had he not, things may well have turned out differently. Keeping his head as a newbie was a bit unexpected and greatly appreciated.

The next day one of the maintenance NCOs found Harry and asked him to come over to the maintenance area. Harry went with him to the rear of the aircraft from the day before. The NCO said, "I wanted to show you this." He pointed up at the back of the number two engine. Harry looked up to see that most of the vanes at the rear of the engine had been at least partially burned off. He could see into the next row, power vanes, and they were in pretty much the same shape. So were the stator (mounted) vanes Harry could see in the third row.

Harry told the NCO, "Looks trashed."

"Big time," he replied. "We'll take it off, put it in a can, and send it back to the States."

Harry told him, "That's good. You know that engine damn near planted me on Nui Ba Dinh a few days ago."

He knew that there'd been a problem but didn't know Harry had been the AC. Harry told him that whoever supposedly fixed it failed miserably, and this time it damn near planted him in a tree line. He said he was glad it wouldn't have the opportunity to kill someone else. He thanked the NCO for showing it to him and left.

# FSB Roy

The 25th Infantry Division, "Tropical Lightning," moved an artillery battery northeast of Cu Chi in the area that FSB Jerry had been. Perhaps the 1st Air Cav had left the area, and the 25th had moved in. Whatever had happened, FSB Roy was not a nice place. It was out in the open flatlands. Of course most of the AO was open flatland. It did not have a well-defined perimeter. There did not seem to be a lot of defensive emplacements, especially given its proximity to Cambodia.

Harry had several missions to FSB Roy, carrying ammo and other supplies. One day when he called with a load, the pathfinder asked if he would back-haul a "water buffalo" (a four-hundred-gallon water tank on a trailer) to Cu Chi. Harry told him certainly.

After he dropped off his load of ammo, he went over to pick up the trailer. The pathfinder was standing on the tank holding the straps and doughnut. Now, an explanation of how a "water buffalo" is rigged for flight is necessary. Fenders run the length of the tank on either side. The clevis hooks for attachment are on the underside of the fenders. Therefore, a special rigging is used to prevent any canvas straps from rubbing on the fenders. The rigging was called "Aeroquip" by its manufacturer. The rigging had chain on one end and canvas straps on the other. The chain was attached to the trailer and the canvas to the doughnut.

Harry hovered over the load, and the FE told him it was hooked, so he began lifting up slowly to tighten the straps and ensure that none had gotten hung up on the fenders. The FE called, "Straps tight, load is off the ground. Five, ten, twenty feet, clear for flight." As Harry continued to climb out and accelerate, the FE said, "Sir, we have a hitchhiker."

"What?"

"The pathfinder who hooked up the load is sitting on the fender."

Harry asked, "Is he secure?"

"Yes, sir. He's sitting on the fender holding onto the straps. He ain't going anyplace."

Harry asked if he was smiling, and the FE told him he seemed very happy. Harry figured he'd had enough of FSB Roy and wanted to go back to Cu Chi. Harry was going to accommodate him. He kept the airspeed down to around forty knots for his comfort, and one didn't want to go fast with an empty water buffalo anyway. They tended to take off on their own and had even hit the bottom of helicopters.

When Harry got back to Cu Chi he called the artillery unit and asked for smoke for the location of the empty trailer. He got the smoke and put the trailer on it. He asked the FE about the hitchhiker. He said that he was off the trailer and waving good-bye to them.

This was the only case Harry had ever heard of with someone hitching a ride on an external load.

Now a footnote to this story. Many years later, in the 1990s, Harry was in Washington, DC, for a meeting of the leadership of his professional association. He and a colleague were sitting in the hotel bar having a beer while waiting for the rest of the group to get together to go to dinner. On the TV over the bar the news was on. An item came on about a news helicopter, a Bell Jet Ranger, which had crashed into the Potomac River. Harry's colleague turned to him and asked, "You used to fly helicopters, didn't you?" Harry replied in the affirmative and was asked what he thought had happened.

Harry was explaining his opinion when a guy sitting several stools down the bar came over. He said, "Excuse me, I heard you say that you used to fly helicopters. Did you fly in Vietnam?" Harry told him that he had. He said, "I have a story for you. I was a pathfinder in Vietnam. I had rigged a water buffalo for a back-haul. After attaching the doughnut, I jumped down and was going around pulling the chain away from the fenders so it wouldn't snag. As I was doing this, I got my hand between the straps just as they came tight. I couldn't get my hand out. The pilot just kept going up so I swung up on the fender, and he took me back to base camp."

Harry said, "Fire Support Base Roy, November 1969."

"Yes," the amazed man said, "How did you know?"

Harry told him, "I was the AC and flying the helicopter. We took you back to Cu Chi. I figured that you'd had enough of that shit-hole Roy and wanted out. I was accommodating you." They had a good chuckle and chatted for a while until the group assembled.

It is a small world.

# CS AT NUI BA DINH

Harry was getting close to the end of his tour. It was 13 December and another hot day in wonderful Vietnam. Muleskinner received another mission to Nui Ba Dinh. Guess who was assigned to fly the mission. Yup! You got it! If it's Nui Ba Dinh, send Harry.

That was OK. However, it struck Harry as strange the other pilots seemed to bow down and pray to Nui Ba Dinh three times a day that they would not get sent to the mountain.

This day it was a different mission. They were to go to Tay Ninh and put a "live track" in the aircraft. Harry wasn't sure what this was but figured it was a roller track for the fifty-five-gallon drums of liquid CS gas that he was supposed to drop on the mountain. Harry had done a lot of different things, but he had never been on a CS drop before.

He and his pilot for the day went out and preflighted the aircraft as usual. Everything looked good, and the FE said that they hadn't had any problems with the aircraft. That's a good thing. They cranked her up and took off for Tay Ninh. Upon landing there, they shut down, and the live track was installed. It was indeed a metal frame with rollers so that they could roll the drums out the back of the aircraft. It was three pieces with two attached to each other in the main cabin and the third installed on the ramp, so it could still be raised and lowered. The plan was to lower the ramp to be level with the cabin floor and slide the drums out one at a time. On the top of each drum was a charge of C-4 explosive with a time-delay fuse. Just before sliding the drum off the end of the ramp, one of the soldiers assigned to handle the CS would pull the pin, starting the timer. It wasn't much of a delay. Just enough to get it clear of the aircraft. The goal was to get it to explode two hundred feet above the ground for maximum, dispersal of the CS.

After installing the live track, they manhandled the drums into the aircraft. There were twelve barrels for three runs of four barrels each. Harry and his pilot both had their gas masks with them just in case. Harry knew of a flight where the second to the last man was pulling the pin on the fuse and the end guy held up the drum because he felt it was too close to the previous one. The guy who had pulled the pin slammed the drum past him and out of the aircraft. It blew up far enough away to not damage the aircraft but close enough to fill the cabin and cockpit with CS. Not a good thing—the crew didn't wear masks. Harry made it very clear to the team handling the drums that no one, but *no one* was to touch the pin on the explosives but the last man.

With everything set and the CS loaded, they again started the aircraft and took off for the mountain. They were to meet up with an air force FAC (forward air controller) south of Nui Ba Din. He would mark the beginning and end of each track with smoke rockets for Harry to fly while the CS was dropped.

Harry flew this mission with his pilot wearing a gas mask. The gas mask used by pilots was the type with a two-foot hose attached to the mask with the filter canister at the end. It was hot and uncomfortable.

As they approached the rendezvous area, Harry called the FAC and received no reply. He set up a large orbit to his left to better see any-thing coming their way. After a couple of orbits he decided to make a call on "Guard." He depressed the mic switch and called, "Short!" A voice came back, "Shorter!" Harry replied, "Fifteen days!" Another reply, "Tomorrow!" What? Tomorrow? Harry called back, "What the hell are you doing out here?" The response was, "Nothing else to do." About this time, Harry spotted an air force OV-10 Bronco FAC plane approaching from the southeast. He went to the other radio and called the FAC. The voice that came back was the same as on "Guard." He and Harry chatted for a couple of minutes; then the FAC asked if he had ever done this before. Harry told him no. So he said he'd fire two rockets, one to mark the beginning of the run, the other to mark the end. Harry said, "Roger that. I'll follow your track."

The Bronco rolled in toward Nui Ba Dinh and fired his first rocket just short of the temples there. The second rocket was just beyond them. He asked if Harry could see them clearly, and Harry responded that he could and was beginning his first run. Harry told the crew on the CS what was going on and said he was beginning his first run. When they were to drop the barrels he would raise the nose and tell them, "Drop!" Harry turned into the mountain and lined up the two smoke rockets. When he was just before the first marker, he raised the nose, called, "Drop!" and the crew rolled out the four barrels for that run.

The runs were to be made at three hundred feet above the target to allow for the barrels to drop and the charge to go off while they were still in the air. This would provide for maximum dispersal of the CS. This also allowed for the aircraft to be above the mountain peak and fly over it before turning for the next run. As Harry turned the aircraft to the left he could see the drop site from his side window. It looked as though he had placed them right on the line and on target. The FAC came on the radio and told him he had done a good job and congratulated him on the placement.

The FAC went in on another run and marked a line that passed over the temple area but at a slightly different angle. Harry followed with his run and again dropped the CS on the new line and on target.

This time when Harry made his turn, the FAC again congratulated him and asked if he wanted to try something different. He said that he would. The FAC said that when he went in on this final run to go in one hundred feet lower. Harry said he'd do that. He wondered where that would put the barrels when they exploded. He knew it would be very close to the ground.

The FAC marked the third line, and Harry went in at the lower altitude and again dropped the barrels on the line and on target. As he turned, the FAC called and said, "Excellent job. You got two secondary explosions. This meant that when the barrels exploded they must have been at ground level and set off other types of explosives in the ground. So Charlie was using the temple area as a weapons cache, contrary to treaty agreement.

Harry felt pretty good about the mission. He had performed a new task with the desired results and blown up a weapons cache as a bonus. Not bad.

Harry and his crew returned to Tay Ninh to drop off the live track and the chemical crew.

# Going Home

Harry was grounded for rotation back to the States around 14 December 1969. This was fourteen days before his DEROS of 28 December. Two things with this. First, Harry would much rather have been flying. Second, if he couldn't fly he was hoping that he'd be able to go home before Christmas. After all, if he wasn't flying, he really had nothing to do.

Harry got a wooden box to send home his "hold baggage." This was baggage that one did not want to have to carry. The box was about a four-foot cube. Now Harry wanted to take the M-16 he had acquired with him. He decided to just leave the small refrigerator for his hooch mate, Al Smith. Harry had acquired a lot of stuff during his time in Vietnam. He had poncho liners (a camouflage blanket that could be tied into a poncho; made a nice sleeping bag), ponchos, cameras, radios, tape recorders, and just a lot of stuff.

Looking at the box, Harry saw that it would be relatively easy to put a false bottom in it. He got some extra wood from boxes that spare parts had been shipped to the company in. He made a bottom that looked just like the one that was in there. He put some nails into the framing at the bottom of the box. He used rubber bands to secure the M-16 in the box so that it would not rattle. He added a bandolier of extra ammunition. He then placed the false bottom in place and secured it with nails just like those already used in construction of the box. Harry examined his work and was very satisfied that it would pass any inspection. He stood up, and there on the wall was his Thompson submachine gun. Damn!

There was no way to disassemble the box without destroying it. He sold the Thompson to one of the other pilots for twenty-five dollars.

With that done, there was really *nothing* to do. Harry just moped around the company area. He checked each day to see if he could get to Bien Hoa to go home. Each day the answer was no. On 24 December, Bob Hope came to Cu Chi for his Christmas USO tour. Harry had seen him during his first tour when he came to Camp Enari for the 4th INF DIV. This time he was too depressed to go see that many guys having such a good time. He stayed in the company area. About the only thing to do was sit in his hooch or lie on his bed and read paperback books. Thrilling.

*Finally*, on the twenty-seventh, Harry was given his orders and a ride to Bien Hoa in one of the company aircraft. When they dropped him off, they did a pedal spiral liftoff, like a corkscrew, and had several smoke grenades hanging from the cargo hook hole. That was really nice!

Harry made his way to the repo-depot and checked in. He asked about traffic through the depot the last few days. The NCO told him that they'd been sending planes out only half-full. Wonderful, just fucking wonderful! Harry's sitting around with his thumb up his ass, and they're sending half-full "freedom birds" back to the States.

The good news was that there were others from Playtex and Pachyderm who were screwed the same way. Harry was glad to have old friends to talk to and travel with.

They spent the night at the depot, and the next morning they were called to a formation where the names for the day's flight were read off. Harry and the others scheduled to depart got on buses and went to Ton Son Nhut airfield terminal. They watched out the window as the Boing 707 taxied up and disgorged a load of fresh troops just starting their tour. Someone had the sense to separate the two groups so the ones going home couldn't harass the newbies.

The plane was refueled, and the troops boarded. Very good to finally be headed home. As soon as the doors were closed, the stewardesses (they were "stewardesses" back then) went down the aisle and sprayed a liberal amount of air freshener into the cabin. The guys were so used to the stink of Vietnam they didn't realize that the smell was even in their clothes. The showers everyone had taken the night before didn't do a lot of good to get rid of the smell.

Takeoff, gear up, flaps in, on the way! By the time the flaps came in, the aircraft had enough airspeed and altitude to be out of the range of the rockets and mortars. More than one freedom bird had been hit on the runway.

Nothing to do until their scheduled refueling at Honolulu, Hawaii. They were given a box lunch with a sandwich, potato chips, apple or orange, a cookie, and a can of pop. The guys talked, played cards, read, or slept. Harry did not sleep on the flight. And it was a long flight. He reflected on all the things that could have injured or killed him during this tour in Vietnam. Enemy artillery, mortars, small-arms fire, "friendly" artillery, other aircraft, his own aircraft, weather, terrain, the pilot in the other seat, just a myriad of things he'd managed to avoid. He felt very lucky to have gotten through it with just some shrapnel in his shin.

They finally arrived in Honolulu. Many of the guys kissed or touched the tarmac of home. They went into the terminal and got something to eat, like a cheeseburger! And real milk! Or, oh my God, a *milkshake*! It was heaven!

Back on the plane for the relatively short flight to Oakland, California, and Travis Air Force Base. More air freshener, another box lunch, and back in the States. At Travis they again went through a pile of paperwork and were given new uniforms and a ride to San Francisco International Airport. Harry caught a flight to Minneapolis where he was met by his oldest sister, Jean, and her husband, Gordy. The rest of the family, his wife, mother, grandmother, and other sister were waiting in Rochester.

A bit over an hour's ride, and Harry was *home*!

# Glossary

**101ˢᵗ Airborne Division** – Screaming Eagles. Shoulder patch is an eagle's head with a rocker above with 101ˢᵗ Airborne. In 1969 based at Camp Eagle (Hue).

**11ᵗʰ ACR** – 11ᵗʰ Armored Cavalry Regiment. Black Horse Cav. Shoulder patch is a shield with red upper left, white lower right and a black horse in the center. No established base. Mobile.

**1ˢᵗ Cav** -1ˢᵗ Air Cav - 1ˢᵀ Cavalry Division (Airmobile). Shoulder patch is a large yellow triangular shape with a black slash and a horse head in the upper left portion. The original air assault helicopter division. Initially the 1ˢᵗ Air Assault Division, it was renamed in 1965 prior to being deployed to Vietnam. In 1969 based at Phouc Vinh, northeast of Saigon.

**25ᵗʰ Infantry Division** - Tropical Lightning. Shoulder patch is a red leaf with gold lightning bolt in center. In 1969 based at Cu Chi, northwest of Saigon.

**4ᵗʰ Infantry Division** – The Ivy Division. Shoulder patch is a white square on end with a green border and four ivy leaves extending from the center. Based at Camp Enari, south of Pleiku.

**7.62 mm** – The NATO approved 7.62 x 51 mm round used by the US forces in Vietnam. Also known as a.308 (caliber) Winchester. This was different that the 7.62 x 39 mm ammunition used in an AK-47. Used in M-14 rifle and M-60 machine gun.

**9ᵗʰ Infantry Division** – Old Reliable. Shoulder patch is an octofoil, red on top, blue on bottom with a white circle in center. Based at Dong Tam on the Mekong River southwest of Saigon.

**AA or AAA–** antiaircraft artillery. Usually 20mm or 40 mm.

**AC** – Aircraft Commander or alternating current. The pilot in charge of and responsible for the aircraft, crew, and mission. Whatever happens it this person's fault – good or bad. The latter is one of the electrical power supplies used in the Chinook at 120 volts.

**AK-47** – The most popular weapon of the Viet Cong (VC) and North Vietemese Army (NVA). It used a 7.62 x 39 mm round so our 7.62 x 51 mm ammunition would not fit in its chamber. This was the same round used in their other rifles. It could fire 600 rounds per minute. The SKS was also popular. It was a semi-automatic weapon with a ten round box magazine. This meant it had to be loaded from stripper clips through an open chamber. It had a rate of fire of around 700 rounds per minute but with reloading it was more like 50.

**altitude** - In aviation it is normally the height above sea level.

**AO** – Area of Operations. The geographical area that was assigned to a particular unit to operate within.

**Assault Helicopter** – Prefix for direct assault helicopter units.

**Assault Support Helicopter** – Prefix for helicopter units supporting direct assault.

**Aussie** – Term referring to an Australian. Both military and civilian Australians were in Vietnam.

**Aviation batallion** – A unit consisting of two or more companies. Normal infantry divisions had an aviation batallion with one lift company and one gun/scout company.

**Aviation Group** – An aviation unit consisting of two or more aviation batallions. The 101st Airborne (Airmobile) group had three battalions of lift and gun/scout companies, an arial rocket artillery company, and an assualt support batallion of three Chinook and one Tarhe (Crane) companies. There may have been more.

**bee hive round** – Common name for an artillery round using flechettes.

**butter bar** – Derogatory term for a second lieutenant, 2LT.

**caliber** – The method used to measure the size of a US bullet. Caliber is the same as inch. A .50 caliber bullet is 0.50 (one half) inche in diameter (across).

**CE** – Crew engineer. This is a position of responsibility in the flight crew. Usually second to the FE (flight engineer). This person was normally stationed at the right door machine gun during flight.

**CG** – Center of gravity. This is the point around which the mass is centered. In an aricraft it must be within certain limits depending on that aircraft. Getting the weight outside of the CG wll prevent full use of the controls to fly the aircraft. Not conducive to longevity.

**CO** – Commanding Officer. The commander in charge of a unit, company, battalion, or whatever. Sometimes referred to as 'The Old Man".

**CPT** – Commissioned officer rank of Captain, O-3.

**CS** - A riot control gas named from its inventors Corson and Stoughton in 1928. Causes burning sensation and tearing of the eyes to the extent that the subject cannot keep their eyes open, and a burning irritation of the nose, mouth and throat mucous membranes causing profuse coughing, mucous nasal discharge, disorientation, and difficulty breathing, partially incapacitating the subject. It has no permanent effects.

**CW2** - Warrant officer rank of Chief Warrant Officer 2, CW2. There were also CW3 and CW4.

**DC** – Direct current. One of the power supplies used in the Chinook at 24 volts.

**density altitude** – Altitude adjusted for pressure, temperature and humidity. Of special concern in Vietnam due to high temperatures and humidity.

**DMZ** – Demilitarized Zone. Zone on either side of the border between North and South Vietnam where there was to be no military activity. The zone was five kilometers either side of the dividing line which roughly followed the Ben Hai River near the 17th parallel. The NVA did not pay any attention to the treaty and this restriction.

**DEROS** – Date eligible or estimated return overseas. The day a soldier left Vietnam for the States. In Vietnam this was one year from the day you left the States.

**Duece-and-a-half** - Very common Army truck rated at two and a hlaf tons. Actually a five ton truck.

**EM Club** – A bar for the use by enlisted ranks, usually below E-5. E-5 and above had NCO Clubs.

**FE** – Flight engineer. This is the enlisted person responsible for the maintenance and operational capability of the aircraft. Universally referred to as "Chief". This person was normally stationed on his belly looking through the cargo door at the load or checking on the equipment in the aft of the aircraft.

**First sergeant** – The highest ranking non-commissioned officer (NCO) in a unit.

**Flechettes** – Small metal darts in artillery rounds or 40 mm grenade launchers used for anti-personnel actions.

**FSB** – Fire Support Base. Remotely located bases for providing artillery fire for support of operations, usually infantry. Most were one battery (six guns) of 105 mm artillery. Some were more, some had 155 mm guns, and others had 175 mm gums.

**GP Medium** – A sixteen by thirty two foot canvas tent with three center poles used for a variety of purposes such as quarters and mess halls.

**GP Small**, a six sided tent with a center pole seventeen feet six inches wide.

**Ground effect** – When a helicopter operates near the ground it builds up additional airpressure under the aircraft thereby increasing lift capability.

**Gunner** – Responsible for the care, cleaning, and operability to the two (sometimes three) 7.62 mm M-60 machine guns. Also assisted with the maintenance of the aircraft. This person was normally stationed at the left door 7.62 mm M-60 machine gun.

**hooch** – Term used for the living quarters in Vietnam.

**hooch maid** – Indigenous personnel that were hired to clean the rooms and do laundry.

**howitzer** – A type of artillery piece characterized by a relatively short barrel and the use of comparatively small propellant charges to propel projectiles at relatively high trajectories, with a steep angle of descent. The 105mm and 155 mm cannons were howitzers.

**IP** – Instructor Pilot. Person responsible to sign off on the capabilities of a pilot or AC.

**JP-4** – Jet petroleum 4. A type of kerosene used as fuel in jet turbine engines in helicopters, jets, etc.

**KIA** – Killed in action. Death as a result of enemy activity. Eligible for a Purple Heart medal.

**M-14** – The 7.62 NATO (.308 caliber) round rifle initially used in Vietnam. It used a 20 round detachable magazine and had a rate of fire of 700 – 750 rounds per minute. There was an optional selector switch that could be added to operate on either semi-automatic (normal) or full automatic (optional).

**M-16** – The 5.56 mm (.223 caliber) NATO round rifle that replaced the M-14. The ammunition was smaller and the rifle much lighter reducing the load for the soldier. It had a build in selector switch and was capable of firing 700-950 rounds per minute.

**M-60** – A 7.62 mm machine gun, capable of firing 500 to 650 rounds per minute. Normally there were two mounted in a Chinook, at the left front window and the right front door. A third could be mounted as a tail stinger on the aft ramp.

**MAJ** – Commissioned officer rank of Major, O-4.

**military time** – The military operates on a 24 hour clock. This eliminates confusion over am and pm. Anything after noon one ads two to the hours. So 1:00 pm is 1300, 6:30 pm is 1830, 10 pm is 2200, etc.

**mm** – Millimeter. It is equal to 0.039 inches. See MILIMETERS to INCHES chart for conversions. Used to measure the size (Diameter) of a round. In the book from 5.56 to 175.

**NCO** – Non-commissioned officer. Enlisted ranks of E-5 and above.

**O Club** – Officers' Club – Anything from a small bar in a 'hooch' to a full service restaurant where access was restricted to officers.

**pilot** – One who flies an aircraft. This is not the person in charge of the aircraft. That would be the pilot in command or aircraft commander.

**pilot in command** – A pilot assigned as in charge of the aircraft but has not yet attained aircraft commander status.

**pressure altitude** – The atmospheric altitude or altitude adjusted for atmospheric pressure.

**PX or BX** – Post or Base Exchange. A military department store where all types of dry goods and appliances were available. Everything from buttons to refrigerators, socks to jackets.

**ranks** – Generally broken down into three groups: Enlisted, Warrant Officer and Commissioned Officer. The Commissioned Officer was further sub-divided into Company Grade (O-1 to O-3), Field Grade (O-4 and O-5), General staff (O-6), and General (O-7 to O-11).

**RPG** – Rocket propelled grenade. A version of a bazooka firing a missile with an explosive warhead.

**rpm** – Revolutions per minute.

**SAS** – Stability augmentation system. Complex system that assisted in stabilizing the aerodynamics of a dual rotor system.

**SOP** – Standard Operating Procedure. Established method of doing a thing.

**SP** – Self propelled. Some of the guns were self propelled with a body and frame using tracks for propulsion. Like an open top tank. Included 40 mm, and 175 mm guns.

**SP packs** – Supplemental pack. Large boxes containing additional items for the troops. Included things such as cartons of cigarettes, paper and pens, envelopes, ball points, candy, gum, soap, razors, shaving cream, tooth brushes, tooth paste, etc. Highly valued by the troops.

**Steel pot** – Term used for a helmet. Comprised of a fiberglass liner with adjustable straps and a steel outer shell.

**Tac E** – Tactical emergency. A dire situation that was supposed to be so important that the loss of the aircraft and crew were secondary to accomplishing the mission. They were supposedly only called with the approval of a Colonel (O-6) or above.

**TACAN** – An electronic ultra-high frequency navigation system which provided a continual indication of bearing and distance from a transmitter. Marines had these devices, not the army.

**vertigo** – Spatial disorientation. A condition where a person believes they are moving in a direction they are not. Highly dangerous for pilots. A pilot must rely on his instruments to overcome the desire to follow what is felt rather than what is.

**WIA** – Wounded in action. Wounds as a result of enemy action. Makes one eligible for a Purple Heart medal.

**WO1** – Warrant officer rank of Warrant Officer, WO1.

# Conversions

Milimeters to Inches      Meters to Feet      Kilometers to Miles

| MILIMETERS | INCHES | | METERS | FEET | | KILOMETERS | MILES |
|---|---|---|---|---|---|---|---|
| 1 | .04 | | | | | 1 | 0.62 |
| 2 | .08 | | 1 | 3.28 | | 2 | 1.24 |
| 3 | .12 | | 2 | 6.56 | | 3 | 1.86 |
| 4 | .16 | | 3 | 9.84 | | 4 | 2.49 |
| 5 | .20 | | 4 | 13.12 | | 5 | 3.11 |
| 5.56 | .22 M-16 | | 5 | 16.90 | | 10 | 6.21 |
| 7.62 (AK-47) | .30 M-14 | | 10 | 32.8 | | 20 | 12.43 |
| 10 | .40 | | 20 | 65.62 | | 30 | 18.64 |
| 20 | .79 | | 30 | 98.42 | | 40 | 24.85 |
| 40 | 1.57 | | 40 | 131.23 | | 50 | 31.07 |
| 105 | 4.13 | | 50 | 164.04 | | 100 | 62.14 |
| 155 | 6.10 | | 100 | 328.08 | | | |
| 175 | 6.89 | | 1,000 | 3,280.83 | | | |

# Time

| Civillain | Military | Civillian | Military |
|-----------|----------|-----------|----------|
|           |          |           |          |
| 1:00 AM   | 0100     | 1:00 PM   | 1300     |
| 2:00 AM   | 0200     | 2:00 PM   | 1400     |
| 3:00 AM   | 0300     | 3:00 PM   | 1500     |
| 4:00 AM   | 0400     | 4:00 PM   | 1600     |
| 5:00 AM   | 0500     | 5:00 PM   | 1700     |
| 6:00 AM   | 0600     | 6:00 PM   | 1800     |
| 7:00 AM   | 0700     | 7:00 PM   | 1900     |
| 8:00 AM   | 0800     | 8:00 PM   | 2000     |
| 9:00 AM   | 0900     | 9:00 PM   | 2100     |
| 10:00 AM  | 1000     | 10:00PM   | 2200     |
| 11:00 AM  | 1100     | 11:00PM   | 2300     |
| 12:00 AM  | 1200     | 12:00PM   | 2400     |

# Afterthought

## Afterthought

**W**riting this book was a real trip-in many ways. For many years I have wanted to tell the tale of what it was like flying Chinooks in Vietnam. Hopefully I have conveyed that.

It was a wonderful journey down memory lane. I wish that I had kept a journal so the items would be in chorological sequence but I tried as best I could with thirty seven year old memories. I know that some of the items are out of sequence but could not find a better placement for them.

Remembering my friends and comrades was pleasant. For the most part they were a great bunch of guys. The things we did together, the things we faced, and succeeded at were rather phenomenal. We were young and crazy. As Joe Galloway said, we were "God's own lunatics." Only a crazy person would get in an aircraft that isn't supposed to be able to fly and yet take it into harm's way. Often times knowing what was waiting for us, we went anyway. Yes, we were certifiable!

The aftermath of the Vietnam War and what the media and politicians did to it and us was unforgiveable. Many of us spent years out of contact with those we served with. Fortunately, many of us have gotten by that and are back in contact with those we were closest to. The Vietnam Helicopter Pilots Association has been very helpful with that. Combat can form bonds like no other experience. I am very grateful to have the friends that I do from my service. They are a great bunch of guys that were willing to give their all.

I learned a lot in the army. Most of it good and valuable information. Duty, honor, country is more than a motto. It affects how one sees and does things. Nearly all my friends and comrades have had successful and productive lives. Again contrary to what the media and politicians tried to make of us.

I found a very successful carrier in health care as a human resources executive. In addition to several other positions, I was president of both my state (Colorado) and national professional associations. I believe I owe this in large part to what I learned in the army and in Vietnam.

My first tour was highly educational. The second was much more so. If one paid attention there was a tremendous amount of a variety of things to be learned in Vietnam. It was the most educational and probably the best year of my life.

I would not do it again.

Made in the USA
Lexington, KY
10 June 2017